Pesos and Politics

Pesos and Politics

BUSINESS, ELITES, FOREIGNERS,
AND GOVERNMENT IN MEXICO,
1854–1940

Mark Wasserman

STANFORD UNIVERSITY PRESS
STANFORD, CALIFORNIA

Stanford University Press
Stanford, California

© 2015 by the Board of Trustees of the Leland Stanford Junior University. All rights reserved.

No part of this book may be reproduced or transmitted in any form or by any means, electronic or mechanical, including photocopying and recording, or in any information storage or retrieval system without the prior written permission of Stanford University Press.

Printed in the United States of America on acid-free, archival-quality paper.

Library of Congress Cataloging-in-Publication Data

Wasserman, Mark, 1946– author.
  Pesos and politics : business, elites, foreigners, and government in Mexico, 1854–1940 / Mark Wasserman.
      pages cm
  Includes bibliographical references and index.
  ISBN 978-0-8047-9154-0 (cloth : alk. paper)
  1. Industrial policy—Mexico—History. 2. Businesspeople—Mexico—History. 3. Elite (Social sciences)—Mexico—History. 4. Investments, Foreign—Mexico—History. 5. Business enterprises, Foreign—Mexico—History. 6. Mexico—Politics and government—1867–1910. 7. Mexico—Politics and government—1910–1946. I. Title.
  HD3616.M43W37 2015
  322'.3097209034—dc23
                                                  2014037756

ISBN 978-0-8047-9521-0 (electronic)

*This book is dedicated to Hudson Theodore Blass,
my beautiful, brave grandson.*

Contents

List of Tables — *viii*
Acknowledgments — *ix*

1. Elites, Foreigners, and Government in Mexico, 1877–1940 — 1
2. Mexican Entrepreneurs — 31
3. Mexico Versus the Seven Kings: The Railroad Consolidation, 1902–1910 — 58
4. Foreign Landowners — 77
5. The Corralitos Company — 112
6. Foreign Mining Entrepreneurs — 132
7. The American Smelting and Refining Company in Mexico, 1890–1940 — 158
8. Conclusion — 181

Notes — *187*
Bibliography — *233*
Index — *249*

Tables

2.1	Inventory of Banco Minero de Chihuahua Stockholdings as of August 1916	37
2.2	Cía Metalúrgica de Torreón: Profits, 1902–1906	47
2.3	Enterprises of Ernesto Madero, 1895–1912	52
7.1	Average Wage Cost at ASARCO, 1931–1937	177
7.2	Estimated Profits at ASARCO, 1900–1925	178

Acknowledgments

Pesos and Politics is a work of two decades, interrupted by the writing of a synthesis about nineteenth-century Mexico, three editions of a textbook, and two document readers. Thus, this book has proceeded in fits and starts. As in the case of most projects that evolve over a long time, the book has taken some twists and turns, sometimes unexpected. For example, two summers each produced a chapter that I had not included in my original plan. Along the way I have accumulated some intellectual debts. John Coatsworth first stimulated my interest in economic and business history. Friedrich Katz pointed me toward the Terrazas family and ultimately foreign investment in the north of Mexico. John Mason Hart pushed me to look hard at foreign investment in Mexico, though ultimately I came to disagree with his conclusions. Michael Adas, much like Hart, incited me to closely examine the impact of developed nations on the less developed world, with similar results. Colleagues at Rutgers, including Adas, Samuel Baily, and John Gillis, taught me that historians should not be afraid to work "against the grain" and should not follow accepted interpretations. Stephen Haber and his "crew" at Stanford forced all historians of Latin America to reexamine their assumptions about economic development and business operations in the region. Carlos Marichal and Mario Cerutti pioneered in the business history of Mexico. Three scholars, Jeremy Adelman, Paul Clemens, and Gail Triner, read versions of the first chapter and provided me with insightful criticism. The National Endowment of the Humanities provided me with a year to research and write, and Rutgers University granted me a valuable sabbatical to finish the manuscript. As always, Marlie Parker Wasserman was my inspiration. I dedicate this book to Hudson Theodore Blass, my grandson, who faces a long, tough fight and who is far more important to me than my lifetime of scholarship.

Pesos and Politics

ONE

Elites, Foreigners, and Government in Mexico, 1877–1940

The relationship between business and politics is crucial to understanding Mexican history, particularly the eras of Porfirio Díaz (1877–1911), the Revolution (1910–20), and the revolutionary reconstruction (1920–40).[1] The ability of the Díaz regime to construct a network of intricate arrangements that tied together the many conflicting interests of the Mexican elite and foreign investors was, with the personal force of the dictator, the very heart of its thirty-five-year rule. The Revolution in considerable part resulted from the breakdown of these Porfirian deals. During the ten years of civil strife that followed the fall of Díaz, businesspeople, politicians, and military struggled to make new arrangements. The Constitution of 1917 restructured government relations with landholders and mineral producers and introduced a whole new array of rules for the treatment of employees. The transformation of business relations that reflected the interests of new elites and newly influential groups, such as workers and peasants, comprised the core of the struggles of the 1920s and was a crucial reason for the ultimate creation of the revolutionary party, the Partido Nacional Revolucionario (PNR), in 1929. The widespread expropriations of land and the government takeover of the oil industry during the presidency of Lázaro Cárdenas necessitated the construction of yet another set of understandings.

Pesos and Politics will combine the most important approaches to the field, such as the study of the composition and behavior of oligarchies, the exploration of the development of the modern state, the examination of the impact of external economic factors, and the emphasis on regional and local politics and consider the relations between businesses, elite, foreign investors, and government from the municipal to the international levels. The extension of the analysis to the regional and local levels will present a better picture of how the interactions between these entities worked on an everyday basis and improve our overall understanding of how Mexican business functioned and how its operations changed over time.

I will argue that throughout the era from 1876 to 1940—begun by Porfirio Díaz and his henchmen Manuel Romero Rubio and José Yves Limantour, continued through the nearly decade of civil war and the postwar state under Alvaro Obregón and Plutarco Elías Calles, and further sustained during the emergence of the one-party state and the readjustment during the presidency of Lázaro Cárdenas—there was an evolving elite-foreign enterprise system. This constantly changing set of arrangements required intricate checks and balances.[2] For the sixty years under study, no one entity—neither the national government/regime, nor any national or regional elite faction, nor the military, nor foreign investors, collectively or individually—was so powerful as to dominate the relationships. For the most part, beginning with the mid-1880s, the state, with its varied strength over time, was the primary entity that maintained the equilibrium between contestants, for its own benefit and theirs. The negotiations and resulting agreements took place within important constraints. Because both the pre- and postwar regimes were committed successively to development, led first by raw material and agricultural exports and then by import substitution industrialization, each of which depended on foreign capital for its success, Mexican governments had to reach a balance that simultaneously attracted foreign entrepreneurs, but did not allow them to become too powerful. Díaz's purchase of the foreign-owned railroads and Cárdenas's expropriation of the foreign-owned petroleum companies were only the most notorious efforts to maintain the equilibrium. In addition, various regimes had to struggle to balance local, state, and national governments. Regional and local elite factions and the political bosses who sometimes represented them were powerful entities that often limited the actual power of national governments. The issue of local autonomy sustained through the entire period. The famous cry of "obedezco pero no cumplo" (I obey but do not comply) during the Spanish colonial period was no less the description of the relationship between the national government and the localities from the 1850s through 1940. Moreover, through almost all of the era, it was a more evenly balanced struggle than historians have assessed. Neither the Porfirian state nor the revolutionary state were even close to omnipotent. To a large extent the course of the Revolution owed to local and regional prerogatives overpowering the national regime.

Local, regional, and national elite and the governments at these levels that they influenced or ran were deeply involved in the struggle to maintain checks and balances with foreign investors. Here, too, the process was more on equal terms than historians have generally asserted. Foreigners did not control the Mexican economy at any point, though they owned a considerable part of it. It is not clear that foreigners received better treatment than native Mexicans, as some have claimed. For example, while some foreign enterprises might obtain favorable consideration at one level of government, they might likely find a less hospitable environment at another. The elite-foreign enterprise system functioned in spite of the sometimes nationalistic rhetoric of various regimes, which served to camouflage the never-ending process of negotiations.

Because Mexican business over the course of six decades is an enormous topic, far too extensive for a book of modest length, this study will concentrate on the three most important sectors of the Mexican economy: mining, agriculture, and railroads.[3] Within these, it will investigate, for the most part, the operations of foreign enterprises and their interactions with elites and governments at various levels. It is my supposition, however, that the histories of foreign companies and individuals do not differ substantially from that of Mexican-owned and -operated enterprises.[4]

At the core of the relationships between Mexican business and politics were the five overlapping sectors that competed and cooperated from the Reform (1854) to the Revolution (1910–40): (1) the Mexican national elite; (2) regional (state) elite; (3) local (municipal) elite; (4) large foreign corporations; and (5) individual foreign entrepreneurs. During and after the Revolution, organized labor and organized peasants joined these five.

MEXICAN ELITES

Mexican elites were in constant conflict. From the Liberal reforms until 1940, three sets of simultaneous, interconnected struggles occurred: local elite fought the efforts of state-level oligarchies to encroach on their autonomy; rival elite factions at the state level clashed to establish their domination; and state elite battled with successive national regimes to maintain regional autonomy.[5] The Mexican national elite, based in Mexico City, controlled the central government and unceasingly sought to extend its influence. For much of the nineteenth century, the national elite divided into two irreconcilable warring groups. After thirteen years of civil war from 1854 to 1867, the centralist Conservatives lost out to federalist Liberals, who in their efforts to modernize the nation soon became centralists. Dictator Porfirio Díaz, who seized power in 1876 and held it for thirty-five years, forged a national elite comprised of military officers, allied with civilian technocrats, the latter known popularly as *científicos*. This coalition encouraged and facilitated enormous foreign investment in order to modernize the nation's economy and maintain its position of power. Díaz and his cronies struggled to push their influence into the regions, but fiercely resistant regional elite forced compromise. A mosaic of deals and alliances formed the basis of the regime. The Revolution of 1910 tore apart the system. For a decade no national group or leader constructed a replacement, foundering on the rocks of regional opposition. In the regions and localities the various revolutionary and counterrevolutionary factions competed and alternated in power, mixing ambitious new freebooters and, at times, remnants of the old guard. During the presidency of Alvaro Obregón (1920–24) a new national elite took shape. Predominantly made up of military officers, it reconstructed a system of compromises similar to those of the Díaz era. In the 1930s, under the auspices of the PNR, government use of military force and patronage restarted the process of centralization. The new regime diminished (but did not destroy) the power of regional elites, employing peasant and worker organizations as political counterweights. Throughout the enduring conflicts between national regimes and regional elite, local elites fought to maintain their autonomy, as well.[6]

The Revolution pushed the prerevolutionary elite from its political place and, in many respects, that elite never recovered.[7] Economically, members of the Porfirian upper class survived in inverse relation to their dependence on land for their fortunes. Some of the old elite flourished in the new order.[8] The new ruling elite derived mainly from the upwardly mobile middle classes and ambitious military officers. Overall, the biggest winners in the Revolution were members of the middle class, who gained access to government, education, and economic opportunity. The Sonoran dynasty—Adolfo de la Huerta, Alvaro Obregón, and Plutarco Elías Calles—epitomized this middle-class triumph.[9]

The current historiography maintains that there was little or no separation between economic and political elite until the Revolution of 1910. Thereafter, the revolutionary regime supposedly split the national power structure into economic and political groups.[10] The revolutionary party pointedly excluded the business sector from its ranks. But my research indicates that these separations did not apply at the state and municipal levels.[11] And, if the careers of presidents Alvaro Obregón, Plutarco Elías Calles, and Abelardo Rodríguez were any indication, the overlap of economic and political interests existed on the national level as well.[12] It is not evident that there was any clear difference between the single political and economic elite of the Díaz dictatorship and the supposedly dual elite that existed during the immediate postrevolutionary war years, 1920 to 1940. There arose from the Revolution a group of military and civilian entrepreneur-politicians whose activities blurred the lines between economic and political elite. As Dudley Ankerson observed of the generals, the difference between them and their predecessors was that "the methods of their plunder became more sophisticated."[13] One observer noted, "The Generals and other officials devote more time to mercantile pursuits than to combating banditry; they . . . attend to their own business first."[14]

These demarcations were also not so clear at the state and municipal levels. Revolutionary leaders behaved much like their predecessors, employing public position for private gain. The revolutionary military, also like the Díaz elite, made money the "old fashioned way," through payoffs, bribes, and padding payrolls. If anything, the "freebooters" of the Revolution may have been better entrepreneurs, more adept at intermingling economics and politics, and more willing to innovate by entering new fields such as industry and gambling. Through 1940 the bifurcation of the elite into economic and political segments did not seem to have taken place at the state and local levels. The lessons learned in the nineteenth century regarding the need to control local politics in order to protect economic holdings was probably more important in the 1920s and 1930s than ever before.[15]

Old and new elite depended on their families for the base of their influence and enterprise. The greatest fortunes of the Porfiriato, such as the Terrazas-Creel, the Madero, and the Molina-Montes fortunes, were founded on extended family ties. Before and after the Revolution the major fortunes of the Monterrey group were perpetuated by family.[16] The revolutionaries were similarly inclined. Thus, the Quevedos and Almeidas used their extended families to solidify their economic holdings and political influence in Chihuahua during the 1920s and 1930s, and the Avila Camachos did the same in Puebla in the 1930s and 1940s.[17] The revolutionaries also relied heavily on their *camarillas*, groups of loyalists with links from the university or local politics.[18]

FOREIGNERS

Foreigners went to Mexico in search of their fortunes from the first years of Mexican Independence in 1821.[19] They also purchased the new nation's public debt and invested in its commerce, agriculture, and mining industry. After an initial boom and bust, during which the losers were primarily Europeans, there was a long period from the 1830s through the 1880s, when investment was almost nonexistent. Foreign invasions, civil wars, and political uncertainty presented risks that were far too high for investors, despite the enormous resources and potential opportunities. There were, of course, foreigners who settled and made good in Mexico during these dark years, such as the American Braniff family.[20] Others, like Irishman Patrick Milmo (Mullins) and American Joseph A. Robertson in Monterrey and John R. Robinson in Batopilas, Chihuahua, made their fortunes in the 1860s and 1870s.[21] Nonetheless, the real boom in foreign investment and entrepreneurship took place after Díaz took power in 1877. The regime, whose motto was "order and progress," attracted people and money from all over the world.

The number of foreigners in Mexico through 1940 never exceeded 1 percent of its population. Prior to 1910 Sonora had the highest percentage of foreigners with 3.5 percent and three other northern states, Chihuahua, Coahuila, and Tamaulipas, had more than 1 percent. Ten years of Revolution decreased the number of foreigners both in absolute and relative terms. Chihuahua, Durango, and Sonora experienced drastic deductions. But the number of foreigners in the north increased by 183 percent during the 1920s.[22]

Of course, the number of foreigners was not nearly as important as the amount of money they invested. Although there is some disagreement about the statistics, especially those concerning the origins of investment in railroads, it is likely that there were about a billion and a half dollars invested from abroad in Mexico in 1912, with a little more than 1 billion from the United States and more than 300 million from Great Britain. By the mid-1920s US investment had risen to 1.280 billion dollars.[23] Foreigners played important roles in the major sectors of the Mexican economy, mining, transportation, and agriculture. By some estimates the value of American investment was twice that of Mexicans in 1910. Americans controlled three-quarters of the Mexican mining and metallurgical industries. Other foreigners owned 80 percent of the nation's industry.[24]

Foreign investment in underdeveloped nations is, of course, controversial. The advocates of the dependency framework maintain that there was an unequal relationship between the great industrialized nations that invested and the less developed countries that received the investment. According to this general viewpoint, the investors, who supplied capital and technology and often management, exploited the recipients, taking their nonrenewable resources from which they obtained enormous profits and returning nothing other than the paltry wages of selected workers and the rents derived by the domestic elite from their ownership of property and their control of positions of authority at various levels of government (through bribes and so on). Therefore, until recently the widely accepted interpretation of the economic history of Mexico since 1850 has been that the nation was a victim of exploitation, most particularly by US capitalists. In that analysis, the Díaz era was the most striking. John Mason Hart goes even further in asserting that the North Americans controlled the Mexican economy at least until 1910 and certainly dominated thereafter as well.[25] During the past decade or so, however, the historiography, it seems to me, has taken two tracks. The first track emphasizing foreign entrepreneurs' exploitation and control has, despite various revisions in interpretations of the era, remained quite strong. But a second track, built by economic historians of Mexico, points out that foreign investment was often unsuccessful in Mexico and that Mexican elites often got the better of foreigners.[26]

The evidence that either Díaz betrayed his country, selling it to the Americans, or realized too late that he had permitted the Americans too much influence, is not so clear as Hart or Ramón Ruiz might have it. The regime was anything but a pushover for Wall Street. Especially after 1900, Limantour and Díaz took a series of measures to encourage European investment to counteract the *norteamericanos*. This angered in particular American oil tycoons. Limantour also instituted higher tariffs to protect domestic industry from foreign competition.[27] The evidence, furthermore, indicates that foreigners received no extraordinary treatment. Díaz favored those who offered Mexico opportunities to develop its economy, foreigners and Mexicans alike. Wealthy entrepreneurs, Mexican or foreign, had access to the highest echelons.

The assumed dichotomy between the dictatorship of Porfirio Díaz (1877–1911) and the Revolution of 1910 influences the study of Mexican business history, particularly with regard to the evolution of the role of foreigners in Mexican economic development. Historians have generally represented the first era by repeating the common complaint of Mexicans critical of the Díaz regime that Mexico was the "mother of foreigners and the stepmother of Mexicans." In turn, historians have characterized the Revolution as a period when foreigners suffered at the hands of rebel armies, which destroyed their property, and were victimized by radicals, who expropriated their lands and mines. The claim that foreigners exploited Mexico and in the process extracted enormous sums from its economy underlies these discussions.[28]

It is the object of this book to build on the recent studies that complicate the analysis of the relationship between business and elites and government in Mexico. First, it sets out to reestablish a more balanced view of foreign investors in Mexico.[29] Most importantly, it asserts that most foreign entrepreneurs in Mexico failed to obtain anywhere near an approximation of great riches. They sometimes earned modest short-term success, perhaps intermittent, but rarely sustained. This claim includes fairly large operations, such as ranches with hundreds of thousands of acres and mining firms with millions in capital, as well as small holders and fly-by-night promoters. Second and closely related to the first, this study proffers that Mexican authorities did not usually favor foreigners, certainly not to the extent claimed by some revolutionaries in 1910 or later. Americans, British, Chinese, French, Germans, and Lebanese were subject to the arbitrary and capricious application of the clearly unsatisfactory body of law concerning business.[30] However, the treatment they received was no more or less than Mexicans endured. Third, I maintain that the Díaz government and governments at the state and local levels most assuredly did not give their nation away to foreigners. On the national level Díaz and his chief aide José Y. Limantour were very much aware of the dangers of upsetting the economic and political balances they so carefully maintained. They were not about to let the foreigners grow too powerful and therefore upset the equilibrium of the system. Mexicans were very much in control of the operations of their own economy.

If the Díaz government was not quite as favorably inclined toward foreigners as historians have concluded until now, then the Revolution and the postrevolution were not as hard on them. On the local level, there were, to be sure, many incidents of extortion, raiding, destruction, and even murder during the years of violence.[31] And there were wide variations in treatment of foreigners from region to region. But on the whole, it was not in the best interests of any of the revolutionary factions to discourage the production of foreign operations or to shut them down. The rebels of all stripes simply needed the revenues and they preferred the population to have employment. During the Madero presidency, those in power were not predisposed to harass foreigners, although the Maderos had competed fiercely against foreigners in various businesses. As Friedrich Katz has discovered, rebel leader Pancho Villa had at times been tough on foreigners—he shot dead Englishman William Benton—but because he initially did not need revenue as badly as his rivals, he facilitated their operations until the Pershing Expedition in 1916, when he rightly perceived the United States had turned against him.[32]

Foreign companies adapted to the ebbs and flows of the civil wars. Those businesses that were well capitalized, adeptly managed, and flexible survived; a few even prospered. In order to endure the conditions of war, foreign companies had to maintain satisfactory relations with whatever group was in power at any particular time, and they also had to have sufficient capital on hand to obtain cooperation. There were clear differences in how the revolutionaries treated small and medium-scale enterprises and the larger companies, favoring the latter. The smaller mines and ranches had far less leverage. But even this pattern was not uniform because those foreigners who had ties of marriage or had otherwise integrated into their communities might have escaped relatively unscathed. Large corporations were not always treated as favorably locally as they were by national authorities.

I maintain that during the Díaz era, the Revolution, and revolutionary reconstruction foreigners in business in Mexico encountered continuous, substantial obstacles, sometimes because of adverse relations with elite or governments at various levels. I also assert that very few foreign entrepreneurs or enterprises consistently earned profits from their Mexican ventures over the long term during the period from the 1880s through the 1940s. Foreigners mostly did not prosper and surely did not grow wealthy. It is impossible to claim that there was never any exploitation—for surely at the very least there were foreign employers who mistreated their workers in some ways—but generally they did not pay less or offer worse working conditions than domestic employers. My conclusions are part of an underlying effort to restore the economic and business history of Mexico to Mexicans. That is, far from being impotent in the face of foreign economic might, Mexicans controlled their own economy.

Most foreign entrepreneurs in Mexico during the period under examination were conspicuously unsuccessful. Traveler Frederick Ober reported in 1882 that "there has been a great concentration of North Americans in Monterrey and the streets of the city are filled with disillusioned adventurers. They came to this country as if it was new, without taking into account too late . . . that the Mexican . . . has an instinct for commerce and a love for luxury as developed as the most talented Yankee. . . . The Americans . . . have not had much luck in business."[33] More than three decades later Nils O. Bagge, a mining engineer, who had spent eighteen years in Mexico, came to similar conclusions. "American engineers . . . found that the Mexican is an extremely shrewd trader and it is undeniably true that a Mexican mine owner asked and usually obtained more money for his property than an American prospector would for a similar property in the United States."[34] Typical of the plight of the foreign entrepreneur was one American adventurer who wrote to the *Engineering and Mining Journal* in 1923: "I read my journal usually in bed, under a mosquito bar, legs of the bed sitting in kerosene to keep off the scorpions, bedding sprayed with fly-on-san to minimize the fleas, and a towel to wipe off the sweat."[35] A glamorous and remunerative life indeed!

Successful foreign-owned enterprises in Mexico during the dictatorship of Porfirio Díaz, the Revolution, and revolutionary reconstruction depended on sufficient capital to purchase necessary equipment and pay for daily operations, competent management, a steady market for minerals or agricultural commodities, accessible transportation, a reliable workforce, and the maintenance of good working relations with local, state, and national authorities. Most foreign companies and individuals lacked at least one and usually more of these required components.

The availability of capital ebbed and flowed according to the economic circumstances. During the early years of the dictatorship of Porfirio Díaz, both domestic and foreign investment funds were scarce. The risks involved in investing in Mexico were too great to attract large sums. There was, however, an inflow of foreign capital to finance the railroads during the 1880s after Porfirio Díaz had taken power and established relative peace and another inflow to underwrite mining after 1890. The long-lasting depression of the 1890s stymied investment, but a massive infusion of foreign funds followed from 1900 to 1907, ending when another depression struck. Obviously, the outbreak of revolution discouraged investments from home and abroad, though not until the full force of the violence occurred between 1913 and 1917. Foreign investment remained minimal for a decade, except in petroleum and mining, areas in which large multinational corporations purchased vast holdings despite the disruptions of the civil war. Political uncertainty continued to discourage foreign capital through the 1930s. The radical Constitution of 1917 and the subsequent, if erratic, land reform and resurgent labor union movement worried potential investors, as well.

Management skills varied widely. Mining and ranching, whether domestically or foreign-owned, were risky enterprises that depended, in great part, on unpredictable weather and geological conditions. A large number of experienced supervisory mining personnel, who migrated back and forth across the border with the United States, were available throughout the era and worked in both Mexican and foreign operations. The Revolution, especially from 1913 to 1917, caused foreigners to flee the country, leaving the mines without supervision. Many of the mines fell into considerable disrepair as a consequence. The uncertainties of the 1920s did not seem to deter foreign mining personnel from Mexico. Ranches had an easier time finding qualified supervisors because they were more likely to hire Mexicans for these positions.

Mining was heavily dependent on world market prices for minerals. These tended to boom and bust. There were severe depressions in the 1890s and from 1907 to 1909, both of which sent ore prices plummeting. Prices were high during the late 1910s as a result of World War I. The market for cattle was predominantly, though not entirely, domestic. Ranchers in the Mexican state of Chihuahua, the location of Corralitos, for example, shipped cattle both to Mexico City and across the border. Because domestic demand was steadier, the boom and busts of the cattle market were not as pronounced as in mining.

Access to inexpensive transportation contributed to the mining boom after 1884. The ten thousand miles of new railroads built in Mexico hauled hundreds of thousands of tons of ores. Spur lines and regional lines that spread out across the mining regions stimulated exploration and revived old camps. The Revolution badly disrupted transportation with the railroads all but shut down for commercial traffic from 1913 to 1917, making it nearly impossible to transport ore to refineries or to the market or to obtain necessary equipment and supplies, most importantly coal.

The workforce for mining and cattle ranching, particularly in the northern part of the country, was a problem for operators. Skilled cowboys and miners were much in demand in the United States and northern Mexico. Wages in the United States were double those in Mexico. In times of economic downturn, labor was less scarce, but demand was lower as well.

Relations between foreign firms and the various levels of Mexican government depended on three sets of circumstances. First, the Mexican elite owned the rich natural resources that foreigners sought to develop and controlled the various levels of government, which regulated economic activities. Second, the native elite, for the most part, was willing to allow foreigners to develop the nation's resources, to participate in a wide range of economic endeavors, and even to dominate certain sectors, most importantly mining. The national elite saw in this a great advantage for themselves. They were ideologically committed to modernizing the country; foreign investment and expertise was the fastest and most efficient way to industrialize. Each group regarded foreign businesses as providing opportunities to augment income through sale and lease of property, bribes, and commissions. Development through foreign investment also preserved elite privilege and the political status quo. Finally, foreigners possessed the capital and technology to exploit the nation's resources, neither of which was available in Mexico.

The relations between native elite and foreign business involved the participation of two (at times three) elite groups—national and state (and local). Arrangements were complicated by the conflicts between elite at the different levels. The treatment of foreigners evolved from widespread hostility through the 1880s to general cooperation during the first decade of the twentieth century to varying degrees of unwelcome in the revolutionary civil war between 1910 and 1917, and harsh treatment in the 1920s and 1930s. Conduct toward foreigners varied according to the interests of the affected elite. Foreign companies usually obtained better treatment from the national government, whose policy it was to encourage investment from abroad, than at the local and state levels. The Revolution brought profound changes to the relations between the five groups. In the decade of civil war, 1910 to 1920, widespread destruction ruined the economic base of much of the elite of the Díaz regime and stripped it of most of its political power. The new national revolutionary elite, learning from the lessons of the defeated Díaz dictatorship, sought to centralize authority through a series of practical strategies, which included the use of the support of the popular classes to overcome strong regional elites. For the two decades after 1920, state and local elite factions fought for political power, the contests complicated by the existence of the remnants of the prerevolutionary elite, emergent popular class organizations, and a resurgent national regime.

Individual entrepreneurs poured into Mexico from Europe and the United States in search of opportunity. They farmed, mined, promoted, and sold. A small minority became wealthy. Most foreign entrepreneurs failed miserably. Much more than the large companies and their employees, they dealt directly with government at the state and local levels, with state and local elite, and with the rest of Mexico's people and society. In the instances of the small- and medium-scale businesses, the operators of which may well have intended to make their permanent homes in Mexico, it was quite clear that to earn success they had to make connections and assimilate. Most likely, they accomplished these by learning to speak Spanish and by marrying themselves or their children into the local society. For the most part, however, investors, small, medium, or large, despite often earning intermittent successes, no matter whether before, during, or after the Revolution, almost inevitably failed.

Perhaps the crucial element for success for small- and medium-scale enterprises was integrating into the local economy and society. But this was not an uncomplicated endeavor. Britton Davis, who had come to Mexico in the 1880s and had had a long career in mining and ranching, advised newcomer Morris B. Parker to "let their politics alone, let their religion alone, let their women alone, and you will have no difficulty."[36] But, for the most part, with the obvious exception of religion, Davis was mistaken. Foreigners quite clearly had to establish political connections in order to obtain subsidies, tax exemptions, mining claims, public lands, and protection. Moreover, intermarriage into local and national elites was often the surest method to acquire such connections.

Along the same lines, Otheman Stevens, writing a few years later, warned that "the American who comes here expecting Mexico and the Mexicans to think as he does, to adapt themselves and their conditions to his idea of things as they should be, can best serve himself by taking the next train home. . . . But the American who comes here and employs some sense and discretion, who does not expect a miracle to happen, who does not believe that Mexico will greet him 'with vine leaves' in her hair, will make good, big money."[37] Stevens was quite correct, but may have been a bit too optimistic.

Foreigners found that there were ways to survive even in chaotic times. E. B. Foster related to the *Engineering and Mining Journal* in 1924 his sure method for getting along in Mexico: "Pay your taxes, dues, etc. Treat the peon and the upper class with the same respect that you would demand for yourself, and you will find that Mexico is no Wild West Show."[38]

Despite the difficulties, there were notable success stories. John Brittingham was for a half-century, spanning the Porfiriato and the Revolution through the 1940s, a linchpin of the impressive domestic entrepreneurship in Chihuahua, the Laguna region of Durango, and Monterrey.[39] Patricio Milmo and Joseph Robertson prospered as founders of the Monterrey group.[40]

There existed a historical division between those foreigners who arrived before the late 1890s and those who came afterward. Assimilating and making connections were least difficult for the Europeans who arrived before the construction of the railroad network during the 1880s. The earliest entrepreneurs did not intend to return home, actively sought marriage, and readily acquired the language.[41] One observer noted that the German community in Chihuahua, leaders in the new industrial life of the region, made "common cause with their adopted land, assumes no airs of superiority, and pays deference to local customs, and ideas."[42] The 142 Germans who resided in Guadalajara in the first decade of the twentieth century also "integrated into the social and economic life" of the city.⁴³ The US consul in Ciudad Juárez in 1906 observed that foreigners in Chihuahua, particularly the Americans, "were intimately associated with Mexicans of all classes in business, socially, and by marriage and friendship."⁴⁴

The extent of assimilation decreased after the numbers of foreigners, particularly from the United States, increased so much after 1898 that they could (and did) isolate themselves among the foreign community and still find success. Those foreign entrepreneurs who located themselves close to the US border, by the first decade of the twentieth century an area thick with norteamericanos, had an increased likelihood of success. But even this was for only a short time. The Revolution and its aftermath put an end to all but the sturdiest and most persistent enterprises; those that had the six attributes mentioned earlier likely survived and the others did not.

The pattern of failure held true for all but the largest investors, such as the Guggenheim family and their smelters' trust, the American Smelting and Refining Company, and the multinational British and American oil companies. Large, foreign companies were an important part of Mexico's economic landscape after the construction of the major north-south railroads in the 1880s. US corporations constructed and managed the important railroads until the Mexican government consolidated them from 1902 to 1911.⁴⁵ Foreign companies were preeminent in the export sector of the Mexican economy (minerals and petroleum) as well as much of the banking system. Despite the tremendous dislocations of a decade of violence, the large corporations continued their crucial role in the Mexican economy through the 1930s. In mining the Revolution actually brought about further concentration in the control of foreign multinationals.

Of course, if the foreign enterprises were not profitable then the issue of exploitation, so prominent in some revolutionary propaganda and in some historical views, is subject to questioning.⁴⁶ I would argue further that even those companies that generated profits did not exploit Mexico. They often built industries where none had existed. They did not usually mistreat their workers, in fact paying them equal to or above the going rate for any region or providing at least as good working and living conditions as the highly dangerous occupation in isolated areas would allow. Miguel S. Wionczek in referring to the electric power industry in Mexico states the situation well:

They came to the country in search of profits on their capital and experience and found and took full advantage of the opportunities afforded by a growing laissez-faire economy. They came to Mexico—they thought—to stay forever and, in their own way, they believed in Mexico's future. They made a large contribution to the growth of the country's economic infrastructure which after the revolutionary upheaval was to serve as a physical base for the next stage of Mexico's modernization, coinciding with the international boom of the 1920s.[47]

GOVERNMENT

The investigations of the policies and actions of the Mexican government with regard to economic development and relations with business over time have focused primarily on three areas: (1) favoritism or discrimination (during the Porfiriato and Revolution, respectively for or against foreign investors and entrepreneurs); (2) attempts to promote economic development through public policy; and (3) informal and formal arrangements, known by political economists as "credible commitments" or sometimes as "crony capitalism."[48]

Underlying these approaches are the differences in view about the role the Mexican state played in economic development. It is my notion that the national government (the state) was a proactive participant, acting as an intermediary or coordinator among the vying groups. The state was never during the period under study powerful enough to impose its economic will and often had considerable limitations on its political power, as well. The primary goal of the state at any particular time was to maintain both Mexican sovereignty and the current regime.

Favoritism/Discrimination

Generally historians have viewed Mexico under the Díaz regime as favorably disposed toward foreigners and the Revolutionary regimes quite difficult for them.[49] I maintain, however, that the Porfirians were not nearly as welcoming as supposed, particularly at the regional and local levels, and that the revolutionaries, for the most part, followed a similar pattern; that is, they were not nearly as hostile, as some believe. Díaz and his revolutionary successors faced the same dilemmas about locating the correct balance between the need for external capital and technology to rebuild and develop the Mexican economy, maintaining national sovereignty, and satisfying vociferous domestic political demands.

Authorities on all levels were acutely aware of the growing clout of foreigners after 1900. The national government moved to curtail the foreign entrepreneurs with new commercial codes and mining laws. Díaz and Limantour moved to consolidate the railroad network to prevent takeover by US trusts. Limantour, for example, was particularly concerned with the possibility that the Fundición Hierro de Monterrey, the nation's major steel mill, would fall into bankruptcy in the depression of 1908 and fall into the hands of the U.S. Steel Trust, proposing steps to keep it solvent with a large order of steel rails and other steel products from the National Railways.[50] On the local level the sentiment was similar, though the execution of policy was, perhaps, a bit cruder. In Chihuahua the local newspaper warned of the threat of the great trusts in Mexico.[51] In 1904 the Chihuahua City Council passed an ordinance requiring that all signs on stores and factories be written entirely in Spanish or in both the foreign language and Spanish.[52] There were also reports that during the Porfiriato local elites resented foreigners because they raised wages.[53] The *South American Journal* revealed that a so-called group of miners publicly objected to the outflow of resources resulting from foreign ownership of mines.[54]

One indication of just how tough the policies adopted by Díaz and Limantour were on foreign businesses was the reaction of Daniel Guggenheim, president of the American Smelting and Refining Company, the largest mining operation in Mexico, to a new mining law proposed in 1908:

> The new mining law is a most concrete example of the apparent desire on the part of the government of Mexico to place an undue burden upon the capital which has already been invested by citizens of this and other countries in Mexico, and which will make it absolutely impossible in the future for such capital to be invested in Mexico.[55]

This was particularly shocking to Guggenheim because of past "most favorable supervision, regulations and laws on behalf of Mexico on behalf of my family."

As the railroad companies and Wall Street financiers discovered during the Mexican government's consolidation of the railroad system, Limantour was no pushover. He was a tough negotiator, meticulously guarding the government's prerogatives. But he seemed fair. In two instances in dealing with Weetman Pearson's interests, his evenhandedness is apparent. In the first, involving financial recordkeeping for the Tehuantepec Railway, he made every effort to accommodate the company, though he questioned its methods quite thoroughly.[56] In the second, he showed himself "stubborn" in refusing to waive taxes on oil tankers because "it was not onerous on such a remunerative business."[57]

There is considerable disagreement among historians about the role that economic nationalism played in the Revolution. One view has it that anti-foreign sentiment abounded and was crucial in motivating people to rebel.[58] However, Alan Knight has maintained that economic nationalism and anti-American sentiment in particular were not widespread in Mexico during the Revolution. Clearly, Chinese and Spaniards were set upon harshly, but other foreigners experienced no worse than Mexicans. Knight quotes US consular reports from Saltillo and Nogales in 1913 and 1915 respectively that "with few exceptions Americans are being well and justly treated by higher authorities . . . there have been no flagrant confiscations of American property, personal or real."[59] He concurs, of course, that there were losses, but that they were limited. US interests were not particularly damaged. In the early 1920s the only difference from the Díaz era was that "the disturbed conditions of recent years appear to have hastened the tendency for properties to be concentrated in comparatively few hands, since the larger companies have been able to secure for themselves a degree of protection not possible to the smaller ones."[60] Of course there were some rebel bands with grudges—the revolutionaries in northwestern Chihuahua certainly had no love lost for the Mormon settlers in their region and forced them out in 1912, for example—but the overwhelming sentiment was not hostile.[61] The foreigners had often brought employment and in the north higher wages.

Treatment depended a great deal on the time and place. A group of forty-four oil executives wrote to US President Woodrow Wilson in 1916 that "it has become almost impossible for an American to do business of any nature in this section of the country because of restrictions placed by the authorities that we believe to be directed primarily against Americans. . . . For a year a series of decrees have made their appearance which have been progressive in that they are consistently becoming more anti-American."[62] This, of course, was an exceptional time because the United States had just invaded Mexico a little more than a month earlier (the Pershing Expedition began on March 14). The myth of mistreatment owed primarily to the loud complaints of Americans, such as the above, affected by the difficulties inherent in warfare. More often than not the Americans exaggerated their losses and the severity of their treatment in the hopes of obtaining compensation from the Mexican government through the mechanism of an international claims commission. Foreigners were not more adversely affected than wealthy or middle-class Mexicans with land, mines, or factories.

Economic Development Policies

Recently, historians, such as Edward Beatty and Sandra Kuntz Ficker, have uncovered evidence that indicates that, although most of governments' actions were ad hoc, both Díaz and the revolutionaries who succeeded him had coherent, if not always successful, economic policies.[63] Neither adhered to any ideological or theoretical approaches, but underlying their policies was the firm determination to develop Mexico through the use of foreign investment and technology, to encourage domestic industry, to maintain a balance of power between foreign and Mexican interests, and to sustain their respective regimes by juggling domestic political demands.

Although the emphasis was on the export economy, the Díaz government, was interested in import substitution and, according to Beatty, actively promoted domestic manufacturing by providing "protection to national industries that would . . . [otherwise] be annihilated by foreign competition."[64] Beatty argues that the goal was development, through the use of foreign capital and technology. But this did not exclude domestic industrialization. Nor did the Porfirian regime give away Mexico, the propaganda of some of the revolutionists of 1910 notwithstanding. Much of the economic reform carried out by the Díaz government, however, aimed to ease the path of foreigners to acquire land, mineral rights, and timber. In order to clear a path for development the Mexican government had to restructure property rights, commercial law, patents, and contracts. It also adopted legislation to facilitate the distribution of public lands and eliminate internal taxes on commerce, all of which benefited both foreign and domestic entrepreneurs.[65] Beatty maintains that the regime's policies with regard to tariffs, patents, and tax exemptions "formed a coherent set of pro-industrial policies designed to encourage investment in domestic production. Their administration, moreover, was generally even-handed, competent, and consistent."[66]

In the tumult of seven years of civil wars and at least two years of them, 1914 and 1915, when there was barely a functioning national government—alternating between Conventionalists (Villa and Zapata) and Constitutionalists (Carranza and Obregón)—we can hardly expect there to have been much well-thought-out policy for economic development. But certainly Villa and Carranza had policies toward foreign companies. Each faction sought to obtain the most revenue without, at least initially, killing the goose that laid the golden egg. In one instance in 1915 Villa advanced the Madera Company of Chihuahua, a lumber mill, 500,000 pesos so that it could pay its bills and continue operating.[67] On the local level there was somewhat less attention paid to the long term and thus some provincial rebels shortsightedly robbed and pillaged.

The Constitution of 1917 was by one measure an all-encompassing effort to retain (at least on paper) or perhaps reestablish the balance between foreign capitalists and the Mexican government. Fred Adams, who was a member of the boards of directors of three railroad companies, a bank, and various other businesses, wrote a memorandum to Weetman Pearson in 1917 outlining the extensive impact of the articles of the constitution on foreign investment, which he attributed to the virtually impossible notion that Mexico could redistribute wealth to its workers and enable its industry to compete on the world market.[68] But his complaints all pointed to the revolutionaries' purpose of attaining the balance of forces.

After nearly a decade of war the reconstruction of the economy was paramount to the revolutionary administrations of General Alvaro Obregón and his successor General Plutarco Elías Calles.[69] This required a delicate balancing of forces and interests. Calles, for example, permitted the International Telephone and Telegraph Company (ITT) to purchase the Mexican Telegraph and Telephone Company in 1925 and renegotiated more favorable terms for the concessions of it and its major rival Ericsson in order to encourage the growth of the industry. Calles, however, at the same time, insured a specified percent of the profits and discounted service for the government.[70]

New to the mix of contestants were labor unions, most importantly, the formidable Confederación Regional de Obreros Mexicanos (CROM), led by Luis Morones, and organized peasant groups. Powerful regional bosses, military officers, and remnants of the oligarchy of the old regime also demanded their due. The clamoring masses, often still armed, demanded land redistribution and improved working conditions. But they all needed sustenance and employment, which required economic development. The latter required investment capital, but neither domestic nor foreign investors would likely have risked their funds in an environment of radical reform.

By the mid-1930s, the Revolution had not fulfilled its promises for reform, especially in the countryside. However, President Cárdenas distributed forty million acres of land, wholeheartedly backed labor union demands for higher wages and better conditions, and underlined the government's control of the nation's resources, all of which the Constitution of 1917 had mandated almost two decades earlier. But Cárdenas, for all his radical innovations, was very careful about keeping the various interests competing for reward in balance.[71]

Credible Commitment

The most recent examination of government economic policies during the period of the Porfiriato and Revolution assesses how these regimes managed economic growth despite the absence of institutions and legal structures that would facilitate development. The governments of Díaz, Carranza, Obregón, and Calles had no structure of institutional or legal restraints. Because they were strong enough to define and arbitrate property rights, there was an ever-present possibility that they would abrogate them for their own benefit. Accordingly, unless these governments could convince investors that they would not act in their own short-run interest by seizing property or levying confiscatory taxes, they would not invest.[72] Lack of investment then would result in limited economic activity and insufficient tax revenues for the government. Consequently the government had to find a way to limit its own actions in order to assure its own long-term survival. The answer to this dilemma, the "commitment problem," in a dictatorship like that of Porfirio Díaz and the postrevolutionary regimes through 1940, according to this interpretation, lay in the fact that investors cared above all for the sanctity of *their own* property rights. They did not require that government protect property rights as a public good or in general practice. With this in mind, the government could set up mechanisms for credible commitments to selected asset holders. "These mechanisms neither require the rule of law nor a stable polity. What they require is credible threats of retaliation by investors."[73] The threat could come from either a foreign power of possible intervention or a powerful political group aligned with investors. Vertical political integration, the blurring of the lines between asset holders and the government, enabled the credible commitment to function.

In Mexico Díaz, with an unstable polity and weak formal political institutions, lacking an administrative structure to collect taxes, having limited possibilities of obtaining foreign loans because of past defaults, and having scarce domestic resources available to finance his government, nonetheless, established "order and progress" by eschewing the protection of property rights globally and instead protecting the property rights of a select group of asset holders and using the rents generated from this selective protection to either buy off or coerce political opponents.[74] In order to obtain the funds to co-opt his opponents, Díaz had to encourage investment. This in turn demanded that Díaz enforce property rights "as private, not public, goods. It also required Díaz to make a credible commitment to select asset holders."[75] Díaz in effect created monopolies for his privileged supporters. Díaz also had to provide asset holders with the means to monitor the government and enforce their privileges. Consequently, the dictator integrated economic elites directly into the governing process and involved regional bosses in businesses dependent on government actions. "He turned potential political enemies into third-party enforcers of the property rights system he was creating with Mexico's asset holders."[76] Díaz's vertical political integration proved quite successful.

With the eruption of revolution in 1910 and the subsequent destructive civil war that ensued until 1920, Mexico once again returned to a condition of regional fragmentation that had existed before 1880. Historians have paid scant attention to economy during the decade of civil wars.[77] The state disintegrated for at least part of the decade; thus, it could not act to protect anyone's property rights. And it certainly could not function as an arbiter or maintain the balance of interests.

The new revolutionary government with General Alvaro Obregón (1920–24) at its head confronted a new set of regional bosses in its attempts to reestablish order and renew economic development. Obregón and his successor Plutarco Elías Calles (1924–28) constructed a "curious coalition of revolutionary generals turned landlords, Porfirian bankers and industrialists, and gangster-led unions" to replace the old Díaz system of vertical political integration (VPI).[78]

The VPI that emerged after 1940 replaced regional bosses with labor unions. The revolutionary government did not, like Díaz, bring businesspeople into politics, but rather pushed government into business. However, the system maintained its base on the selective enforcement of property rights for a privileged sector. The mechanisms were similar to those of the Díaz regime, as well. One national bank, Banco de México, obtained a monopoly on the issuance of currency and provided capital for powerful politicians (Obregón and Calles, for example) and loans to the government. Banco de México acted as "a punishment coordination mechanism" to keep the government from acting as a predator.

The difference between my elite-foreign enterprise system and the notions of credible commitment and vertical political integration revolve around two aspects of political economy in this period in Mexico. First is the evenness of the balance of competitors. I maintain that no group, neither regional nor national elites, nor foreign investors, nor the government at any level, was strong enough to dominate the others. This meant that no group could enforce a credible commitment. Most important, perhaps, was the inability of any national government to ensure favorable treatment of any enterprise at the state or local level. Second, I posit a more proactive role for the state (national government). According to one critic, the VPI model "virtually excludes the state and is insensitive to the changes in its role," and the "VPI model takes the state out, replacing it with coalition between the dictators and groups of asset holders . . . in a balance that does not account for historical evolution."[79] In the elite-foreign enterprise system the state is an active participant-intermediary.

Clearly, credible commitment is a rather ingenious analysis of the Díaz and revolutionary regimes. My positing of an elite-foreign enterprise system does not preclude regime self-limitation by means of the implicit threat of retaliation by its clients. Commitment is one part of the construct of checks and balances. It is part of the triangular relationship among national, state (or regional), and international interests.[80]

ELITE AND FOREIGN ENTERPRISE

The following factors governed the relations between Mexican elites and foreign business. First, the former owned the rich natural resources that foreigners sought to develop and controlled the various levels of government, which closely regulated economic activities. Second, Mexican elites often were willing to allow foreigners to develop the nation's natural resources, to participate in a wide range of economic endeavors, and even to dominate certain sectors, most importantly mining. The national elite saw in this great advantage to themselves. Its members regarded foreign businesses as providing opportunities to augment income through the sale and lease of property, bribes, and commissions. They were ideologically committed to modernizing the country. The use of foreign investment and expertise was the fastest and most efficient way to industrialize because it preserved elite privilege and the political status quo. Finally, foreigners possessed the capital and technology to exploit the nation's resources, neither of which was available in Mexico.

The relationship between foreign entrepreneurs and Mexican elite proceeded roughly as follows. An individual foreign entrepreneur or representative of investors from abroad arrived in Mexico in search of potentially lucrative mining or agricultural property. Often the foreigner acquired the services of a local promoter, knowledgeable about available mines or ranches. The next order of business was to purchase or lease a promising property from its local owner. The foreign entrepreneur hired a local or in the case of larger companies both a local and a Mexico City-based intermediary, usually a lawyer, with connections to the relevant authorities. The most famous of these were the científicos around Porfirio Díaz and José Yves Limantour and the partners in a number of firms in the capital that negotiated for such companies as the railroads and the American Smelting and Refining Company. The intermediary not only arranged for the sale of the property but also favorable treatment from various levels of government in such matters as taxation and concessions. The foreign firm retained the intermediary on an annual basis to ensure continued cooperation. Given the likelihood of long, costly litigation in the Mexican courts over disputed mining claims and property boundaries, it was imperative to obtain ongoing representation by well-connected intermediaries. It was common for foreign companies to place important government officials or their kin on their payrolls and boards of directors or to funnel stock to them. Mexican property owners usually sold outright, but occasionally they obtained stock in the company formed to exploit the mine or ranch or earned royalties.

Corruption, or at least what some historians have labeled corruption, in its various guises was an integral part of the system of relations among elite, foreign enterprise, and government. To some observers it was the essence of the Díaz administration and the single party state that followed after 1929.

Jesús Silva Herzog, the economist, bemoaned the corruption that accompanied the establishment of the one-party state: "Politics degrades and corrupts everything. . . . Politics is the easiest and most profitable profession in Mexico. . . . Immorality is most alarming in the Federal Public Administration, in the states and in the municipalities."[81] It is more than a little difficult to come up with direct evidence of corrupt practices. Businesspeople and politicians rarely admitted wrongdoing. But we do have some documentation. In 1903 Pedro Martínez del Río, one of the prominent Mexico City-based intermediaries between foreign companies and the Díaz government, remarked to his clients, the Douglas mining interests based in Arizona, that he thought that their attorney Calero had "allowed himself to be engrossed by legal arguments instead of securing other support, as I suggested to him."[82] Clearly Martínez del Río believed that they were wasting their time by going through bureaucratic channels and should use bribery to garner support.[83] Almost a year later, he wrote that Douglas had asked him

> to give Calero my assistance in Government circles and authorized me to engage the services of anyone that I might think desirable and to spend such sums of money as might be convenient in order to insure a successful issue. I accordingly engaged the assistance of a prominent lawyer who had the entrée with several judges of the Supreme Court, and besides this I personally took the matter up with the President and Minister Limantour.[84]

There is indication that the Revolution did not alter the way to conduct business. When during the Madero administration in April 1912, the Aguila Oil Company, controlled by Englishman Sir Weetman Pearson, who had been a favorite of Porfirio Díaz, had experienced some rough treatment from the revolutionaries, the manager of Pearson's interests in Mexico, John B. Body, wrote after meeting with Enrique C. Creel, a member of the company's board of directors, that "undoubtedly we must take action to counteract the effect of these agitations. It will cost a considerable amount of money to do so, but it is quite necessary."[85]

Another such instance emerged in a letter from an official of the Mexico Mines of El Oro, in the state of Mexico in 1922, who wrote:

> We have three judges here who are generally elected from the working class, and who have to return to work again after their year of office unless they have succeeded in laying away sufficient money in their own term of office by some means. . . . We propose as soon as the new set tale office to arrange that a certain sum, about 100 pesos, be paid monthly to each of them. Grafting is most distinctly universal in Mexico, but we have never done anything for judges here.[86]

It is obvious from this correspondence that the company had long practiced this form of bribery.

A mine manager writing in 1926 put it this way:

> I frequently give small gratuities to various officials in recognition of prompt and satisfactory service; as for example, to a certain local railway official when he sees that I get empty railroad cars when I need them. Also, I make fairly liberal contributions—entirely aside from local taxes—to funds that are collected personally by various officials of the pueblo . . . and to some other worthy causes. Frankly, I make no attempt to oversee disbursement of these funds. Nor do I know if any books are ever kept. I have also made "loans" for which I have no notes, and which will never be repaid.[87]

During the Revolution, the old system of influence peddling crumbled temporarily. Foreigners had to negotiate individually on an ad hoc basis with successive military commanders. Unfortunately for the foreign investors, none of these military honored the agreements of their predecessors. The Revolution was so fragmented and conditions so changeable that inevitably entrepreneurs' expenditures did not prevent the destruction of their properties. Business confronted an impossible bind. If a company paid taxes to one faction, the next group did not recognize the payment. Furthermore, whoever the current victor regarded previous tax payments as aiding and abetting the enemy.

The treatment of foreigners evolved from widespread hostility through the 1880s to general cooperation during the first decade of the twentieth century to varying degrees of indifference or unwelcome in the revolutionary civil war between 1910 and 1917, and sporadic harsh treatment in the 1920s and 1930s. At the regional and local level, conduct toward foreigners varied according to the interests of affected elites. Foreign companies usually obtained better treatment from the national government, whose policy it was to encourage investment from abroad, than from local and state levels. Foreigners, for example, often met hostility from local elite against whose economic interests they competed.

The Revolution brought profound changes to the relations between the five competing groups. In the decade of civil war, 1910 to 1920, widespread destruction ruined the economic base of much of the oligarchy of the Díaz regime and stripped it of its political power. The new, national elite, learning from the lessons of the defeated Díaz dictatorship, sought to centralize authority through a series of practical strategies, which included the use of the support of the popular classes to overcome strong regional oligarchies. For the two decades after 1920, state and local elite factions fought for political power, the contests complicated by the existence of remnants of the prerevolutionary elite, emergent popular class organizations, and a resurgent national regime.

From 1910 to 1920 it was crucial that any business operators, foreign or Mexican, get along with local authorities, who in times of highly uncertain conditions at the state and national levels, controlled their environment, regardless of policies promulgated from above. If one backed the wrong side, one paid dearly. In the aftermath of the fighting after 1920, when for more than a decade the central government struggled, often unsuccessfully, to reestablish some sort of working control of the economy and rebuild from the damages of war, enterprises more than ever had to maintain good relations with local and state authorities. That was not easy because many of the states endured strife between competing elite factions. In many areas there were radical demands from industrial workers for improved conditions and pay and from agrarian organizations for redistribution of lands from large estates.

The evolution of the Mexican state during the 1920s and 1930s was critical for its relations with foreigners. The Sonoran dynasty and its successor Cárdenas confronted several dilemmas. First, the economy was, if not in ruins, damaged by the travails of nearly a decade of warfare. It had not grown or experienced significant investment since 1913. Second, the transportation infrastructure was badly dislocated by the fighting. Third, agriculture needed to meet the demands for food. Fourth, people demanded employment after returning from the military. Fifth, international relations were shaky because of unpaid debts, damages to the property of foreign citizens, and irate investors. Sixth, the victorious freebooters wanted their rewards for brave services rendered—this meant everything from their own haciendas to government posts and local fiefdoms. Seventh, peasants and workers demanded land and better wages and labor conditions to fulfill the goals for which they had fought. Eighth, people in the countryside wanted to retain local autonomy, the "liberty" of their fight for "land and liberty." As is readily noticeable, the solutions to these problems were often contradictory.

Obregón and Calles put their fingers in the dike. Wherever strong pressure arose, they would yield, thus temporarily patching the wall. Land reform went ahead only in the face of demands from armed peasants, such as in Morelos or in areas where loyalty to the Revolution was too evident to ignore. They entered into an arrangement with the Confederación Regional de Obreros Mexicanos and its leader Luis Morones for higher wages in return for political support. Gradually it became evident that the place of the new regime, the national government, was to act as an intermediary, to insert itself between the constituents who demanded reforms and land redistribution and their goals. It was crucial to make the demanders beholden to the regime, not simple social or legal justice, for the achievement of their goals, thereby earning their loyalty thereafter. The revolutionary regime became the arbiter of all disputes. And the bureaucratic processes, often quite purposefully complicated, required to fulfill the demands became the source of considerable revenues and the bureaucracy of fulfillment became the source of enormous patronage.

This ad hoc approach to the various interest groups allowed Obregón and Calles to muddle through, but two crises led the revolutionary regime to a more permanent solution. First, the Cristero rebellion (1926–29), mainly in western Mexico, caused in great part by Calles's unrelenting persecution of the Catholic Church, shook the regime to its core. Second, Obregón, after winning election to a second term in 1928, fell to an assassin's bullets. Calles, the incumbent president, scrambled and found a series of temporary presidents to fill out the new six-year term. But he realized that the regime could not succeed in the long term without bringing the regions and their general-bosses under centralized control. His solution then was to organize the official party, the PNR, and to establish a one-party state. Instead of relying on one leader as had the Porfiriato and as the current regime would have had Obregón lived, the new mosaic of political arrangements would pass through the party.[88] Although many studies have concluded that the PNR and its successors (the Partido Revolucionario Mexicano, or PRM, and the Partido Revoluciónario Institucional, or PRI) became virtually omnipotent, recent investigations centered on the local level have revealed a far less powerful entity (and far more vicious), most especially before 1950. The PNR had to negotiate with many groups, peasants, workers, industrialists, bankers, and foreigners in order to maintain political and economic equilibrium, much the same as Díaz had before 1911.

CONCLUSION

The elite-foreign enterprise system, originated by Díaz and carried through after a difficult ten-year interval by the post-civil-war state under Obregón and Calles, and then readjusted through the evolving one-party state, established checks and balances.[89]

No one group was so powerful as to dominate the relationship. The state, with its varied strength over time, was the primary entity that maintained the equilibrium between contestants, for its own benefit and theirs. Both the pre- and postrevolutionary regimes were committed successively to exports and import-substitution industrialization, each of which depended on foreign capital for its success. Mexican governments, then, had to reach a balance that attracted foreign entrepreneurs but did not allow them to become too powerful. Díaz nationalized the foreign-owned railroads and Cárdenas expropriated the foreign-owned petroleum companies to maintain the equilibrium. Pre- and postrevolutionary governments, too, had to struggle to balance local, state, and national governments. The issue of local autonomy sustained through the entire period. For almost all of the era it was a more evenly balanced struggle than historians have assessed. The Revolution itself was to a large extent owed to a resurgence of local and regional prerogatives.

The Cárdenas regime was, perhaps, the last gasp of the elite-foreign enterprise system, for Cárdenas tried to even the balance between the industrial bourgeoisie and labor unions, between large landowners (including revolutionary generals) and peasants, and between foreign investors and the government. The result was that the balance tilted to the national government, which as the ultimate arbiter grew stronger and stronger. The checks on Díaz and a series of revolutionary leaders from Francisco I. Madero through Abelardo Rodríguez by regional elites eroded, though they did not disappear entirely, leaving the national government, the one-party state, much more powerful than ever.

The evidence to be presented is anecdotal. Most foreign farmers, ranchers, planters, and miners did not leave memoirs or any other records. Consequently, there is always the possibility of skewed samples. History may have recorded the "losers" better because they complained to their consular agent or congressional representative. Certainly this was true of some of the most notorious cases, such as William Benton and Rosalie Evans. I have no substantive cumulative or comparative statistics, so it is not possible at this point to have a sense of what exact percentage of foreign businesses were profitable. Nor can we determine if the foreigners collectively were more or less profitable than their domestic competition. What we do come up with is a sense that Mexicans in fact controlled their economy from the 1880s through 1940. Foreigners did not exploit the country. (At least no more than any other businesses would have in trying to make a profit.) And Mexicans established, sometimes shakily, sometimes unplanned, a system of relations among foreigners, elite, and government (and later unions and peasant organizations) that maintained checks and balances on all parties. Whether this system turned out best for the long-term economic and political development of Mexico is a subject for another book. Now let us turn to specific examples of how the elite-foreign enterprise system operated.

TWO

Mexican Entrepreneurs

Family firms were at the core of Mexican entrepreneurship from the nineteenth century through the mid-twentieth century. Founded by exceptional patriarchs, who often were influential in politics and government, as well as business, these kinship groups commonly allied with other similar, important groups in their own region or neighboring regions in major undertakings, such as banking and manufacturing. The families were enormously resilient, some of them contesting the regime of Porfirio Díaz and then surviving the Revolution and revolutionary reconstruction. Although the founding patriarchs were often humbly born and began their labors in the crafts, as small merchants, soldiers, or modest ranchers, they almost always came to base their wealth on land ownership. Those most likely to outlive the Revolution, however, were diversified (commonly on both sides of the northern border) into other sectors. The crucial elements to long-term success were political connections, best to be had at all levels from local to national, but sufficient if just on the local or regional levels; economic diversification in order to avoid the risks of individual sectors such as ranching, farming, mining, industry, or banking; the willingness to work with foreigners to obtain access to capital and technology; and competent leadership after the patriarch.

The system of relations among the national government, state or local elites, and foreign businesspeople both before and after the Revolution was based on the Mexican elite's ownership of the nation's exploitable resources and control of government at the various levels, and foreign entrepreneurs' possession of capital and technology. In a typical case, a Mexican landowner would sell a mining or agricultural property to a foreign individual or company. In order to facilitate the negotiations the foreigner hired a local representative to arrange purchase or lease and to obtain the needed tax exemptions, concessions, and subsidies. Usually, the foreigners also required representatives at each level of government.[1] Regional elites similarly had to contract the services of local representatives in order to conduct business in other regions and in Mexico City.

A half-century of disruptions after independence had taught Mexican (and other Latin American) elites the necessity of acquiring political power, at least to the extent that allowed them to control their immediate environment. Control of local government was crucial to protect their haciendas, mines, and commerce from extortion, robbery, and erratic law enforcement; control of politics at the regional level provided even more security. Throughout the nineteenth century, local elites therefore fought bitterly to maintain local and state political power to protect and expand their economic holdings. It is not the least surprising that the four greatest tycoons of the Porfiriato—Luis Terrazas, Enrique C. Creel, Evaristo Madero, and Olegario Molina—were state governors for extended periods. Political influence was no less important in the aftermath of the revolutionary civil wars between 1910 and 1920, as prominent generals and politicians such as Aarón Saenz, Alvaro Obregón, Plutarco Elías Calles, and Abelardo Rodríguez used their positions to enhance their fortunes.

During the Porfiriato, the family-based regional entrepreneurs, like the Terrazas-Creels, the Maderos, the Molina-Montes, and various groups in Monterrey and the Laguna (Coahuila and Durango), sometimes contested with and at other times shared power with an influential circle of Mexico City headquartered intermediaries, known as the científicos, who virtually monopolized access to national government largesse. Added to the mix, too, were state-level camarillas, best illustrated by the group around the Sonoran triumvirate, headed by Ramón Corral, Díaz's widely despised vice president, and regional bosses, such as General Bernardo Reyes of Nuevo León. During the civil wars between 1910 and 1920, these various groups scrambled to survive. The Madero family, of course, most notably, reached for national power, as did Reyes, but neither ultimately succeeded. Others, like the Terrazas-Creel and Molina, went into exile. A few, most obviously Montes in Yucatán and most of the Monterrey entrepreneurs, stayed throughout to protect their interests. In the aftermath of the Revolution, the Porfirian entrepreneurs struggled against and negotiated with new groups of generals, politicians, and businesspeople.

E. Alexander Powell in 1910 summed up the feelings of many foreigners who conducted business in Mexico during the regime of Porfirio Díaz: "All the great financial deals in which the government is interested pass through their [científicos] hands and are molded by them. . . . Among them [científicos] numbered the presidents of the leading banks of the republic and the foremost corporation lawyers; between them they control the national finances and the avenues of trade."[2] This tight-knit inner circle that greatly influenced the dictator was comprised of José Yves Limantour, the group's leader, Ramón Corral, Enrique C. Creel, Guillermo Landa y Escandón, Joaquín Casasús, Fernando Pimentel y Fagoaga, Pablo Macedo, Rosendo Piñeda, and Hugo Scherer. Powell pointed particular venom at the Compañía Bancaria de Obras y Bienes Raíces, the Bancaria, which he called "a very convenient cloak for the grafters."[3] Not only has the general historiography concurred with this assessment until recently, but also it has extended the interpretation to the Revolution and revolutionary reconstruction periods (1910–40).[4] During the Revolution and reconstruction the names changed, but the new regime maintained a similar structure of insider deals. The Revolution replaced the científicos with shifting inner circles attached to each president, consisting of old school chums, military cronies, and blood relations. The revolutionary camarillas, as they are known, were equally as skilled at using political influence to enhance their economic interests as the Porfirians had been.[5]

This chapter will focus on the interactions of elites, foreigners, and government through the lens of two major family business networks, the Terrazas-Creels, as represented by Enrique C. Creel, and the Maderos, led by Evaristo Madero, two of the major entrepreneurial clans of the Porfiriato that survived the warfare of the 1910s and flourished in the postrevolutionary era. I have chosen these two because they offer differing examples of relations with other elite groups, national regimes, and foreigners. Creel was, perhaps, the preeminent intermediary between elite groups in the north (centered in Chihuahua, the Laguna, and Monterrey), between foreigners and northern elites, and between foreigners and the national regime. He was, to be sure, a facilitator (fluent in Spanish and English), but he was not a pushover or lackey of either foreign interests or the Díaz dictatorship. Evaristo Madero, no less an extraordinary businessperson, contrastingly, was not an intermediary, nor was anyone in his family. He cooperated with foreigners to some extent (although apparently only when in partnership with Creel), but as often as not was in direct, not necessarily friendly, competition with them.

ENRIQUE C. CREEL

No figure better reflected the close relationship between business and politics under the Díaz dictatorship, the Revolution, and reconstruction than Enrique C. Creel. Not only was Creel the second-in-command and the national and international representative of Mexico's most powerful regional political family and the son-in-law of Luis Terrazas, the nation's largest landowner and cattle rancher, but also he was himself the country's leading banker, perhaps the most influential Mexican representative of foreign capital, and one of the nation's most important industrialists. Creel was squarely at the fulcrum of the crucial events in business and politics for nearly fifty years. He was a member of the Monetary Commission of 1903, governor of Chihuahua from 1904 to 1910, headed Díaz's secret service along the northern border in 1910 and 1911, served as Mexican ambassador to the United States in 1910 and Díaz's secretary of foreign relations in 1910–11. After many years in exile during the Mexican Revolution, Creel returned to act as an important economic advisor to President Alvaro Obregón during the 1920s. We can learn much about the relation between business and politics during both the prerevolutionary and postrevolutionary eras by examining Creel's career.[6]

Enrique Creel was an unusual figure in Mexican business and politics, because he was both a very successful entrepreneur and an intermediary. Creel and his father-in-law mastered the arts of business and politics in the rough-and-tumble world of the northern border. But just as important as his dominance of Chihuahua's state government was his ability to profit from the influx of foreign investment after 1880. He adeptly used the capital and technological expertise of foreign entrepreneurs to expand his family's holdings. Unlike his contemporaries among the elite, because he had his own firm capital base, Creel did not negotiate with foreigners from a position of weakness.

Born in Chihuahua in 1854, the son of the US consul in Ciudad Chihuahua, Reuben W. and Paz Cuilty de Creel, Enrique showed an early aptitude for business, establishing himself as a merchant of note by the time he was twenty-three.[7] In 1880 he married Angela Terrazas, the daughter of Luis Terrazas, then the political boss of Chihuahua. It was a partnership of enormous profit for all concerned. For Creel the marriage brought access to his father-in-law's enormous capital, widespread family connections, and political clout. For the Terrazas, the alliance drew into the family a brilliant, ambitious young man, who led them into new economic areas, diversifying them from their traditional bases in land and cattle. Their varied holdings were the most important reason that the family survived the revolutionary years and flourished during revolutionary reconstruction.[8]

Marriage was an important political and economic tool of elite families in Mexico. They often injected "new blood" in order to acquire allies, financial backing, and social standing. In the north it was not uncommon for elites to bring foreigners into their families in order to obtain needed management or technical expertise. The Terrazas were particularly adept at strategic marriages, forging connections with virtually every important family in Chihuahua and much of the north. Luis Terrazas and Carolina Cuilty de Terrazas's dozen surviving children and seventy-one grandchildren created a vast network of familial ties.

THE BANKER

Creel earned his great prominence as a banker and international financier. As the overseer of the Terrazas banks, he supervised 200 million pesos in assets, almost one-fifth of the nation's total bank assets in 1910. He had substantial interests in banks in Chihuahua, Monterrey (Nuevo León), Mexico City, Guanajuato, Sonora, and the United States. He became the coordinator of various Mexican and foreign banking groups. With

José Y. Limantour, Díaz's minister of the treasury, Creel was the fulcrum of finance in Mexico.

His base was Banco Minero de Chihuahua. Founded with four partners in 1882, the bank, under Creel's supervision, grew from a modest investment of 100,000 pesos to a giant with 23.2 million pesos in assets in less than three decades. During that time, it earned more than 6 million pesos in dividends for its shareholders. By 1910 Banco Minero was Mexico's fourth-largest bank with branch offices all over northern Mexico. It was a major underwriter of foreign mining companies in Chihuahua and financed several native-owned industrial concerns.[9] As we see in Table 2.1 below, Banco Minero was at the very core of the northern network of investors into the Revolution.[10] These figures from 1916 reveal only a fraction of its influence because the bank had suffered enormous losses after 1911.

There were also substantial investments in the Batopilas Company, the Helena Mining Company, the Minas de Cobre Magistral, and the National Exchange Bank of El Paso.

Creel played a crucial role in coordinating native and foreign banking interests. He was associated with the Sonoran elite as president of Banco Mercantil de Cananea.[11] In partnership with Mexico City lawyer Joaquín Casasús and several Monterrey entrepreneurs, he founded Banco Mercantil de Monterrey in 1889.[12] Creel was also a large stockholder in Banco Oriental de México and a board member of Banco de Guanajuato.[13]

His most ambitious projects were two large banks in Mexico City. Creel founded Banco Central Mexicano in 1899 to provide "a mechanism in Mexico City" for state banks of emission to circumvent the currency monopoly of Banco Nacional. By 1910 it had become Mexico's second-largest bank, with assets of 90 million pesos.[14] In addition, Creel set up Banco Hipotecario de Crédito Territorial Mexicano, which had 38 million pesos in assets in 1910, to furnish long-term, low-rate mortgages to finance the modernization of agricultural properties.[15]

Creel's banking enterprises well illustrate the connections between business and politics prior to the Revolution. Political influence was crucial in building the Terrazas financial empire. As governor of Chihuahua, Luis Terrazas granted himself and his son-in-law a state charter for Banco Minero in 1882. He then defended the bank from the provisions of the national commercial code promulgated in 1884, which would have canceled its charter. The Díaz administration eventually compromised and granted

TABLE 2.1. Inventory of Banco Minero de Chihuahua Stockholdings as of August 1916

Company	Stockholdings (in pesos)
Compañía Cervecería de Chihuahua	97,000
Rastros de Torreón y Parral	18,900
Caja de Ahorros	50,000
Banco de la Laguna	96,000
Bancaria de Fomento y Bienes Raices	104,000
La Equidad, SA	12,000
Compañía Harinera de Chihuahua	16,900
Gran Unión de Licores	20,000
Perforadora Mexicana	29,000
Guarantee Trust	100,000
Minera La Reina	19,000
Minera La Juárez	17,000
Harinera del Golfo	37,500
Sindicato de Estudios	21,350
Cía Agrícola La Peregrina	137,500
Cía Agrícola Colonizadora	50,000
Compañía Eléctrica y de Ferrocarriles de Chihuahua	1,612,135
Pan American Railway	25,000

Source: Inventory of Banco Minero de Chihuahua, Aug. 31, 1916, CD 2, File 161, Papers of Enrique C. and Eduardo J. Creel, Centro de Estudios Históricos Mexicanos, CARSO.

the bank a new federal charter in 1888. Creel obtained state tax exemptions for all the family's banks. After he became governor in 1904, Banco Minero lent the state large sums to finance his administration's ambitious program of public works. Interest payments allowed the bank not only to survive but also to prosper during the severe depression that badly affected the rest of the Mexican banking community from 1907 to 1909.[16] Banco Minero was an important political tool in that it could provide financing for Terrazas-Creel's old allies and bring new allies into the fold.

Under Creel's leadership Banco Minero underwrote foreign mining companies. Most importantly Banco Minero financed Alexander Shepherd's

Batopilas enterprise. Banco Minero had helped get Shepherd started.[17] In 1899 Shepherd owed Creel 500,000 pesos on a signature loan. Creel was worried about Shepherd's ability to repay because the former was at odds with his shareholders at the time.[18] The company, which was constantly in debt, to the point in 1902 that Shepherd, unable to obtain further capital from his stockholders, mortgaged his house in Washington, DC, to raise funds. Despite Shepherd bringing "some uneasiness" to Banco Minero's board of directors, the bank stood by him.[19] Nonetheless, a decade later Creel called in a loan to Shepherd's son for the San Gil mine.[20] Banco Minero handled all of Batopilas's silver shipments for more than twenty-five years. It also paid the company's bills.[21]

The Terrazas-Creel banks fit into the general pattern analyzed by Noel Maurer for Porfirian banks, for they lent money mainly to family members, family-operated companies, and the family's business partners and political allies.[22] But Creel banks also invested in foreign-owned enterprises, such as Batopilas. "Insider lending," a very common occurrence in the United States, was, Maurer argues, a logical solution to the problem of the lack of information available about prospective lenders. He maintains that banks were engines of economic development, "not merely in spite of insider lending, but because of it."[23] The banks enabled Porfirian elite entrepreneurs to raise capital from investors in Mexico City and abroad, through selling stock in their banks that would then lend to their companies. Investors were aware that in buying bank stock they were in effect putting their funds into the enterprises of the members of the banks' boards. Interlocking memberships of the boards of directors served as a monitoring mechanism for the banks. The system proved quite profitable.

THE INTERMEDIARY

Creel was at the center of the intricate interplay of regional, national, and foreign economic interests during the Porfiriato. Although in exile during much of the Revolution, he returned in the 1920s to work behind the scenes in reconstructing the family's empire, participating in the formation of at least one of the nation's most important postrevolutionary economic groups. Prior to the Revolution he conducted business in four overlapping areas. In Chihuahua and along the northern border Creel brought together the capital of the local elite and border entrepreneurs, most of whom were North Americans. His second financial nexus was among the industrialists and landowners based in Monterrey and the Laguna region of Coahuila and Durango. Third, Creel worked out of the national capital to coordinate the interests of regional, Mexico City-based, and foreign investors. Lastly, Creel was a highly valued representative of large foreign corporations. He was one of the most visible of the científicos.

In the north Creel partnered with a number of foreigners, such as prominent border merchants Max Krakauer, Gustavo Zork, and Ben Degetau, speculator Max Weber, and mine manager Britton Davis, primarily through the El Paso-based Guaranty Trust and Banking Company and the Compañía Eléctrica de Ferrocarriles de Chihuahua, which provided electricity to Ciudad Chihuahua.[24]

Creel's connections with the Monterrey and Laguna elite centered on the Compañía Industrial Jabonera de la Laguna, S.A., and Banco Mercantil de Monterrey. Jabonera, as it was called, was organized in 1898 by the Terrazas-Creel, Juan Brittingham, a North American, and Tomás Mendrichaga, a Monterrey industrialist, landowner, and president of Banco Mercantil, as a cooperative venture joining the interests of cottonseed producers and processors. The company manufactured cottonseed oil, soap, and, most important, glycerin, a crucial element in high explosives. Although after 1902 a bitter dispute arose between the Laguna cotton planters and the company over the low prices for cottonseed, the Jabonera was typical of Creel's ambitious efforts to coordinate the business activities of various regional elites and to extend his family's economic empire beyond Chihuahua.[25] Creel, Mendrichaga, and Joaquín Casasús, a prominent científico and well-known fixer, founded Banco Mercantil in 1899. The bank served as the fulcrum of the axis between the Terrazas-Creels and Monterrey and included, among others, the Maderos.[26]

Creel perhaps reached his peak putting together Banco Central, Banco Hipotecario, and Compañía Nacional Mexicana de Dinamita y Explosiva, which joined together powerful regional, national, and foreign groups. For example, Banco Central's board of directors included northern industrialists Francisco Madero and Juan Brittingham, Mexico City wheeler-dealers Fernando Pimentel y Fagoaga, and Joaquín Casasús, and French entrepreneur Donato Chapeaurouge. J. P. Morgan and Company and Deutsche Bank and other foreign investors supplied half the capital.[27] Banco Hipotecario brought together the same mix of financial interests.[28]

The Compañía Nacional Mexicana de Dinamita epitomized the profitable combination of regional, national, and foreign interests and the importance of political influence during the Díaz era. Established by the Terrazas-Creel, Brittingham, the Financiera por la Industria en México (a consortium of Mexico City-based investors), and the Société Centrale de Dynamite of France, the company obtained a concession to manufacture dynamite in Mexico. With the cooperation of the Mexican government—the sons of both José Y. Limantour and Porfirio Díaz were on the board of directors—which raised the tariff on imported explosives and exempted the company from all import duties, the new trust acquired a monopoly on dynamite sales. With no competition the company set high prices that increased the costs for mining companies.[29]

Creel was the linchpin of these enterprises with a keen grasp of the role of politics in business and an uncanny ability to bring together disparate interests in order to raise capital; he was also fully capable of running the businesses themselves. It was no wonder that he was at the center of finance during the Porfiriato. He was the "man to see" in starting a business in Mexico "known for his ability and integrity" and for his knowledge of Mexico's resources.[30]

Creel was not the arch-typical intermediary. His resources were so enormous and his political power so strong that he did not play a subordinate role. In Chihuahua, there was no possibility of circumventing the Terrazas-Creel, even if you had direct access to the dictator himself. The American Smelting and Refining Company, Arthur Stilwell, the railroad tycoon, and William C. Greene, the copper skyrocket, had to pay dearly for his cooperation. The Mexican Central Railway paid him 50,000 pesos a year to sit on its board.[31] Giant ASARCO had to buy land from the Terrazas for its smelter near Ciudad Chihuahua.[32] Greene bought two mines for more than 800,000 pesos in order to acquire an enormous concession to mine and cut timber in western Chihuahua, while Creel was governor of the state.[33]

ENTREPRENEUR

Creel was a risk capitalist as well as an intermediary, employing his considerable financial and political resources to his advantage. He had ready capital in Banco Minero de Chihuahua and other banks and an eager network of coinvestors among the northern elites. His extensive political connections enabled him to obtain tax exemptions that increased profits. Creel also followed a distinct strategy in establishing his industrial empire. Recognizing that although he was an excellent manager, he did not have technical expertise, Creel hired foreigners to run the daily operations of many of his businesses. He took over a failing metal foundry in Ciudad Chihuahua and through shrewd management and an infusion of capital transformed it into the Compañía Industrial Mexicana, one of the largest and most modern metal fabrication facilities in Mexico.[34] Creel was successful in mining by both working mines and selling them to foreigners. He turned the Río Tinto mines in northern Chihuahua into moneymakers after several foreign firms had gone bankrupt.[35] Creel worked the Mercedes mine in Santa Eulalia and produced 500,000 pesos in ore.[36] He was a shrewd negotiator. In 1906 he leased his La Reina mine to the Mexican Mines Syndicate with a promise to purchase for the following terms: 10 percent of the silver mined with guaranteed rent that escalated from 100 pesos a month initially to 1,000 pesos a month in the third year. The foreigners were to buy the mine for 250,000 pesos within three years. If they did not purchase it, all improvements would remain with the owner. The company failed to buy the mine, and the Madero's Compañía Metalúrgica de Torreón took over the lease in 1908.[37]

At the turn of the century, perhaps taking his cue from businesspeople in the United States, Creel tried to establish trusts in flour milling and meat packing. He built a near monopoly in flour milling in Chihuahua, but he could not extend it elsewhere.[38] Creel also purchased the concession to operate the stockyards in Mexico City, but he was unable to establish a monopoly over beef distribution, eventually selling out at a profit to a foreign company.[39]

THE REVOLUTION

Like the rest of the Terrazas extended family, Creel suffered enormous losses during the Revolution, but his holdings were diverse and extensive and he consequently survived the storm.[40] While in exile, he struggled mightily to salvage what he could and to honor his debts. He spent a substantial amount of time seeing to the ramifications of the Carranza government's takeover of Banco Minero and the default of his insurance company La Equidad, S.A. Creel also worked hard from Europe and the United States to recover what he could of his extensive landholdings, lost to government intervention under both *villista* and *carrancista* rule. By his own estimate, Creel lost 5 million pesos in damages to his properties.

The first setback came in 1912, when the acting governor of Chihuahua, Felipe Gutiérrez, levied a forced loan on banks and individuals in the state on behalf of rebel Pascual Orozco, who had taken up arms against Francisco Madero. The Terrazas-Creel group put up more than 300,000 pesos or about 25 percent of the loans.[41]

Under the government of Pancho Villa from 1913 to 1915 in Chihuahua, the state confiscated the Terrazas-Creel estates and took over many of their businesses. By 1915 and 1916 Creel was burdened with heavy debt, especially to the National Park Bank in New York. The Mexican government takeover of his property tied up almost all his assets. He estimated his property was worth 2.5 million pesos, but he would have been satisfied to get a million for it. His only available asset was apparently the family house in Mexico City, but that was owned by his wife.[42] The biggest blow landed in 1916, when the Constitutionalists looted Banco Minero and then revoked its charter.[43] As late as the mid-1920s, the Mexican government still owed the bank more than a million pesos in loans.[44]

Although he lost most of his land, he kept the core of at least four Chihuahua haciendas, together extending over 185,000 acres, or approximately 10 percent of his earlier holdings.[45] In addition to his vast Chihuahua properties, he also was a principal in the Compañía Agrícola de la Torre and the Compañía Agrícola Colonizadora, which owned the Hacienda San Nicolás de la Torre in Querétaro and the Hacienda El Rusio in Veracruz, respectively, which were evidently not under government control, but heavily mortgaged, in default, and for sale. The de la Torre company owed Banco de Hipotecario de Crédito Territorial 950,000 pesos.[46] In 1917 the family had extensive contacts with Carranza in order to get its property disintervened.[47]

On behalf of Banco Minero, Creel undertook two major deals to liquidate its holdings. First, in 1918 he arranged to sell the bank's stock in the Alvarado Mining Company, El Refugio Mining Company, Montana Coal and Coke, the Esmeralda/Parral Mining Company, and the Compañía Carbonífera de Sabinas to A. J. McQuatters, a North American investor in

Chihuahua, for US$1,175,000.[48] Second, Creel unloaded the Huerta government bonds he had purchased in 1914.[49] Creel also sold off the Compañía Mineral El Magistral to ASARCO.[50] In 1915 he tried to unload his stock in the highly profitable Compañía Industrial Jabonera de la Laguna.[51]

Throughout the Revolution, the family maintained its headquarters in Mexico City, through Creel's sons and Francisco C. Terrazas, in El Paso, where the manager of Banco Minero, Juan A. Creel, Enrique's brother, lived, and in Los Angeles, where Creel resided most of the time. Creel's sons established Creel Hermanos during the Revolution to conduct business in Mexico and in California. Initially the firm had a million pesos, which it deposited in Banco Central. However, the revolutionary government confiscated the money in 1915.[52] In 1912 Eduardo J. Creel returned to Mexico City, setting up a mercantile firm Eduardo J. Creel y Compañía.[53]

Creel's sons retained control of a number of important businesses in Chihuahua, including the Compañía Eléctrica y de Ferrocarriles de Chihuahua. Creel had US$1.5 million invested in the company, which the government took over in February 1914. Then, during the desperate days of 1915, Creel offered it to ASARCO for US$350,000, but the giant corporation declined.[54] By 1917, however, the company was earning a profit, which the management reinvested in the railroad it operated.[55] The Creels also invested in properties during the Revolution, such as in 1914 in the Compañía La Peregrina, S.A. But by 1920 the enterprise owed Creel US$300,000; he tried to sell his stock, but he was unsuccessful.[56]

Creel returned to Mexico in the early 1920s, becoming an important financial adviser to the Obregón government. Many of his recommendations provided a basis for the regime's fiscal and monetary policies during the decade. He wrote and spoke widely on public finance. He died in 1931.[57] The Creel and Terrazas families received compensation for their expropriated lands, later regained a considerable part of their holdings, allied with new, emerging entrepreneurs, and once again became powerful in business and politics through to the present day.[58]

THE MADERO FAMILY

The Madero family, based in Coahuila and Monterrey, was at the center of the crucial network of northern entrepreneurs who were so important to the Mexican economy from the mid-nineteenth century through the Porfiriato, Revolution, and revolutionary reconstruction. Evaristo Madero, like Luis Terrazas, built a great empire through entrepreneurship and familial and political connections. In 1910 the *El Paso Morning Times* referred to him as a "Mexican Croesus," the largest cattle owner other than Luis Terrazas with a personal fortune estimated at US$20,000,000.[59] The Maderos owned the largest Mexican-owned smelting operation in Mexico, were important agriculturalists in the Laguna region of Coahuila, and were involved with the Terrazas and the Monterrey interests in many industrial and banking concerns.[60]

Unlike the Terrazas-Creel, the Madero's influence in regional politics was not omnipotent and their relations with foreigners much more ambiguous and sometimes contentious. Although their influence reached into the highest echelons of the national government, the family consistently ran afoul of dictator Díaz and by no means held sway in Coahuila or La Laguna. Although their closest partners outside the family were foreigners, like Juan. F. Brittingham and Patricio Milmo (Mullins), at the same time they competed fiercely against foreigners in at least three businesses, guayule and cotton farming and smelting. Because they did not have control of state government, their bargaining position in their rivalry with foreigners was not nearly as powerful as that of the Terrazas. Apparently, the Maderos joined with foreigners only when the Terrazas-Creel were involved as well. Unlike Creel, no Madero family members functioned as intermediaries.

The patron of the family, Evaristo, born in 1828, like both Luis Terrazas and Enrique Creel, was a prodigy. His father died when he was five. He married at nineteen. Evaristo began his career as a freighter along the recently drawn border between Mexico and the United States. At first he operated mule and wagon trains out of Villa Guerrero and Rio Grande in Coahuila, soon moving on to trading contraband silver bullion, wool, and hides across the border in return for dry and manufactured goods. His wife Prudencia brought him into a very important Nuevo León family, the González Treviño.[61]

Evaristo Madero earned a fortune in border trade, in particular generating enormous profits from Confederate cotton during the US Civil War in the 1860s, when the Union navy blockaded southern ports, leaving only outlets through Mexico to export to markets in Europe. In his illicit trade Madero benefited from the protection of Santiago Vidaurri, the political boss of Nuevo León and Coahuila. Much like Luis Terrazas, who used the huge revenues from cattle sales to create a diversified economic empire during the 1880s, Evaristo used the income from his mercantile business to buy land and expand into industry and banking. His first investments were to obtain for US$300,000 a huge ranch in Coahuila that included an old winery, then a number of flour mills and a textile mill. From the late 1860s to the 1880s he saw an enormous opportunity in the Laguna region, buying the haciendas El Rosario and San Lorenzo and moving to Parras.

Like the Terrazas, the Maderos relied heavily on their family connections. Evaristo Madero had eighteen children, and between them his children, grandchildren, and great-grandchildren numbered 124.[62] Many married into prominent families. Most important were his own marriage into the González Treviño, important landowners and politicians in Nuevo León, and his daughters' marriages to Antonio Hernández and Viviano Villarreal. He also had marriage ties to the Monterrey families Zambrano and Sada Muguerza. With nine sons and numerous sons-in-law, he had a substantial pool of managers to succeed him.[63]

The Madero family also had widespread contacts. Evaristo carried on an extensive correspondence with José Y. Limantour, the finance minister and head of the científicos.[64] The Maderos had close relations with the Terrazas, as well. For example, in 1904 Evaristo accompanied Luis Terrazas on a tour of the latter's properties in the company of General José María de la Vega, the military zone commander, Daniel Madero, and many members of the Creel and Terrazas families.[65] The Monterrey elite, consisting of the Garza, Muguerza, Sada, Milmo, Rivera, and Calderón families were their steady allies.

MINING AND SMELTING

The Maderos first became involved in mining in 1868 in Zacatecas. However, their most important mining and smelting venture was the Compañía Metalúrgica de Torreón, a smelter, which the Maderos organized in 1900 and began its operations in 1902 with 1,250,000 pesos capital, increased to 1,750,000 pesos in 1903, 3.5 million pesos in 1904, and 7 million in 1907. The company was very profitable. It declared dividends of 18 pesos in 1902, 14 pesos in 1904, 12 in pesos in 1905, 12 pesos in 1906, and 6 pesos in 1909. It declared no dividends in 1907 and 1908 in order to set aside a reserve fund for the early redemption of company bonds. Its annual profits were excellent. (See Table 2.2 below.) In 1905 the Compañía Metalúrgica de Torreón was regarded as one of the most prosperous enterprises in Mexico.[66]

The Maderos spent huge sums first in order to ensure that the smelter in Torreón had sufficient ores to process, second to supply the smelter with fuel (coal) to operate, and third to provide lead for processing ore. The Madero brothers bought the Los Remedios mine in 1901.[67] Their Compañía Metalúrgica purchased the Americana mine in Terrazas, Chihuahua, from F. McDonald and the Dale brothers for 100,000 pesos in 1903.[68] Ernesto Madero purchased a coal mine in San Juan de Sabinas owned by Guillermo Beckman and Arturo Longe in 1905 for US$1 million.[69] Ernesto Madero was also a shareholder in the Compañía Carbonifera de Sabinas, S.A.,[70] which in 1907 was the largest coal producer in Mexico. The Mexican Mining and Industrial Corp., Ltd., of which científico Hugo Scherer was president, with stockholders in Europe, was also involved.[71] They bought two important lead-producing properties in 1905 and 1908.[72]

The family expanded its operations through the first decade of the new century and were quite willing to expend large amounts in purchasing and modernizing new holdings. Gustavo, Francisco, and Ernesto Madero also operated a copper field of "immense wealth" in Santa Bárbara, Chihuahua.[73] The Maderos with their partners paid US$200,000 for the option to the property of the Compañía Minera Ramón Corona de Naica in 1907.[74] By 1913 Alberto Madero and A. González were partners in 150 claims in Cusihuiriachic, Chihuahua.[75] In 1908 Madero Brothers took over the Mexican Mines Company, near Cusihuiriachic.[76] In 1909 they leased the Las Cuadras mine in Santa Bárbara, expanding and updating the plant.[77] The Compañía Metalúrgica de Torreón owned the San Diego mill in Santa Bárbara, Chihuahua, one of the most technologically advanced in Mexico.[78]

As the Compañía Metalúrgica expanded its plant to smelt silver, gold, and copper ores,[79] the enterprise helped to revive mining in both Hidalgo de Parral in southern Chihuahua and in Coahuila.[80] Eventually the family's holdings extended into Nuevo León, Zacatecas, and Durango.[81]

Enrique Creel had for the most part shied away from operating his mining properties, usually employing foreigners to run them or leasing or selling them to foreign companies. The Maderos, by contrast, were quite willing to operate their own properties. They competed directly with giant

TABLE 2.2. Cía Metalúrgica de Torreón: Profits, 1902–1906

Year	Profits (in pesos)
1902	280,979
1903	701,049 / 404,344
1904	629,369
1905	700,944
1906	775,386

Sources: *Mexican Herald*, Aug. 16, 1910, p. 9:4; and James Hyslop Collection, Box 2, University of Texas, El Paso.

ASARCO in the smelting business. Most notably, the family refused to join the smelters' trust. In 1904 the Maderos reportedly rejected an offer from ASARCO for the Torreón smelter. ASARCO made a new offer in 1905, but, according to the *Engineering and Mining Journal,* ASARCO initially offered only one-half of what the Maderos asked.[82] ASARCO offered US$4.5 million in October, but the Maderos held out for US$5 million.[83] In 1909 there were, once again, rumblings that the Guggenheims were buying the Torreón smelter, but these turned out to be rumors.[84] The Terrazas-Creel family had threatened to build a smelter in Ciudad Chihuahua in 1906, but, of course, then they sold their concession to ASARCO. Smelting required large capital outlays for equipment; Creel and Terrazas were unwilling to expend such sums in competition with ASARCO (the smelters' trust) and the Maderos. The Maderos had undertaken their venture before the organization of the trust at the height of the mining boom. They made considerable profits and were unwilling to sell out to the foreign giant.

AGRICULTURE

The Maderos reportedly owned seven million acres of land.[85] Family members owned large guayule haciendas in San Luis Potosí, Coahuila, Zacatecas, Durango, and Chihuahua.[86] The family formed a series of land companies for their holdings. The land company Madero y Hernández, with partners Francisco Madero and Antonio V. Hernández, operated at least a dozen haciendas from 1887 to 1894. The Compañía de Terrenos y Ganados de Coahuila, S.A., owned more than one million acres, with 700,000 pesos capital. The Negociación Agrícola y Ganadera de San Enrique, S.A., with 75,000 acres and 360,000 pesos in capital, ran several ranchos in Coahuila. The Compañía de Tierras de Sonora owned more than 1.5 million acres in Sonora around Ures, Hermosillo, and Altar.[87] In partnership with Edward Maurer, Inc., the Maderos owned the Compañía Explotadora Coahuilense, organized in 1905, which grew and sold guayule.[88] Evaristo's son Alberto Madero was the administrator of the enormous Zuloaga haciendas in Chihuahua, having married into that family.[89]

The Maderos took on another powerful US trust, as they had in the smelting industry, in the production of guayule. The Rockefellers' Continental Rubber Company after 1905 held a virtual monopoly in the Laguna. The US company had powerful allies in Porfirio Díaz and Enrique C. Creel. Local politicians, such as Governor Miguel Cárdenas and Práxedis de la Peña, had sold out to Continental with huge profits. But the Madero family was not intimidated. When the rubber trust lowered its prices to drive the Maderos from the industry, Francisco Madero bristled that he "was not afraid of Continental. If they put the prices so low that we cannot sell, we will stop our factories."[90] During the downturn in 1907 the family was caught with a large stock of guayule and thus needed to borrow capital abroad to finance its overhead. With Limantour's help, the Maderos avoided bankruptcy.[91]

The Maderos had another run-in with foreigners when they tried to purchase about 20 percent of the holdings of the Compañía de San Marcos y Pinos, located near Monclova. W. B. Cloete and Roberto Symon had bought two tracts with a total of 1.5 million acres in the mid-1880s from the Sánchez Navarro family. It appears that the Maderos through their Compañía Merced sought 250,000 acres of this land to grow guayule.[92] Cloete complained to Díaz that the Maderos had taken "menacing actions."

The Maderos were also cotton farmers and thus deeply involved in water-rights disputes on the Nazas River in the Laguna region. The area's land was fertile, but it required irrigation. Water rights to the Nazas were crucial. In the 1880s disputes grew violent as planters in Coahuila and Durango fought over water. A foreign company, the Compañía Tlahualilo, obtained a concession in 1888 that usurped much of the river's water. Again the Maderos were in the forefront of the struggle against a large foreign company.[93]

Lastly, the Maderos were vintners. In 1893 Evaristo Madero purchased the San Lorenzo hacienda, which had produced wine since the sixteenth century. He introduced European vines and techniques.

The Compañía Industrial Metalúrgica de Torreón and the large land holdings were family enterprises. These were the great profit centers for them. The Maderos in addition were involved in two major businesses that were crucial to the network that spread over northern Mexico with anchors in Chihuahua, the Laguna (Coahuila), and Monterrey, the Compañía Industrial Jabonera de la Laguna and three banks, Banco Mercantil de Monterrey, Banco de Nuevo León, and Banco Refaccionario de La Laguna. These companies interwove the interests of the Terrazas-Creels, the Maderos, the Monterrey groups, and various large landowners and merchants in the three regions.

COMPAÑÍA INDUSTRIAL JABONERA DE LA LAGUNA

During the last half of the nineteenth century there was an agricultural boom in the Laguna area of Coahuila that arose from the emerging market for cotton created by the textile industry in northern and central Mexico and from the construction in the early 1880s of the Mexican Central Railroad that ran through the region. The Laguna became the major cotton-producing zone in the country, generating 75 percent of its production.[94]

The boom brought together an entrepreneurial network, consisting of Enrique C. Creel and Juan Terrazas (Luis's son) from Chihuahua, Monterrey merchants and manufacturers, Patricio Milmo, an Irish immigrant, Francisco Belden, Tomás Mendirichaga, and Isaac Garza, held together by Terrazas confidante Juan F. Brittingham, an American. They formed the Compañía Industrial Jabonera (CIJL) in 1898 at a time when, as we have seen, Creel attempted to establish a series of trusts in two other agro-industries, meat packing and flour milling. The CIJL was a venture to monopolize the production and use of cottonseed from which derived oil to make soap and explosives.

The Compañía Industrial Jabonera de la Laguna, under the management of Juan F. Brittingham, was a very profitable enterprise.[95] As it turned out, the original contract with the Laguna cotton planters assured low prices for the cottonseed, while prices for the products derived from it, such as glycerin used in explosives, rose sharply. The CIJL sold its glycerin exclusively to the Compañía Nacional Mexicana de Dinamita y Explosiva, the explosives monopoly operated by a consortium of elites led by Brittingham and Creel. Soap was not as profitable, but the company had a contract with the Pullman Company to provide soap for all the railroad cars in Mexico.[96] In 1902 the Jabonera's dividend was 1.3 million pesos. In 1909, after two years of economic downturn the Jabonera was the only factory in the Laguna flourishing and employing a large workforce.[97]

However, a bitter dispute arose between the planters, who were substantial stockholders as well as suppliers, and the CIJL over two issues. First, there were reports that the company used cheaper materials other than cottonseed oil in its soap, thus diminishing the demand for cottonseed and adulterating the product. Second and more important, the planters sought a readjustment of the price the company paid for the cottonseed. Many of the planters had in their efforts to expand or improve production raised additional capital by selling their stock in the CIJL or using their stock as collateral for loans. They believed that the CIJL exploited them. The leading producers, the Luján and Purcell families, sought relief by claiming that the contract applied only to the lands in production in 1898, not any additional lands put into cultivation after that date. The Terrazas-Creels and Brittingham resisted these efforts by the planters. When the conflict inevitably ended up with Díaz, the dictator stalled on a decision, favoring the Terrazas-Creels.[98]

The role of the Madero in this drama is somewhat puzzling. On the one hand, they were major stockholders in the CIJL and partners of the Terrazas-Creels in important banks and other ventures.[99] If the planters won out, it would have likely bankrupted the CIJL, thus rendering their stock worthless. A victory, too, might have jeopardized their working relations with Creel, one of the most powerful persons in the country. On the other hand, there were contemporary reports that the Maderos were trying to purchase the lone competitor of the CIJL, La Unión, which paid higher prices for cottonseed in order to run CIJL out of business.[100] They also apparently played an active role in trying to influence the Díaz administration in the planters' favor. Whatever bitterness arose from the contract, the Maderos continued to work with the Terrazas-Creels, buying mining property from them and continuing as partners in various other ventures.

INDUSTRY

Madero y Compañía established the Fábrica de Hilados y Tejidos "La Estrella" in the 1870s. It became a major textile plant and large employer in the area. The business became the base of the Compañía Industrial de Parras, S.A., in 1902, and merged with four other textile plants.[101] La Estrella had a major setback when a fire in July 1909 resulted in a US$300,000 loss.[102] There were also holdings in a winery, bricks, food processing, guayule processing, and printing. They were shareholders in many of the major industrial enterprises in Monterrey as well, such as the Compañía Fundidora y Afinadora "Monterrey," S.A., the Fundidora de Fierro y Acero de Monterrey, S.A., the Fábrica de Vidrios y Cristales de Monterrey, S.A., the Fábrica de Cartón de Monterrey, S.A., and Compañía Ladrillera "La Unión," S.A.[103] We can get a sense of just how extensive the family's involvement in industry from Table 2.3, which lists the businesses in which Ernesto Madero, the oldest son of Evaristo's second family, participated.

BANKING

The northern network revolved around the Compañía Industrial Jabonera de la Laguna and three major banks.[104] As early as 1892 the Maderos were partners in Banco de Nuevo León.[105] In a decade its capital grew from 600,000 pesos to more than 2 million pesos. Banco Mercantil de Monterrey, S.A., was founded in 1899 in Monterrey, capital of the state of Nuevo Leon and home of many of Mexico's largest and most dynamic industrial enterprises. Creel was its second-largest stockholder.[106] The bank brought in eight of the ten great families of Monterrey as shareholders (Madero, Ferrara, Rivero, Milmo, Hernández, Sada-Murguerza, Zambrano, and Garza).[107]

TABLE 2.3. Enterprises of Ernesto Madero, 1895–1912

Name	Business	Type of Participation
The Mexican Mining and Industrial Co., Ltd.	Mining	Board of Directors, shareholder
Cía Harinera del Golfo, S.A.	Flour milling	President, shareholder
Molinos de Cilindro de Monterrey, S.A.	Industry	President
Ernesto Madero y Hermanos	Textiles, commerce	President
CIJL	Soap	Shareholder
Fábrica de Vidrios y Cristales de Monterrey, S.A.	Glass	Founder, shareholder
Compañía Metalúrgica de Torreón, S.A.	Smelter	Founder, president, shareholder
Compañía Harinera de Chihuahua, S.A.	Flour milling	Shareholder
Compañía Fundidora Afinadora Monterrey, S.A.	Industry, mining	Shareholder
Compañía Carbonato, S.A.	Mining	Shareholder
Compañía Minera La Fraternal, S.A.	Mining	Shareholder
Compañía Minera Azteca, S.A.	Mining	Shareholder
Compañía Minera Dolores de Guadalcázar, S.A.	Mining	President, shareholder
Compañía Fundidora de Fierro y Acero de Monterrey, S.A.	Industry, mining	Shareholder
Compañía Restauradora de Guadalcázar, S.A.	Mining	Shareholder
Negociación Minera Santa María de la Paz	Mining	Shareholder
Compañía Carbonífera de Nuevo León y Coahuila, S.A.	Mining	Vice president, shareholder
Empresa Editorial de Monterrey, S.A.	Textiles	Shareholder
Salvador Madero y Compañía	Industry, commerce	Manager
Compañía Minera del Carmen, S.A.	Mining	Shareholder
Compañía Explotadora Coahuilense, S.A.	Agriculture, industry	Vice president, shareholder
Compañía Industrial de Parras, S.A.	Textiles	Secretary, shareholder

Source: Mario Cerutti, "Empresariado y banca en el norte de México (1870–1910): El Banco Refaccionario de la Laguna," in *La banca regional en México (1870–1930)*, ed. Mario Cerutti and Carlos Marichal (Mexico: El Colegio de México and El Fondo de Cultura Económica, 2003), p. 198.

Like CIJL, Banco Refaccionario de la Laguna, founded in 1907, brought together landowners, industrialists, and merchants.[108] The bank had among its shareholders foreign investors, including a number of Spaniards, old-line merchant houses, which had in the era before banks provided capital for the cotton planters, and the Terrazas-Creels. Brittingham, as he had been with the CIJL, was the primary organizer. With 6 million pesos capital, it began operations in 1908 in the midst of a severe economic downturn. Major disputes over the water rights of the Río Nazas and the prices for cottonseed paid by CIJL pitted many of the shareholders against each other. Nonetheless, with the support of both President Díaz and Limantour, the bank raised the necessary capital.[109] Banco Refaccionario de la Laguna cooperated closely with other regional banks, many of which were stockholders in it.[110]

THE REVOLUTION

On the eve of the Revolution, the Madero family appeared to be a bit shaky, though given their enormous assets, truly serious difficulties appeared unlikely. The fire at "La Estrella," the closing of the textile factory La Amistad, and the limited operations of the San Diego mine were huge blows.[111] In testimony before the US Senate, Manuel L. Luján claimed that the Maderos were bankrupt before the Revolution and that there were judgments against them in Mexico City in the amount of US$25,000 to $100,000.[112]

The Revolution brought on hard times for the Maderos. Although Evaristo's grandson, Francisco I., had won the Revolution in its initial stage, defeating Díaz in May 1911 and succeeding to the presidency in the fall, the family's economic holdings were battered. For example, in July 1911 eighty workers went on strike at the Compañía Explotadora Coahuilense, the guayule operation.[113] The Torreón smelter closed in 1912.[114] "La Estrella" closed in 1913.[115] In addition to the assassination of both Francisco I. and Gustavo in 1913, the family endured a sustained effort on the part of Venustiano Carranza, the victorious revolutionary chieftain, a fellow Coahuilan, to destroy its economic base.[116] Carranza confiscated Madero property in 1915.[117] The carrancistas confiscated the Compañía Explotadora Coahuilense in 1915.[118] Another of the properties taken was the Fénix flour mill. Consequently, the Maderos ended up selling a substantial portion of their holdings to foreigners. In 1916 they sold the Torreón smelter to the Peñoles Company, a German firm.[119] ASARCO purchased 51 percent of the Rosita Coal Fields in Coahuila, paying the Madero estate US$1.5 million in 1919.[120] The government of the state of Coahuila seized the Compañía Industrial de Parras, S.A., which incorporated the "La Estrella" textile plant, in 1915, but returned it less than two years later.[121] At least part of the family fled Mexico after the assassinations in 1913. Daniel, Evaristo, and others escaped to Havana on a US warship.[122]

Nonetheless, family members continued to be involved in mining during and after the Revolution. Alberto Madero, working from El Paso in 1915, had a mining claim in Villa Ahumada.[123] Evaristo owned a molybdenum mine in Coyamé, Chihuahua, in 1916.[124] The family was involved in the Negociación Minera Jesús María Mining Company, through Ernesto Madero and Brothers, in Saltillo in 1921.[125] Alberto Madero, still working from El Paso, had two properties in the Colorado Mountains near Tres Marías, Mosqueteras, Chihuahua, in 1923.[126]

Because some of the heaviest fighting of the Revolution took place in the La Laguna area around Torreón, transportation was badly disrupted. In 1914 Pancho Villa occupied the region and the major cotton haciendas. Villa operated the plantations in order to generate revenue for his army. The Compañía Jabonera needed cottonseed to produce glycerin and soap. The two interests joined to yield an arrangement whereby Jabonera bought Villa's cotton, for which he paid cash at the US border. Villa made sure to deliver the cotton. Brittingham, who negotiated the deal, paid well under market value. He then shipped the cotton to desperate, war-ravaged Europe for an enormous profit. Villa soon figured out that Brittingham had taken advantage of him and extorted forced loans of US$350,000.[127] The Jabonera survived the Revolution, apparently quite well, yielding its shareholders dividends and appreciating stock prices.[128] But because of the conditions during reconstruction after 1920, the company converted into a cooperative dominated by farmers. It sold its assets to the Jabonera de la Laguna Sociedad Cooperativa Limitada for two million gold pesos (one million US dollars). Brittingham stayed as manager for two years. The Jabonera lent the cooperative one million pesos to start up operations.[129] The Dupont Company through its subsidiary Dinamita Hércules set up the Compañía Mexicana de Explosivos and in 1925 bought the Compañía Nacional Mexicana de Dinamita y Explosivos.[130]

Banks were among the chief targets of the revolutionaries, for they were repositories of ready cash. The officers of Banco Mercantil de Monterrey, S.A., in 1913, sent millions of dollars worth of gold bullion to the United States to keep it from falling into the hands of the various fighting factions. The Terrazas-Creels had early on shifted their monies from Banco Minero to Mexico City, but later lost the funds to the carrancistas. The Obregón government, struggling as ever to reconstruct the damaged economy, made a concerted effort in 1921 to revive banking. In January 1921 it returned twelve banks to their prerevolutionary owners. Two of the five that were able to reopen were Banco Mercantil de Monterrey and Banco de Nuevo León. According to the *Boletín Financiero y Minero*, these banks had transferred substantial funds out of the country during the early stages of the upheaval and thus were not damaged as badly as others by the seizure of specie by Carranza.[131]

BUSINESS AND POLITICS

Over the long term, the Madero did not prove as adept as the Terrazas-Creels in asserting their direct political influence over their home state. This proved detrimental to their economic interests. Both Evaristo Madero and Luis Terrazas had opposed Díaz when he took power in 1876. Luis Terrazas was governor of Chihuahua and Evaristo Madero was governor of Coahuila from 1880 to 1884, when Díaz left the presidency for one term. Díaz pushed them both out when he returned to office in 1884. Personal relations between the dictator and the two patriarchs were never warm and were sometimes contentious, though never overtly. Both Terrazas and Madero from behind the scenes supported rebellions in the early 1890s, which forced Díaz to realign his treatment of them. In Chihuahua, the Terrazas's main rivals lost influence when Díaz negotiated the installation of Miguel Ahumada as governor. Ahumada proved an amenable compromise. But the Terrazas returned to direct control of Chihuahua in 1902 with the election of Luis Terrazas as governor once more.[132] The Maderos, however, while they helped force out one of the rival camarillas in Coahuila, could never recapture the governorship.

The Maderos did not lose all their influence, however, for they remained the leaders of one of the three contending camarillas in Coahuila. Their strong economic base and their widespread family and business connections assured they would continue as a formidable force in the state. The family also maintained close ties with José Y. Limantour, although unlike Creel, no Madero was counted among the inner circle of the científicos. Evidently, the Madero family and their allies held sway in the municipal government of their home base in Parras. The rebellion in 1893 eventually brought a compromise, much as had evolved in Chihuahua, with a trusted agent of the Díaz regime acceptable to the dissidents (in this case the Maderos and their allies) installed as governor. The Coahuilan example, however, developed somewhat differently, because General Bernardo Reyes, then the political boss of Nuevo León, was assigned the task of reestablishing order. Reyes never more than tolerated the Madero group.[133] During the 1890s the Madero camarilla had access to high political offices in the state, but their cronies were under tight leashes.[134] In 1905 the Madero camarilla allied with the científicos to undermine Reyes by ousting his chief ally in Coahuila, Governor Miguel Cárdenas.[135]

In 1905, at the height of their economic power and evidently taking lessons from the Terrazas-Creels' successful restoration three years earlier, the Maderos decided to challenge Díaz indirectly with científico support in Mexico City. At the time Reyes's relations with Díaz were shaky—the dictator saw him as a rival, and thus vulnerable—and the Madero war chest was full from their booming cotton, guayule, mining, and smelting operations. There was no hint of the downturn that occurred two years later. The Maderos allied with their former enemies the Garza Galán camarilla (that they had helped oust in 1893) against Cárdenas. A new group joined the old camarillas against Cárdenas, the Club Democrático Benito Juárez, made up of young professionals, led by none other than Evaristo's grandson Francisco I. Madero.[136] Of course, the challenge failed. The disillusionment of the young Madero subsequently resulted in his leading a nationwide opposition party against Díaz in the presidential election of 1910. Thereafter the Madero family resumed its tenuous relationship with Díaz and Reyes. Not all was lost, however, for the family retained its connections with Limantour. And both Díaz and Limantour assisted their Banco Refaccionario de la Laguna in 1908. But we should note that the Maderos were not the linchpin investors in the bank.

According to W. S. Langston, Díaz, although he allowed the Maderos to greatly prosper, did not favor them in any economic disputes.[137] On different occasions, for example, Díaz declined to order lower taxes for the Maderos's textile plants.[138] Because the Madero camarilla, many of whom were cotton planters, had opposed Governor José María Garza Galán, he dragged his feet in defending their interests against the Tlahualilo Company.[139] They obtained their revenge, however, succeeding in ousting him in 1893.

CONCLUSION

Enrique C. Creel and Evaristo Madero were, of course, exceptional cases. One could argue that their examples can yield only limited conclusions about Mexican elites. That both families were clearly products of the northern border region in close proximity to the United States, also, perhaps, lessens their use as models of elite behavior. Furthermore, each family achieved extraordinary success and as such may have been outliers. But the excellent studies of the Monterrey elite by Saragoza, Mora Torres, and Cerutti, and the examination of other elite in Yucatán and elsewhere show many similarities.

Although the two families differed considerably in their approaches to entrepreneurship, they fit into the framework of the elite-foreign enterprise system in their own particular ways. They epitomized the checks and balances of the Díaz version of the system. The dictator was powerful enough to keep them from controlling their state governments, but not sufficiently strong enough to eliminate them from competition. The national government sometimes favored their economic interests, while in other instances stymied them. The Terrazas and Madero families for their part built enormous economic holdings that made them too strong to defeat. They also kept on probing, on occasion financing rebellions against Díaz, generally funding the local and regional opposition to keep the dictator off-balance and maintain leverage for their constant negotiations. The Terrazas chose to pretty much end their rivalry with Díaz after 1902, as Creel became integrated into the científico group and assumed a cabinet post. The Maderos, some of them perhaps reluctantly, ultimately challenged Díaz when they discerned weakness. Each family also was buffeted by the Revolution, suffered egregious losses in terms of business and human life, but, nonetheless, survived and later prospered. They bided their time, allied with other groups, as they had during the Díaz regime, used their economic clout to obtain influence, and adapted to the new rules of the revolutionary regime.

THREE

Mexico Versus the Seven Kings
The Railroad Consolidation, 1902–1910

In an exposé of the railroad industry in *Cosmopolitan* in 1907 Charles Edward Russell claimed:

> The seven kings of our railroad system looked down to Mexico and it found favor in their sight. They said it was a good thing and they would push it along. They owned shares in many lines; they were building and planning many others. Here was Mr. Rockefeller with his Mexican Central Railroad and Mr. Gould with his Mexican National and Mr. Harriman with his new line to the Mexican Pacific coast. How fine it would be if they were to combine their interests and possess all the country![1]

He surmised that the "great Black Hand" of the railroad business, the group that controlled Rock Island, "an extraordinary group of financial bandits that in ten years . . . has put together the greatest railroad system in the world" and in so doing produced quantities of "fictitious" bonds and watered stock, were also "in line for a slice of Mexico." Rock Island planned to build a new system through Mexico to Panama. The scheme was to divide Mexico between the "harmonious seven kings." Once the combination was in place, nothing would be left for others and the kings would have free rein to "exploit the people and draw dividends."

In response Porfirio Díaz, president of Mexico, through José Yves Limantour, his secretary of the treasury, "in ways so carefully concealed that the seven kings never heard of the matter" purchased the majority of the stock of the Mexican railroads. Emissaries in Europe and the United States had quietly obtained stock. According to Russell, the Mexican government, having observed the creation of the railroad trust in the United States, had determined "that no such power should gain domination over Mexico."[2] Confronted with the vast capital of the seven kings, the Mexican government had "merely bought enough stock of each principal railroad to secure its control." Limantour, when he announced the government's actions, declared that "the government had been driven to the step by the growing danger that the Mexican railroads would be absorbed by the American railroad trust."[3] "The object . . . was to defeat a combination which, if it had been realized, would have jeopardized the country's interests and restricted the liberty of the public powers."[4]

Russell further observed that the Mexican government, though discrete, had begun the process in 1902 with its purchase of the Tehuantepec Interoceanic Railroad, buying the company's bonds on the open market. At the time, the government also asserted that it had moved to "prevent pools and trusts it felt it could not regulate nor control."[5] Díaz and Limantour had carried out the other, later transactions for the same reasons.

The consolidation of the Mexican railways from 1902 to 1910 was in many ways the culmination of the Porfirian tripartite economic system in which Díaz and Limantour (and their agent, the national government) deftly balanced the interests of the national elite, local and state elites, and foreign entrepreneurs. It is my supposition that the consolidation came about as a reaction of the Díaz regime to the increasing dominance of US investors in Mexico. Specifically, the dictator feared the concentration of railroad ownership then taking place across the border would spread south and adversely affect Mexican sovereignty, limit his own political space, and inhibit economic development. Trusts, while perhaps acceptable, and in some instances encouraged, in other domestically owned industries, such as meat packing, cement, and steel, were too dangerous to permit in transportation. In short, the possible invasion of the US railroad magnates had the potential to unbalance the carefully calibrated Porfirian elite-foreign enterprise system, so painstakingly constructed over three decades.

Railroads were the core of Díaz's economic development strategy. They were, after mining, the second major investment area for foreigners. They had the greatest impact of any sector on the nation's economic growth. Export-oriented development, the core of Díaz's plans, relied heavily on access to relatively inexpensive transportation. Furthermore, Mexico could not industrialize without an internal transportation system that would enable it to build domestic markets.[6]

The railroads were essential to the dictator's political survival as well. The coercive mechanism of the Porfirian regime depended on quickly moving its small army over long distances.[7] Díaz had purposefully allowed his military to shrink in size. Without the railroads he could not hope to defend his regime against armed opposition.

Thus, Díaz confronted a major dilemma after the turn of the century. The specter of trusts in the United States loomed. It was taking an enormous effort on the part of the US government to rein in monopolies in the great industries, including railroads. Díaz, however, was not able to take on the giant US enterprises directly because foreign investment was the engine that drove the Mexican economy. An attack on the railroads might have very well caused foreign capital to flee. Foreign investment was notoriously fickle; any hint of trouble would end the flow of capital.

BACKGROUND

During the early years of the Díaz regime, Mexicans regarded foreign investment warily, for the country had endured two major foreign invasions in three decades (the United States in 1846–48, and France in 1861–66). In the 1870s several notable US entrepreneurs, including Ulysses S. Grant and W. R. Palmer, tried unsuccessfully to obtain concessions to build railroads. Their proposals met with emotional responses, such as this by Alfredo Chavero in the Mexican Congress: "You, the deputies of the states, would you exchange your beautiful and poor liberty for the rich subjection which the railroad would give you? Go and propose to the lion of the desert to exchange the cave of rock for a golden cage and the lion of the desert would reply to you with a roar of liberty."[8] Moreover, Díaz's relations with the US government were quite difficult in his early years. Border disputes delayed recognition of his government by the administration of Rutherford B. Hayes.

Eventually, however, Díaz had little choice but to reconcile with his northern neighbor and to encourage its investment capital. His refusal to recognize the debts of Maximilian's government had closed off credit and investment from the only other potential sources in France and Great Britain. After some initial foot-dragging, then, Mexico opened its doors to foreign capital to build its desperately needed railroads. Díaz went so far as to declare that foreigners should be given "generous hospitality and be permitted to enjoy the guarantees that the laws provide."[9]

In the last year of his first term in 1880 Díaz granted charters to the Mexican Central, the Mexican National, and Mexican Southern railroads. His successor, Manuel González (1880–84), supervised the expansion of the railway network from one to six thousand kilometers. The national government underwrote construction with millions of pesos in subsidies.

The terms of the railroad concessions, nonetheless, reflected the continued wariness that Mexicans had for US entrepreneurs. The railroad charters included the following: the railroad, unencumbered, would revert to the nation after ninety-nine years; upon reversion experts would appraise the railroad's equipment and property and the company compensated accordingly; railroads were subject to government inspection; the government was to fix freight and passenger rates; the railroads were to provide free mail service; the government was to receive a 60 percent rebate on passenger and freight service for military and federal employees on official business. The concessionaires received a number of important privileges: duty-free importation of equipment and materials; the right to condemn and acquire property for auxiliary facilities; exemption from most taxes; construction subsidies, based on mileage built; and monopolies on their routes.[10] The government sought in these concessions to limit foreign economic power.

Despite the necessity of permitting the inflow of foreign investment, Mexicans continued to worry. Limantour was among the first to warn against the increasing economic influence of the United States. On taking office in 1893 he admitted his fear of Mexican economic dependence on its northern neighbor. Limantour in 1899 hesitated in arranging an important government loan from the United States because of similar concerns, though again necessity prevailed.[11]

The powerful railroad companies were no easier to control in Mexico than they were in the United States. As a result, the Díaz government again attempted to bring the railroads under closer supervision in 1899 through a new Railroad Law. Concessionaire companies were to fall under the jurisdiction of Mexican laws, maintain headquarters in Mexico City, and maintain a local board of directors. The Mexican government was to regulate the issue of stocks and bonds, and a commission was to oversee rates. Companies were to furnish monthly reports on finances and operations. The national government also tried to encourage the construction of railroad lines that would foster the domestic market; the need was for east-west lines that connected the Pacific coast and the Isthmus of Tehuantepec to the interior.[12]

THE THREAT

By the turn of the century the danger of consolidation was unmistakable. First, there were a number of major efforts to establish trusts in Mexico in various industries by both Mexicans and foreigners. Some of the great US trusts had turned their attention to Mexico. Second, the concentration of railroad ownership in the United States had increased in the first decade of the twentieth century, led by E. H. Harriman.[13] Finally, the weak financial status of many Mexican railroads (like those in the United States) made them vulnerable to takeover by US companies. The flow of capital from the north was about to overwhelm Limantour's modest attempts to curtail the power of the railroads.

The evidence of trust building in Mexico was considerable. The *New York Times* reported in 1901 the efforts of the recent consolidations of factories in the tobacco and soap industries and the attempts of the major breweries and cotton manufacturers to form trusts.[14] US trusts were also expanding into Mexico. The most important example was the Guggenheim Exploration Company, a subsidiary of the American Smelting and Refining Company, "the smelters' trust." The Guggenheims' ASARCO owned almost every smelter in northern Mexico and it controlled the price of silver.[15] Other US-based trusts, such as Standard Oil, the Wells Fargo Company, the American Rubber Trust, and the Sugar Trust, also operated in Mexico.[16] Limantour acted to forestall one effort to form a trust in 1901 when he abolished tariff quotas on grain in order to break up a potential grain monopoly in Mexico City.[17]

The concentration in the ownership of US railroads began in 1894, when in the middle of a prolonged economic depression one-third of both the mileage and the capitalized investment of these companies was in receivership.[18] As the nation emerged from the harsh depression that started in 1890, E. H. Harriman began to build his immense empire with the reorganization of the Union Pacific. By 1906 he controlled virtually all access to the US Pacific coast.[19] Harriman came to control the stock of between 12 and 25 percent of the railroad mileage in the United States. William Z. Ripley described the era: "1901 witnessed the spread of the consolidation movement over into the field of transportation. Great Railroad companies were bought and sold almost like eggs over the counter."[20]

The Mexican railroads were vulnerable to takeover by US tycoons, precisely for the same reasons US railways had been susceptible to consolidation: their financial condition was precarious. Both the major lines, the Mexican National and the Mexican Central, were in distress. The Mexican National had been bankrupt in 1887.[21] The Mexican Central generated enough revenues to pay the interest on its debt in only five of the years from 1889 to 1907.[22] The first to fall was the Interoceanic Railway of Mexico, a conglomeration of several failed existing lines and concessions, which went into temporary liquidation in 1896 barely five years after opening its main line.[23]

The most important cause of the railroads' financial problem was the steady decline of the peso in relationship to the US dollar and the British pence. The Mexican peso worth 76.74 US cents in 1891 was worth only 42.16 US cents in August 1903.[24] In the same period the peso fell from 27.80 pence to 19.68 pence.[25] The railroads had to pay for their imported equipment, remunerate some foreign employees, and service their debt in gold (the equivalent of the US dollar), but their operating revenues were in silver (Mexican pesos). The falling exchange rate thus badly damaged earnings.

In 1901 the threat of the US tycoons grew too strong to ignore. The *New York Times* reported that the recent takeover of the Mexican Central by W. L. Stow was only the preliminary to ambitious plans, whose participants included the Guggenheims, J. P. Morgan, and Standard Oil, to control Mexican commercial and industrial development. The rumors warned of an impending merger between the Central and National companies.[26] In the same year, the Atchison, Topeka, and Santa Fe lost control of the Mexican Central line to a group headed by Henry Clay Pierce, who had close ties to J. P. Morgan and John D. Rockefeller of Standard Oil. Harriman was also a new shareholder.[27] The Central acquired the Monterrey and Gulf line and access to the Gulf of Mexico through Tampico. It also purchased the Coahuila al Pacífico Railroad, which connected the Central and National near Saltillo, Coahuila.[28] The operators of the National worried that the Central would acquire the International and with it control over railroads in northern Mexico except the National. The major shareholder in the International was E. H. Harriman.[29] The National thereupon bought controlling interest in the International through an agreement with Harriman.[30] In March 1901 Speyer and Company acquired a large stake in the National, which the *New York Times* reported was meant to assure the entrance of the Southern Pacific into Mexico.[31]

The National's finances were ruinous, however. It had undertaken an immense project to convert its track from narrow to standard gauge. At the same time, the company was involved in costly litigation over its earlier reorganization in 1887. These added to an already enormous debt.[32] Tycoons Jay Gould and Harriman joined with Speyer and Company and Kuhn, Loeb & Company to reorganize the National once again into the National Railways of Mexico (Ferrocarril Nacional de México). The new company then negotiated an end to rate competition between it and the Mexican Central. The new National bought up a number of small lines in the north from 1902 to 1904, adding almost one-third more to its track miles.[33]

On their face, these events might have seemed merely the normal course of business. However, it became clear to Limantour that intensified competition would escalate costs and lead either to ruin or merger of the two major railroads. Neither outcome was acceptable.[34]

THE MERGER

Limantour acted to forestall future mergers when he outbid both the Central and National for the Interoceanic. He placated investors by insisting that he had no intention of taking over the nation's railroads. The government sought only to prevent a "few large financial groups" from obtaining control.³⁵ Díaz was a bit more forceful, asserting that he was "always most attentive to the interests of the majority of Mexican citizens" and would "break up monopolistic alliances which alter the economic laws governing prices."³⁶ Limantour maintained that the government had undertaken this effort to "protect Mexico from the American railroad magnates and their consolidations" and to ensure "the economic independence of Mexico."³⁷

Limantour began the process when he purchased US$5 million of second debenture stock (4.5 percent) of the Interoceanic in 1903. Limantour then began to negotiate through the financial house James Speyer & Company. Limantour first offered to exchange the government's shares in the Interoceanic and cash for majority interest in the National.³⁸ Speyer owned only 17 percent of the National's stock, and neither the government nor the banker wanted to buy more on the open market. Consequently they devised a complicated scheme whereby the government obtained for a moderate price a majority of the voting stock of the National. Limantour settled for an exchange in which the government acquired 47 percent of the shares, enough to transfer effective control of the line.³⁹ The cost to the government was US$9.5 million.⁴⁰ The deal obtained for the government control of three lines, the National, the Interoceanic, and the International.

Limantour negotiated aggressively to maintain Mexican supervision over the new enterprise. Although he stated in 1905 in a letter to Speyer & Company that the "purpose of my Government [is] to harmonize, as far as practicable, the interests of said companies [the National, the Interoceanic, and the International] with those of other railroad companies in the Republic . . . not to interfere with the immediate management of the railway lines. . . . The interference in the private management is absolutely opposed to my ideas,"⁴¹ the secretary proposed at the same time that the company's board locate in Mexico City. Limantour carefully monitored management, at one point in 1905 insisting on the ouster of an executive whom Speyer had recommended.⁴²

The secretary also sought to move the offices of the new company to Mexico City, maintaining that "natural judgment indicates that the vigilance and management are more efficacious when exerted at the place where the business is established," and to assure that the majority of directors were located in Mexico City.⁴³ Speyer objected rather strenuously to these proposed changes, threatening to abstain from naming its allotted members of the board of directors.[44] The banking house was especially concerned that the "position of the New York directors had become a purely nominal one."[45] The current board, according to Speyer, consisted of the Mexican counsel of the company, two salaried officers, and four Limantour appointees, who were unknown to investors abroad. The bankers also complained that although Limantour was "personally controlling its policy in every way," he was neither an officer nor a director of the company.[46]

Limantour believed that the core of the disagreement with Speyer & Company originated in its inability to understand the changed circumstances. According to the secretary:

> The Mexican government had two very precise aims in buying the shares of the National Railroad. One of them was to prevent its merger with other large railroad companies; by doing so it was serving the high interests of the country, as it transformed the railway in a true national enterprise and opposed the monopoly of the means of communication, one of the most disastrous if handled by strangers. The other one was to improve the credit of the Mexican railway enterprises, by setting up a barrier against the construction of parallel lines and against ruinous competitions that cause the stock of said enterprises to be quoted at ludicrous figures.[47]

The tone of the correspondence though civil reveals considerable tension. Limantour was adamant about the Mexican government's control.

From 1904 to 1906 the financial condition of the Mexican Central deteriorated, triggering the second stage of the railroad consolidation.[48] Limantour feared that if the Central could not service its substantial debt, a US company would acquire it. The secretary of the treasury was especially concerned with the specter of Standard Oil, whose associate Henry Clay Pierce ran the Central and whose agent Kuhn & Loeb was deeply involved with Mexican railroads.[49] Limantour explained his reasons for purchasing the Mexican Central in a speech before the Congress on December 14, 1906:

> When in 1903 the Government acquired a majority of the stock of the Mexican National it was thought that it would not be necessary to take any further steps in that direction. But the circumstances have changed.... At that time the object had in view was to defeat a combination, which, if it had been realized, would have jeopardized the country's interests and restricted the liberty of the public powers....
>
> ... and had it not been for unforeseen circumstances, the Government would have been satisfied with having secured control of the Mexican

National and would have done nothing toward securing a controlling interest in the other railways. But the persons and firms interested in the Mexican Central were at that time in a particular situation, due in part to difficulties of a financial nature . . . , and in part to the apprehension which they entertained that . . . the interests of the two systems might in time come into collision. . . . There are three main arguments. . . . First to avoid friction between different corporations when the two are competing lines or when one of them fears being antagonized by a concern in which the Government holds a contributing interest; secondly, to avoid the absorption of the properties, not controlled by the government, by one of the great railway systems of the United States; and, thirdly, the prospect of realizing considerable economies through the consolidation of all the great railways under a single management.[50]

As a result, Limantour proposed to buy the Central and form a new company incorporating the railroads. James Speyer advised against the merger with the Central. Instead he thought that the Central "should be cleaned up and reorganized separately." And only after it could pay for its fixed charges should the government consider its acquisition.[51] Speyer subsequently changed his mind, however, and provided considerable assistance for the subsequent consolidation.[52]

Some of the Central bondholders, long without interest payments, objected. One representative of the dissidents summarized: "Shall the transfer of their control to your government be effected through injuries to bona fide investors who have loaned their money for the development of Mexico, or for the benefit of so-called financiers whose sole interest consists in covering the exorbitant transactions" described in past correspondence.[53] Others raised the issue of overcapitalization of the new consolidated company.[54]

The negotiations to merge the recently constituted National and the Central were long and difficult. The worldwide depression that struck in 1907 created the worst possible conditions for the undertaking. Nonetheless, working with Speyer & Company, Ladenburg, Thalmann & Company, Hallgarten & Company in New York, and a number of banks in Europe, the Mexican government reached an agreement.[55] The Mexican Congress enacted the necessary legislation on December 26, 1906, and the government and the banking houses completed negotiations at the end of March 1908. On February 11, 1909, the Mexican Central Railway Company, Limited, turned over its assets to the National Railways of Mexico and the same day the National took over operations.[56] In June 1910 the National assumed control of the Mexican International and the Mexican

Pacific.⁵⁷ The National bought most of the shares of the Pan American Railroad soon thereafter.⁵⁸

There were three major concerns for the various participants in the consolidation. First, the Mexican government insisted on obtaining a voting majority of the stock in the new company. The initial capital of the company, the National Railways of Mexico, was to be 460,000,000 pesos (US$230,000,000). The government received 512,723 shares in return for its shares in the National and an additional 637,000 in return for its legal and financial support and its guarantee of the General Mortgage Bonds to be issued. The total of 1,250,023 shares was a voting majority. A board of directors of twenty-one members, not more than nine who could reside abroad, was to run the company.⁵⁹

Second, the bondholders and shareholders sought assurances of future appreciation of their holdings and payment of interest and dividends. A consortium of banking and investment houses agreed on a readjustment plan for the debt of the merged companies. Finally, the government and shareholders needed to believe that the combined railroads would have sufficient resources not only to operate but to expand and improve its assets.

Two issues of bonds, one of US$225 million, secured by the company's stock, and another of US$160 million, guaranteed by the Mexican government, were to buy up the bonds of the old companies, to construct or buy new lines, and to make betterments on existing lines.

CRITIQUE

There were four major criticisms of the consolidation with the Central. First was the analysis that the resulting company was enormously overcapitalized. Second, there were accusations of corruption. Third, some observers believed the transaction was too favorable for the foreign banking houses that negotiated the deal, and for the stock and bondholders. Finally, critics saw the merger as a financial failure.

The National and Central together had stock worth nearly US$250 million. The new company had stock valued at US$400 million.⁶⁰ *Moody's Magazine* in 1907 commented that merged railroads' poor construction and badly kept equipment, its poor physical condition, and low profitability did not warrant its high capitalization.⁶¹ There was a difference of more than

US$100 million between the stock value of the combined old companies and the new company. There was a difference of US$116 million between the bonds of the old companies and the bonds of the new company. Even though these funds were not issued immediately and some stock-watering was normal in such cases, the overcapitalization was considerable.[62]

The allegations of corruption focused on Limantour. One was that Limantour and his brother, with insider knowledge of the government's plan to buy the Mexican Central, supposedly bought up the shares of the lines at low prices and then sold them at higher prices to the government, making US$6 million.[63] Banco Nacional (or French banks) reputedly lent the Limantours the funds to carry out these transactions.[64] Writer Carlton Beals claimed that 50 million pesos disappeared during the transactions (presumably into the hands of the Limantours). He also charged that Pablo Macedo, later vice chair of the board, stole 3 million pesos.[65] John Kenneth Turner, the North American muckraking journalist, reported that Limantour and Pablo Martínez del Río, who managed Banco Nacional, bought railroad stock and went to Díaz with a proposal for merging the railroads, which the dictator rejected. Limantour then turned to E. H. Harriman, who sent to Díaz his agent S. M. Felton, who persuaded him to approve the scheme. Harriman also purportedly convinced Henry Clay Pierce to sell him control of the Mexican Central if the deal succeeded. In return for his help Harriman received from Limantour a special concession and subsidies for his Southern Pacific line on the west coast of Mexico.[66] Edward I. Bell told a slightly different version of events. According to him, Harriman originated the scheme on a secret trip to Mexico to see Limantour in 1902. Harriman sought control of the Central, but he was concerned about the government's control of access to Laredo without which his project could not succeed. He therefore proposed consolidation. Limantour turned down the deal, but then he set out to arrange it himself.[67]

Needless to say, the accusations of corruption are hard to prove. Nonetheless, Julio Limantour was a partner in the banking house Hugo Scherer, which was involved in the merger. And it is clear that both Limantour and Díaz permitted unethical transactions when it suited the purposes of the regime. Certainly the members of the inner circle of científicos around Limantour were not unwilling to use insider information to enrich themselves.

In addition, some critics believed that the railroad consolidation was a scheme meant solely to bail out powerful foreigners from their bad investments. The threat of foreign takeover, according to this reasoning, was imagined, for in fact from 1897 to 1908 the amount of US capital invested in Mexican railroads shrunk 50 percent—US$53.8 million in 1908 alone.[68] Considerable differences exist in the evaluation of the finances of the consolidation. Nicolas d'Olwer maintains that the acquisition was quite inexpensive for the government, costing less than 22 million pesos.[69] Limantour claimed that he paid only 0.5 percent over the market price for National shares, enabling him to pay the bankers for their risks.[70] In the transaction the participants exchanged stocks and bonds on a par value basis, but of course, the stocks and bonds sold at far less than par value on the market. The holders of the old stocks and bonds received in addition US$1,100 for each US$1,000 of old holdings. The bonds were sold at 94 to 95 percent in the issues of May 1908 and June 1909.[71] Given the financial conditions of the time, these were not unreasonably deep discounts.

The banking houses that acted as readjustment managers received substantial remuneration. In April 1908, the new company sold several million dollars in bonds to them at 88 percent of their par value and well below the market value.[72] Of this cash US$400,000 went to Speyer & Company for financial services rendered over ten years and US$6,086,700 went to the banking consortium to cover the expenses of the readjustment and other services. This amounted to a commission of 1.75 percent for the interest bonds exchanged and 0.75 percent for the stocks and income bonds.[73]

The question about the mergers' financial success or failure is impossible to answer, for the Revolution, which broke out in late 1910 and lasted for a decade, caused enormous damage to the railroads and badly disrupted the economy. From 1908 through 1910 the merged line generated enough revenue to pay both its expenses and interest on its debt.[74] The new company paid dividends to the holders of its First Preferred Shares, ranging from 1 to 4 percent from 1908 to 1912. The owners of other stocks in the company received no dividends.[75] In 1910 the railroads were judged "prosperous."[76]

Limantour had hoped to pay for one group of the bonds with operating revenues, but of course the Revolution destroyed any possibility of that.[77] For the second group of bonds, Limantour claimed that the only government obligation was a moral guarantee.[78]

Roger W. Babson evaluated the National Railways in 1911 for *Moody's Manual*. He found that the unexchanged securities and bonds of the combined National and Central consumed in fixed charges 31.4 percent of its gross earnings, doubling the acceptable figure of 15 percent. In 1910, too, fixed charges took up 77.4 percent of net income, surpassing the acceptable level of 50 percent. Surplus available to pay dividends on First Preferred stock amounted to 9.2 percent of gross earnings; the ideal would have been 17 percent. The surplus did not provide sufficient funds to declare a full dividend for the Second Preferred shares. Common stock received no dividend. The trends in 1910, however, were better, with an increase in earnings per mile, a decrease in total capitalization per mile, and a decrease in fixed charges and other expenses as a percentage of gross revenues.[79] The trends were mixed for 1911, the first six months of which the Revolution affected. Babson considered the bonds of the National Railways a safe investment, so long as the civil unrest did not worsen. He judged the First Preferred stock "fairly attractive" because there was only a small number outstanding, and as a result, the company would have less difficulty generating surplus funds to pay its dividends. Second Preferred shares he labeled "speculative," which made the bonds and other securities more attractive than they would have been. When we analyze the fiscal indicators, the performance of the merged company was decidedly mixed.

Some observers have concluded that in reality the consolidation changed little, for the railroads remained in North American hands, the "yanquis" still operated the lines, and the public cost was high in terms of the potential increase in public debt.[80] S. M. Felton, the president of the Mexican Central, regarded the merger more positively:

> The merger plan is a new experiment in the direction of government ownership, and one that appeals to all thinking peoples, having many advantages over direct operation such as exists in Europe.... The government influence will only be felt in the direction of preventing inner railroad construction and in using the resources of the company for the development of the republic and furnishing railway facilities where they do not exist.... The start in Mexico has been made early enough to prevent a repetition of the enormous waste of money that we have seen in this country through the construction of parallel and competing lines. The concentration of so large a mileage into one control should produce large economies in operations.[81]

The newly constituted National Railways (FNM) expanded its transportation holdings and embarked on a much-needed, ambitious program of capital improvements. In July 1909 the company acquired the Mexican Pacific.

The next month it took over Wells Fargo's express business in Mexico. In January 1910, the FNM leased the Mexican Southern.[82] The acquisitions continued with the purchase of shares in the International, the Veracruz to Isthmus, the Veracruz to Pacific, and the Pan American Railroad lines in later 1910.[83] The FNM also invested large sums in betterments and new equipment, some 19,088,454 pesos during the fiscal years from 1908 to 1911.[84]

CONCLUSION

Despite the public pronouncements of Limantour and the contemporary observations of Russell, which are quite clear that the government undertook the consolidation most importantly to prevent the takeover of the nation's railroads by US robber barons, historians have offered alternative analyses of the causes and consequences of the government takeover. Each, to my mind, fits into the framework of preserving the delicate balance of economic forces that comprised the Díaz system. The three most perceptive additional interpretations as to why the Díaz regime undertook to purchase control of the railroad system are: first, that it was a bailout of foreign capitalists from a series of losing investments, in order to assure future infusions of funds into the Mexican economy; second, that it resulted from the interaction between the development of the railroad companies and the national government's railroad policies; and third, that it was part of an overall strategy to centralize control over the economy, which also included asserting control of banking and credit and the particular targets of centralization were the powerful economic groups based in northern Mexico.

First, some observers have claimed that the consolidation was aimed to bail out foreign capitalists from a series of losing investments, in order to assure future infusions of funds into the Mexican economy. The corollary of this view is that in the end the foreign financiers kept both financial and operational control over the new National Railways of Mexico. Lorena May Parlee has argued that the government "decided to cooperate with the U.S. trusts. As a partner in their ventures, the government hoped to retain a certain degree of influence and control over the companies."[85] She maintained that, despite the government owning the majority of shares in the FNM, control of the company actually lay in the hands of the primary creditors, who could take over if the company failed to pay the interest on its debt. There is no overt evidence to support this supposition. The Limantour correspondence with the banking houses cited above certainly contradicts the notion he was in any way not in control. In fact, the foreigners sometimes complained he had too much control.[86] Moreover, although the list of creditors in the consortium put together by Speyer & Company reads like a *Who's Who* of US and international financial institutions, we do not know how unified they were in their objectives and how much actual influence Speyer exerted on their behalf.[87] The fact that the negotiations were quite obviously difficult may indicate that the Mexicans were not willing to give up too much in the negotiations with Speyer and the other bankers. There is some peripheral evidence in the area of labor relations that indicates that the Díaz regime had taken the reins. In 1909 Limantour ordered the official language of the railroads to be changed from English to Spanish.[88] He also ordered that preference be given to qualified Mexicans over foreigners in employment.[89]

Second, other analysts look at the merger as a result of the interaction between the development of the railroad companies and the national government's railroad policies. Arturo Grunstein has maintained that the formation of the National Railways of Mexico was the result of the "historical process of interaction between the government and the railroad industry over time."[90] He identifies a series of crucial issues, such as how the railroads as private enterprises responded to the industry's enormous fixed costs and cutthroat competition. Along these lines, Grunstein explores whether there were strong internal pressures for consolidation among the railroads as privately owned companies. He also looks into government reactions, in the form of its policies, toward these two recurrent problems.

According to Grunstein, the Díaz government during the early 1890s opposed the railroads' obvious solution to their destructive competition, pooling arrangements, which brought about substantial increases in freight rates.[91] The Secretaría de Comunicaciones y Obras Públicas, established in 1891, was supposed to regulate rates, but proved ineffective. Although it was evident that pooling increased revenues and thereby eased the railroads' financial woes, the Díaz government, responsive to the interests of shippers (most likely the large mining companies and cattle ranchers), continued to oppose pooling. Eventually, in 1895, the cooperative agreements between the railroads dissolved because both the National and Central lines accused the other of violating the pact. A rate war ensued, but the railways reached a new arrangement in 1896. The government in this instance did not object. Grunstein concludes that the Díaz administration exerted "a degree" of regulatory control over the railroads and at least in principle opposed rate fixing, but that its main goal was to protect important foreign investments, such as the railroads. It was more likely, however, that Díaz and Limantour faced a somewhat more delicate dilemma in balancing the demands of shippers, some of which were foreign mining companies (the American Smelting and Refining Company, for one) or perhaps influential cattle ranchers. During the early 1890s, Díaz fought against a number of regional rebellions, which may have made him more receptive to the complaints of shippers. Once he quelled the uprisings, the dictator was freer to support the railroads through inaction.

Grunstein is convinced that Limantour gradually came to the conclusion that railroad competition was too costly, initially because he believed the government had to use scarce resources for subsidies to support too many lines, but later also because he saw the adverse financial impact of rate competition on the companies. In the Railroad Law of 1899 the government formally accepted pooling and rate fixing, although the Secretaría de Comunicaciones y Obras Públicas continued to have oversight. The Díaz government, then, was willing to permit cooperation, but maintained its supervision.[92] To that end it established a Tariff Commission. Once again, Díaz and his right arm Limantour walked the tightrope between competing interest groups in a delicate balancing act.

As Limantour gradually realized the detrimental effects of having too many railroads and too much competition, Grunstein asserts that the railroad companies simultaneously came to understand that the structure of the railway system in Mexico posed insurmountable obstacles to any cooperative arrangements in the long term.[93] The only way to end disastrous competition was consolidation. Both the Central and National in 1901 began to acquire other lines. The Central came to control the routes to Tampico, and the National maneuvered to monopolize access to the United States from northeastern Mexico. In 1902 the rivalry focused on the Interoceanic, which was the only possibility remaining for the National to gain access to the Gulf of Mexico. Grunstein argues that while the two major lines scrambled to expand, their financial bases crumbled under the strain of the devaluation of silver. Limantour concluded that railroad competition in the form of parallel lines and cutthroat rates, often in areas that could barely support a single line, wasted scarce resources and doomed major foreign investments to unsatisfactory yields.[94] Consolidation, perhaps through bankruptcies, would be the inevitable result. Collaterally, Mexico's financial credibility would suffer as well. It was at this point that the threat from the US robber barons emerged and spurred Limantour to act. The secretary of the treasury argued that the existing legal structure provided no means to prevent the private consolidation of the railroads.[95]

Grunstein's interpretation of the process by which Limantour came to his policy of consolidation of the railroads under government auspices is perceptive as far as it goes. When we take the railroad consolidation in a wider context, the actions of Díaz and Limantour make even more sense. Díaz carefully built a system of balances between various interest groups with himself at the center. Politics and economics were intimately intertwined. The great merger of railways was another component of the remarkable tightrope act.

Third and finally, historians assert that the consolidation was part of an overall strategy to centralize control over the economy, which also included asserting control of banking and credit; the particular targets of centralization were the powerful economic groups based in northern Mexico. Parlee maintains that the centralization of the Mexican economy began when Limantour took over as *secretario de hacienda* (secretary of the treasury) in 1891. He reordered import and export duties, established new taxes, abolished the *alcabalas* (internal tariffs between states or municipalities), reformed the banking system, and limited the states' ability to borrow and tax.[96]

Parlee points to the reorganization of the Mexican National in 1901, when three important northern entrepreneurs, Miguel de Iturbe of Sinaloa, Juan N. Navarro, and Ernesto Madero of Coahuila joined the railroad's board in Mexico City, as evidence of the growing influence of the northerners. The Madero family was at the center of two major economic groups in the north, the Laguna-based and the Monterrey-based industrialists. The Central counted among its board members, Enrique C. Creel, the son-in-law of Luis Terrazas of Chihuahua, the largest cattle owner in Mexico, and Pablo Martínez del Río, another prominent northern landowner.[97] She also discerns connections between northern interests and the two big US investor-owned lines. For example, the Madero family sold their Coahuila al Pacífico line to the Central.⁹⁸ There is no doubt that the Monterrey group and the Terrazas family had enormous economic power. Díaz, however, in his usual method, sought to divide them. He sent General Bernardo Reyes, the political boss of the Monterrey region, arguably his most logical successor, to a diplomatic post abroad. At the same time, Díaz permitted Luis Terrazas to triumphantly return to the governorship of Chihuahua in 1902, after years of being at loggerheads. The Monterrey industrialists were left alone. Nonetheless, when the railroads merged, the new company did not include any of the northerners on its board.⁹⁹ It is not clear what this meant, for Creel was on his way to Mexico City to serve the Díaz government first as ambassador to the United States and later as secretary of foreign relations and was, thus, ineligible for the FNM board. Regardless, trying to fend off the northern onslaught would have fit into the careful balancing act Díaz and Limantour created.

Although some contemporary critics and later historians have questioned whether the Mexican government was actually in control of the National Railways, the formation of the National Railways of Mexico was a masterful accomplishment. Confronted with the specter of growing trusts in the United States, the movement of the "Seven Kings" of US railroads into Mexico, and the deteriorating financial situation of the nation's railroads, which made them increasingly vulnerable to takeover, Porfirio Díaz and José Y. Limantour sought to maintain the delicate balance within their carefully constructed tripartite system. Díaz and Limantour constructed a relatively inexpensive solution to the railroad dilemma that in the short term because of the Revolution eased the railroads' financial straits, prevented takeover by the US trusts, and maintained good relations with foreign investors. In purchasing the railways, the Díaz regime did not "sell out" its nation, but rather reestablished the checks and balances of its economy.

Díaz, Limantour, and the revolutionary leaders that followed them tried mightily to maintain the difficult balancing act between elite, foreign enterprise, and government, not only with the railroads but also, as we will see in the succeeding chapters, in the other two major sectors of the Mexican economy—agriculture (landholding) and mining.

FOUR

Foreign Landowners

The influx of foreign investment into Mexican land from the 1880s onward was enormous. John Mason Hart has estimated that US citizens owned a hundred million acres, comprising 22 percent of the nation's territory.[1] In trying to assess the operations and impact of foreign landownership historians have encountered considerable impediments. Government documents are incomplete and often unreliable; as a result, obtaining aggregate data on the plight of foreign agricultural enterprises is difficult. There are also very few records from foreign farms and ranches.[2] We are left primarily with anecdotal evidence from scattered sources. However, these are sufficient to leave us with a rough pattern over the course of sixty years between 1880 and 1940. This chapter explores the place of foreign landowners in Mexico from the Porfiriato through the Revolution until 1940. I shall argue three points. First, most foreign landowners failed. In order to obtain success, foreign-owned ranching enterprises in Mexico during the dictatorship of Porfirio Díaz, the Revolution, and postrevolutionary era required all of the following six circumstances: sufficient capital to purchase necessary equipment and pay for daily operations; competent management; a steady market for agricultural commodities; accessible transportation; a reliable workforce; and the maintenance of good working relations with local, state, and national authorities. Most companies and individuals lacked at least one and usually more of these required components. Even with all these, however, it was very difficult to make money. The largest of the operations, with millions of acres and millions of pesos invested, were often at best only erratically profitable. A number of the agricultural colonies and lumber enterprises were spectacular failures. Second, despite the ownership of vast tracts of land, foreign companies and individuals did not dominate agriculture. The prevalent historiography about foreign landholders in Mexico during the era from 1880 to 1940 is insufficiently nuanced. The Porfiriato did not favor foreigners to the extent proffered by the official history of the Revolution, nor did the Revolution treat foreigners as badly as some historians have maintained. Further complicating our assessments and the contemporary situation, governments during and after the Revolution were inconsistent in their treatment of foreign landowners. Because governments at the different levels did not always agree on their attitude toward a particular enterprise, conflicts were common.[3] For example, although the Díaz regime favored the immigration of foreigners to farm and ranch, the welcome did not always extend to the state and local levels. Thus, checks on the influence of the foreign landholders were built into the system. Third, it is not at all clear that foreign landowners were the villains that historians and revolutionaries have sometimes depicted. Foreign landholders invested tremendous amounts in a capital-intensive sector. Expenditures on irrigation, transportation, fencing, housing, and equipment greatly enhanced the countryside and production, though not always to the extent that made these enterprises profitable. Most of the foreign landowners constantly poured funds into their properties, adding to their value and to the local economy, rather than siphoning off funds to their stockholders abroad. Moreover, there is evidence that indicates that foreign landowners paid their workers better and provided more benefits than their Mexican counterparts. Certainly, they treated their labor force no worse.

Foreign agricultural investment was of several kinds: individuals who sought to farm or ranch in agricultural colonies or as individuals or families; speculators, who sought to develop communities of small farmers; religious settlements seeking sanctuary; large investors, both corporations and individuals, which obtained vast tracts; and lumber companies.

BACKGROUND

During the Díaz era, foreign farmers and ranchers came in two waves, the first with the spread of the major north-south railroad lines during the 1880s, and the second with the extension of the railroads east and west to fill in the gaps in transportation after 1900.[4] The Díaz regime made foreign investment an integral part of the development strategy mapped out by the dictator and his advisors. There were, however, a number of obstacles for foreigners who sank their money into Mexican land during the Porfiriato. First, foreigners not infrequently bought property involved in long-standing conflicts with neighboring villages and *hacendados*. To complicate matters further, documentation on boundaries was often unclear. It was not unusual for haciendas and villages to contest their land and water rights for decades. Second, local authorities, often landholders, were not always pleased to have foreign competition. Foreigners were willing to spend enormous sums on transportation, irrigation, fencing, and equipment that most Mexican farmers could not afford. Foreigners commonly, though not always, paid their employees better than the locals, which caused unending resentment among Mexican landowners. In addition, foreign agricultural enterprises often had to pay local police and other officials for cooperation.

During the decade of warfare between 1910 and 1920, foreign landholders suffered considerable damages. Raids took away livestock, harvests, supplies, and equipment. Military operations got preference on the railroads, so it was nearly impossible to ship produce or livestock to market. There were many instances of foreigners taken hostage for ransom and several cases of murder. The losses as reported to the Mexico-United States Claims Commission were enormous, though it is likely that the Americans exaggerated them. Foreigners commonly found themselves caught between the various warring factions, having to pay taxes or extortion to one side or another, depending upon which invaded their property at the time. In some areas radical generals carried out land reform by expropriating foreign-owned properties. By March 1917, according to one American consul, only the Palomas Land and Cattle Company continued to run herds of cattle along the northern border, for the rebels had cleared out the other ranches.[5] Stolen crops and equipment, as well as damaged fences and irrigation took a heavy toll. From the beginning of the Revolution, revolutionaries coveted foreign property for land reform. Pressures for land redistribution built up during the 1920s and exploded under President Lázaro Cárdenas (1934–40). But foreigners were not singled out for either better or worse treatment than Mexican landowners. It was the particulars of the specific circumstances that determined the extent of expropriations or depredations rather than citizenship.

The early 1920s brought a flurry of land redistributions in response to local challenges from the villages that had provided many of the soldiers who had fought the Revolution and the de la Huerta rebellion in 1923 and 1924, which presented a severe threat to the postrevolutionary regime. President Alvaro Obregón had little choice but to redistribute land in order to gain support to balance more than half the national army that revolted against him during the de la Huerta uprising. Reform was erratic during the Maximato (1924–34), when Plutarco Elías Calles ruled with little sympathy for land redistribution. In the years before Cárdenas in Coahuila, for example, the American consul reported that there were still at least eight American individuals or companies that owned more than 100,000 acres in the state.[6] In the Yaqui Valley of Sonora 45,000 of the 125,000 acres under cultivation in 1934 were owned by Americans, who maintained that without exception they had been treated fairly. A few had become Mexican citizens. Two Americans were on the board of the regional Farmers' Cooperative.[7]

According to the calculations of John J. Dwyer, from January 1, 1927, through October 6, 1940, the Mexican government legally expropriated 6.2 million acres from at least 319 American property owners; approximately 1.8 million acres were agricultural lands, 3.6 million for livestock, 450,000 for timberlands, and 300,000 unclassified.[8] Almost two-thirds of the compensation claims filed by the American owners were under US$50,000, and 85 percent were less than US$100,000. Most American landholders held small or medium-size estates (or the government expropriated parts of larger properties).[9] During the Cárdenas era, two hundred Americans lost 5 million acres, a little more than 10 percent of the total expropriated during his presidency. If Hart's calculations are correct that Americans owned 22 percent of the land and Dwyer calculates they only accounted for 10 percent of the expropriations, then, of course, Americans suffered proportionately less than Mexicans in the land reform.

Through all of the civil wars and rebellions, the struggle to maintain equilibrium between the Mexican elite, foreigners, and government continued. The pressure on the revolutionary regime for restitution of allegedly stolen lands was unending and maintained the long-standing conflicts between haciendas and pueblos. During the presidencies of Alvaro Obregón and Plutarco Elías Calles, the crucial counterweight to the demand for land redistribution was the need for reconstruction. Both leaders recognized the necessity to rebuild the agricultural sector, primarily to feed the population. There was a desperate need for expertise, which the large landowners could provide. A second counterweight was the need to mollify the United States. US policymakers distrusted the revolutionary regime and at times refused to recognize its legitimacy. Any move against the property of US companies was sure to damage relations between the two nations. Obregón and Calles were especially careful in their dealings with US landowners. This all changed, of course, after Cárdenas's term began in 1934.[10] Almost all of the foreign-owned ranches lost lands.[11] The pressures for land redistribution were too strong to delay any longer.

The havoc wreaked by a decade of warfare and twenty-five years of on-again-off-again agrarian reforms is difficult to measure because the extent of the reforms and their impact varied according to time period and region. Agrarian reform depended on local circumstances, on just how strong the demands from the pueblos were and the inclinations of political bosses.

Nonetheless, for foreigners, Mexican land, like mining, seemed to be a source of unending possibilities. No matter what the downside—the lack of water, the inhospitality of local officials, resentment by competing Mexican farmers, civil war, agrarian reform—optimistic foreigners continually sought their fortunes.[12] The outbreak of a revolution in 1910 did not initially deter these optimists, and the intensification of warfare did not stop some hardy souls from coming to Mexico during the 1910s. Even the threats of expropriation did not deter foreigners from investing. Some stayed the course through the 1940s and came to prosper when the post–World War II boom came.

If we turn to the six elements of successful landholding by foreigners in Mexico, we can discern just how difficult it was to make a living in agriculture, let alone reap great profits. Although there were, to be sure, foreign farmers who at times prospered, the majority were failures in the long term. The obstacles were considerable.

CAPITAL

Precise statistics for investment in land are difficult to obtain. The two main sources—newspaper accounts and claims placed before the various claims commissions—were unreliable. Certainly, foreigners expended hundreds of thousands of pesos in purchasing land. For example, the Union Trust Company, owned by Texas cattlemen, bought one million acres from the Asúnsolo family in Chihuahua in 1909 for US$500,000 (one million pesos).[13] William C. Greene reportedly expended US$1.25 million dollars to acquire 2.5 million acres in Chihuahua and Sonora for his lumber operation.[14] In addition, the capital investment in livestock breeding, irrigation, mills, and other infrastructure was considerable. Farms and ranches needed substantial capital because good seed, fences, irrigation, and breeding stock were costly. The Corralitos Company poured hundreds of thousands of dollars into its stock, fencing, and irrigation. Other farmers and ranchers invested similarly. Many of the large haciendas constructed fences around their property, sometimes covering hundreds of miles. The cotton plantations of the Laguna in Durango and the vegetable farmers of the Yaqui Valley in Sonora required huge capital investments in irrigation. Ranchers like the Hearsts and Bentons introduced expensive new breeds of cattle. The owners of the larger operations, such as Hearst, Palomas, and Corralitos, sometimes seemed to have unending resources to sink into their estates. Others, like the Richardson Construction Company and Cargill Lumber, never had enough capital available to succeed. Smaller operators with more modest capital resources struggled to improve their equipment and water supply. Even with the difficult experiences of the Revolution, foreigners were willing to expend large sums for property. For example, a German-Russian syndicate bought the 1.4 million-acre Mesilla hacienda, forty miles south of Saltillo, Coahuila, in 1920 and proceeded to invest US$1.2 million in irrigation projects.[15]

MANAGEMENT

Competent management was, perhaps, relatively easy to acquire, but foreign managers were often out of their element in Mexico. W. M. Ferris, who managed the vast Hearst estate San José de Babícora from 1922 to 1931, maintained that "to be successful as a manager of any important business in Mexico during the troublous twenty years following the Revolution of 1910, a man had to be something of a diplomat, lawyer, and almost a prophet, as well as a businessman."[16] Few foreigners could fulfill these requirements. Hearst's first manager, socialite Jack Follansbee, for example, spent most of his time in New York City rather than at the ranch.[17] The foreign-owned ranches were never as expertly run as the Terrazas or Madero estates.

MARKET

The market for livestock depended on the availability of cheap transportation, the status of US tariffs, and the growth of Mexico City. The estimates for exports to the United States, the largest market for Mexican cattle, are incomplete. Between the 1870s and 1910s the price for Mexican cattle in the United States varied from thirteen to twenty dollars.[18] Conditions fluctuated rather sharply over the years. In 1871 the US consul in Chihuahua observed that prospects for cattle ranching were dim because there was no suitable market, but by 1879 exports began to rise.[19] The beginning of construction of the Mexican Central Railroad promised to open up both Mexico City and US markets. Four years later the *Chihuahua Enterprise* noted that demand for cattle was spurring investment interest.[20] Demand caused prices for cattle to rise to sixteen to twenty dollars per head in 1884.[21] The completion of the Mexican Central Railroad in the mid-1880s opened the US market to Mexican cattle and a boom ensued. According to Manual Machado, between 1881 and 1892, Mexico exported 4.5 million pesos' worth of livestock, or 375,000 pesos per annum.[22] (At twenty dollars a head that amounts to 18,750 per year; at thirteen, just over 28,000.)

US capital poured into northern Mexico to take advantage of the potential of cattle ranches. The US Consul General reported that "our citizens . . . hold extensive grazing ranges in various states, and two or three years ago were in a fair way to make large profits. They not only had a considerable market in the interior of Mexico, but also could export to the United States. . . . There was a large demand in the United States for range cows and bulls." The investors planned to take advantage of the lower costs in Mexico.

The US Congress ended the boom abruptly with the enactment of the US McKinley Tariff, which effectively cut off the US market, eliminating more than half the market for cattle.[23] Demand and prices recovered in 1895 when the United States returned the import tax on cattle to what it had been prior to 1890.[24] Mexican exports of cattle then increased markedly from 1895 to 1897.[25] In 1898 the US consul at Ciudad Juárez claimed that the northern herds were almost exhausted because of export demand in the United States and Cuba. But when the United States increased the tariff by three dollars per head in 1897, exports fell again and remained depressed through 1909. Led by rises in the domestic and Cuban markets, another real boom occurred in 1910 and continued through the first three years of the Revolution.[26]

Although from 1914 through 1919, the disruptions of war made it impossible to calculate export statistics, we know that in 1910 Mexico had 5,142,524 head of cattle and by 1923 there were 1,750,305 head remaining. It is likely that many of these cattle found their way to the United States as contraband. With the end of World War I in Europe and the economic downturn in the United States that followed, demand for Mexican cattle declined. In addition, the Mexican government instituted a tax on cattle exports in order to force ranchers to restore their herds. Exports recovered in the late 1920s and maintained a steady rate through the first years of the Great Depression.

WORKFORCE

The availability of the manpower necessary to operate foreign-owned ranches and farms does not seem to have arisen very often as an issue. What is highly controversial is the foreigners' treatment of Mexican peons, sharecroppers, and tenants. According to critics, like John Mason Hart, Americans in particular accomplished the transition to the "new commercial and industrial export agricultural complex . . . through the extreme violence and repression of the rural masses needed to carry out land consolidation."[27]

While certainly there were cases of foreigners mistreating their employees, the scattered evidence indicates rather that foreigners commonly adopted the practices of whatever region in which they farmed or ranched. The wages and working conditions they offered were no better or no worse than what Mexican landowners provided. As Friedrich Katz has outlined, agricultural working conditions during the Porfiriato varied sharply according to the specific area, north, central, or south.[28] Thus, in the north, where American investment concentrated and where competition for skilled cowboys (vaqueros) was intense, wages tended to be higher than in the rest of the country. In the far south, where labor was also scarce, employers used coercion, even to the extent that conditions equated to slavery. There is considerable circumstantial evidence indicating that generally foreigners raised wages and working conditions. First, the region where foreign investment was largest, the north, also had the highest wages. Second, there were common complaints from Mexican landowners that foreigners had offered wages that upset long-standing traditions of exploitation. The most common complaint, especially in the north, though mostly in the mining camps, was the higher wages paid to foreigners and the unwillingness of some foreign companies to promote Mexicans to supervisory positions.

RELATIONS WITH THE GOVERNMENT

In terms of their relations with various levels of Mexican government and elites, foreign landowners sometimes experienced rougher handling by local or state authorities than the federal government during the Díaz era, the Revolution, and revolutionary reconstruction. Although the Díaz regime had the reputation of welcoming foreigners and treating them favorably, the newcomers not infrequently encountered difficulties. Rival elite and middle class resented them. Local authorities did not always concur with national government policies. Landowners met resistance from local villages, which had conflicting, long-standing claims for land and water. Titles and boundaries were often incomplete or inaccurate.

The opposition of local authorities was an obstacle nearly impossible to overcome. For example, the Paul family, German immigrants, settled in Coahuila in 1893 at San Pedro de las Colonias and they encountered no problems for more than a decade. In 1905 Emilio Paul bought two abandoned properties in Coahuila, investing 350,000 pesos. When his first year yielded a cotton crop worth 40,000 pesos, it appeared that Paul was on the verge of success. However, his plantations bordered on the holdings of Francisco Madero y Hijos, which also wanted the properties. The Maderos offered to buy the land for what it had cost Paul. When he refused, the new *jefe político*, Mariano Viesca Arizpe, harassed him. In response, Paul wrote to President Díaz for assistance.[29] The governor of Coahuila subsequently intervened in the matter, reporting to Díaz that the property in question had been subject to litigation before Paul had purchased it. Although Paul's "cavalier" attitude had exacerbated relations with his neighbors, the governor promised to find a solution to the dispute.[30] Local officials were a thorn in the foreign entrepreneur's side during the era of reconstruction. The president of the Campeche-Laguna Corporation, which operated a 609,000-acre chicle plantation, complained bitterly, "I just have to fight daily to save what little I can. Every government official is bitter to the core against all Americans, and they are willfully and deliberately placing every obstacle in their power against our interests."[31] Local authorities were not always hostile. The governor of Chiapas reported to Porfirio Díaz in 1907 that the foreigners in his region, who owned most of the coffee plantations, "do not have difficulties with local authorities," and with the blessing of local authorities they could flourish.[32]

Problems on the local level were not limited to government officials. Agitation by pueblos against haciendas, of course, existed long before the Revolution. Generally, however, the prevalent historiography has not explored these conflicts in the context of foreign investment before 1910. Foreign landowners often faced stiff opposition from neighboring villages. The pueblo of Palomas, Galeana District, Chihuahua, for example, contested land claims with the Wood-Hagenbarth Land and Cattle Company in 1907.[33] Often the foreigners merely inherited the conflicts from the previous Mexican owners. Foreigners bought properties unaware of disputed boundaries and dubious documentation.

The outbreak of the Revolution and the ensuing disruptions took a heavy toll on foreign and Mexican property owners. The government of Francisco I. Madero did not pursue land reform, choosing instead to follow slow-moving legal procedures to restore disputed lands to the villages that had rebelled. The pugnacious pueblos in Chihuahua and Morelos in particular had little patience for the courts to return lands stolen from them by surveying companies and greedy planters. In the civil wars that followed Madero's ouster and assassination, the rival factions regarded foreign landholders as supply depots to support their armies. Soldiers needed the crops and livestock to feed themselves. Whether the landowners turned their commodities over through payment of taxes or extortion or robbery, the result was the same. There were a few radical military who expropriated haciendas. Villa took over the Terrazas estates, for example. Some villages overran abandoned or undefended haciendas, as well. The Constitution of 1917, of course, significantly undermined foreign property rights.

A series of dangerous rebellions during the 1920s and the importance of regional political bosses, such as Tomás Garrido Canabal in Tabasco, Adalberto Tejeda in Veracruz, and Saturnino Cedillo in San Luis Potosí, diminished the authority of the national government.[34] Presidents Obregón, Calles, Emilio Portes Gil, Pascual Ortiz Rubio, and Abelardo Rodríguez focused on reconstruction and repair of US relations, but local commanders and politicos had to respond to the demands and protests of the pueblos.[35] Often local public opinion overrode the presidents. President Cárdenas, with the worst of the Great Depression over and US relations far more favorable, turned toward far-reaching agrarian reforms. The power of the state governments remained considerable as in the case of Sonora, where the relatively conservative governor Román Yocupicio blocked much of the Cárdenas program in his state.[36]

Foreigners protested strongly against agrarian reforms and employed any and all tactics to avoid losing their land, including violence, much like their Mexican counterparts. They used the courts, often obtaining *amparos*, claiming that the government treated them unfairly. They claimed that there were irregularities in the agrarian censuses (which determined who was eligible for land grants), improper classification of lands as eligible for expropriation, noncompliance with the laws regarding dotation of lands nearest to petitioning villages, and failure of local authorities to prevent squatters from occupying land long enough to legally claim the right to petition for ejidos.[37] Some of the larger operations hired their own *pistoleros* to defend their property. The laws allowed division of the properties into smaller, legal units, so American landowners subdivided. Ruben Bruce, for example, bought the Hacienda de Santo Domingo in 1881. Confronted by the uncertainties of the Revolution, his heirs sold the property to the Southwestern Land and Cattle Company in 1912. To avoid expropriation in 1934 the company divided the 180,000 acres into six entities.[38]

Rivalries notwithstanding, large Mexican and foreign landowners were perfectly willing to join forces when necessary to fight land reform. In Coahuila, for example, in 1933 Mexican and American cattle raisers formed the Coahuila Cattle Raisers Association.[39] In the late 1930s the Cárdenas government, worried that the recovery of agriculture, particularly livestock raising, was in jeopardy because of the agrarian reform, changed tactics and instituted policies that granted writs of *inafectabilidad* that protected large estates from expropriation.

INDIVIDUAL HOLDINGS

The histories of individually owned and operated ranches reveal varied success because of their owners' inability to fulfill the required six criteria, with the most important difficulties arising from being unable to fit in with the local environment. We see a pattern in which individuals and corporations invested large sums in the purchase and improvement of their properties, looking toward long-term yields, building irrigation systems, constructing fences and roads, and introducing new livestock breeds. The results during the Porfiriato were mixed. Some of the larger operations, like Hearst's San José de Babícora, flourished. Others made money but poured it right back into the property. Still others failed entirely. The Revolution brought widespread ruin to many large landowners, foreigners and Mexicans alike. Even the biggest operators found themselves raided and robbed. Disrupted transportation shut off access to markets. The result was widespread abandonment, stagnation, or failure. In the aftermath of the Revolution and the beginning of economic reconstruction during the 1920s and 1930s foreign property holders confronted the threat and the reality of agrarian reform. Some smaller operators may have avoided the various waves of land reform, but many were adversely affected. The larger holdings with their more extensive resources held off losing their property, sometimes for decades. Nonetheless, few, if any, escaped. Many lost everything.

Perhaps the most notorious case of an individual foreign landowner in the period under study was that of William Benton, an Englishman, who met his premature end at the hands of Pancho Villa in 1914. Benton was part of the second wave of heavy investment after 1900. He acquired three haciendas that together extended over 300,000 acres near Santa Isabel in Chihuahua, paying at least 200,000 pesos. The land included good pasture with water. He raised 5,300 head of cattle and cultivated 6,000 acres in corn, beans, and wheat.[40] One family member later claimed that the hacienda generated 100,000 pesos a year and its potential was to produce considerably more.[41]

Benton was widely unpopular because of long-standing disputes with his peons and the neighboring pueblo Santa María de las Cuevas. He used hired gunmen to evict tenants from his property, and he fenced off his land, preventing the neighboring villagers from grazing their cattle as they had traditionally. To make matters worse he took over lands belonging to Santa María de las Cuevas. He evidently had Chihuahua state authorities on his side, for a bodyguard of *rurales* allowed him to run roughshod over the region.

The outbreak of the Revolution changed the balance of power in the region. Benton first encountered Pancho Villa in 1912, when the general had demanded a forced loan. The belligerent Benton refused.[42] Villa then took arms, ammunition, and livestock from the Benton ranch. After the coup by General Victoriano Huerta in 1913 that overthrew the government of Francisco Madero, Villa—unusually amenable—advised Benton to leave the country, for he could not guarantee the Englishman's safety. Villa promised that he would not expropriate Benton's land, but neither would he protect him from the local villagers. The conflict heated up, when the villagers took some of Benton's cattle and resumed grazing their cattle on the disputed land. Benton demanded payment for the lost cattle and the expulsion of the villagers from his land. Villa offered to buy the hacienda. When Benton personally confronted Villa on February 17, 1914, there was an altercation and Villa killed Benton.[43]

The Benton heirs, including his widow and children, held on to the property through the Revolution.[44] However, the agrarian reform of the 1920s and 1930s jeopardized the ranch. The Bentons lost nearly 100,000 acres to agrarian reform through 1937.[45] In 1925 Ian Benton proposed that the family exchange Los Remedios for another property, the Hacienda San Lorenzo, formerly part of the Terrazas estate, then controlled by the Caja de Préstamos para Obras de Agricultura y Irigación.[46] At one point the Bentons secured the approval of this plan from Governor Francisco R. Almada and a representative of Calles, Francisco Quijano, who was willing to "cooperate at a price."[47] But the plan evidently foundered when the Bentons could not get the cooperation of Secretary of Agriculture Luis León or the head engineer of the Caja de Préstamos.[48]

The original holdings were mostly lost. But one family member, former British military officer Ian, William's son, leased property in the Santa

Clara Mountains in 1920. He bought Aberdeen-Angus cattle to improve breeding. He eventually moved his operation to the 100,000-acre Sueco Ranch, buying rich grazing land once part of the vast estate of the Terrazas family, which he acquired in 1933 using his connections. He invested heavily, building wells and fencing. He died in the 1950s with a reputation for producing high-quality breeding stock.[49]

The Benton case shows us how elite, foreigners, and government interacted throughout the era. The Englishman enjoyed excellent relations with the Terrazas-Creel family, the dominant political group in Chihuahua during the Porfiriato.[50] The stationing of a detachment of rurales on his property indicated state and national government support. The Bentons also got some backing from the state government and President Calles in its effort to exchange their property for another ranch in the mid-1920s. But, of course, intergovernmental disagreements stopped the transaction. The family apparently reestablished its connections to the ruling group during the 1930s, allowing Ian Benton to purchase a new hacienda from the Caja de Préstamos. The Bentons' connections had not sufficed to fend off the pueblos in the 1920s, but were enough to obtain new lands and remain in Mexico. The Bentons were at the heart of the postrevolutionary conflict between local pressures for agrarian reform and the national government's push to rebuild agriculture, which required considerable capital and expertise.

Of course not all foreign landowners suffered tragic demise; others survived the Revolution only to endure endless struggles with local authorities. Dr. M. F. Bauchert successfully rode out the Revolution only to encounter difficulties in the late 1920s amid the resurgent agrarian reform in Chihuahua. Bauchert had come to Mexico in 1898 as a dentist under contract with Alexander Shepherd and the Batopilas Company. Later that year, he established a private practice in Ciudad Chihuahua. He acquired a ranch in Aldama, which endured considerable damage during the Revolution. Bauchert had to leave Mexico for short periods in 1913 and 1915. He practiced dentistry in El Paso until 1920, when he bought a new ranch in Allende, Jiménez, Chihuahua, the Hacienda Valsequillo. Its 82,000 acres were a "veritable paradise," well watered with excellent pasture and timber, where he raised a variety of crops and rented out part of the property for grazing. In May 1928 the local Agrarian Commission notified him of its intent to expropriate a strip of land along the river that ran through his ranch for the ejidos of the village of Matamoros. Bauchert believed that former General Ernesto García was behind his difficulties, for the two were in legal dispute over unpaid rents. At the same time, local agrarians who had petitioned to take his property cut timber from both the disputed lands and the property recognized as belonging to Bauchert. In 1929 both the governor and the chief of the local agrarian commission ordered the agrarians off the property. Despite the victory against the expropriation, he had lost considerable timber and a year's rent.[51] Bauchert lost at least two more sections, totaling about 12,500 acres, by 1937.[52]

Again in the Bauchert case, the attitude of the authorities was crucial and not uniform. In this instance a local military commander made life miserable for Bauchert, despite the efforts of the governor and the local agrarian commission, which found in his favor. His local connections did him little good during the Cárdenas reform.

Not all foreign landowners persevered as did the Benton family and Dr. Bauchert, despite large investments. Captain A. B. Urmston owned the 206,000-acre Hacienda de San Pedro in Galeana District, Chihuahua. He was unable to recover from the setbacks of the 1910s and eventually sold out, probably at a substantial loss. Urmston and a partner acquired part of the property in two installments in 1891 and 1895, and he then bought out his partner a year later. Urmston lived on and operated the hacienda from 1890 to 1909, investing great amounts in houses, saw mills, fencing, and irrigation. By the time he retired to England in 1909, he had fifteen thousand head of cattle and one thousand horses. Together the livestock alone were estimated to be worth nearly US$400,000.[53]

The revolutionaries ravaged his property. Rebels first raided San Pedro in 1912, and in the ensuing years they took horses, cattle, corn, and merchandise. By May 1920 only three thousand head of cattle and perhaps fifty to one hundred horses remained. The revolutionaries had stolen more than ten thousand head of cattle, which the manager claimed were worth US$285,000. The rebels also damaged the property. These losses were in addition to the US$200,000 in operating expenses incurred from 1912 to 1920.

Urmston nearly sold the property in 1912 for US$600,000, including the livestock, but the outbreak of the Orozco rebellion against Madero aborted the transaction. After many other attempts to sell, Urmston finally sold San Pedro to C. K. Warren for US$170,000 in 1924. Urmston's claim against

Mexico for his losses was US$772,000. The claims commission, however, awarded only US$50,000.⁵⁴ Captain Urmston cut his losses. It is interesting that Warren, who had owned other property in Chihuahua since the Porfiriato, chose to acquire additional land even in the face of the onslaught of agrarian reform.⁵⁵ Evidently the lure of the land was still strong.

John R. Blocker's experience matched that of Urmston. He went to Mexico in 1898, starting out renting a ranch in Coahuila, subsequently purchasing the 125,000 acres in 1900 and then another 362,000 acres in 1909. Blocker later told the Fall Committee that he had projected to have had clear profits of US$500,000 per year. Initially, Blocker had excellent relations with the authorities. During the Díaz administration, he claimed that "nobody was ever treated any nicer than we were."⁵⁶ The first years of the Revolution his property was untouched, most likely because he had purchased 237,000 acres of his holdings from the Madero family. But after Madero's overthrow he endured raids for seven years. At one point, General Marcelo Caraveo took one hundred twenty horses and ten mules, killed forty hogs and all the chickens, and slaughtered a number of cattle. Blocker also had to pay a ransom to a carrancista major for his foreman. In 1920 Blocker had not earned a cent from the land in five years and the ranch lay idle.⁵⁷ Like Urmston, Blocker's large investments were lost and the Revolution undermined the value of his property.

Sometimes even the cooperation of local officials was not enough to assure the protection of foreign properties. James D. Sheahan was one of five partners who purchased 362,000 acres near Jimenez, Chihuahua, for US$350,000 in 1903, and over the next six years he invested another US$300,000. He grew grain on a third of the ranch and grazed blooded, registered stock on the rest. The ranch employed 350 people, most of whom were Mexican peons who worked the land on shares. In one instance the ranch rented several thousand acres to José Chávez, who in turn subleased it to peons. The ranch provided housing and a school, and it refurbished the church. Sheahan encountered no trouble with authorities or bandits until 1914, when the carrancistas demanded livestock and took the harvests. In 1917 the ranch appealed to the US consul, who got the local military commander to send troops to protect the harvest. Unfortunately, the fifty troops dispatched to protect the ranch got drunk and burned down much of the property. By the time of the Fall Committee hearings in 1920, Sheahan assessed the ranch as a "total wreck."⁵⁸

Another victim of the Revolution was the Tabasco Plantation Company, which had purchased more than 250,000 acres on the Coatzalcoalcos (pronounced: ko-ats-al-ko-al-kos) River, in Veracruz and Tabasco, producing cacao, rubber, and bananas. The company invested US$300,000 in the land and another US$1.5 million in a sugar mill to create what its owner boasted was "the finest plantation in the state of Veracruz." For its enormous investment it earned a paltry US$500 a month in rent for pasture. The extortion of the company by the revolutionaries started in 1914. The next year a band of soldiers settled on the plantation and took whatever they wanted. The conditions worsened under the Carranza regime, when the company was "harassed to the point of exasperation." The company was "badgered, shanghaied, and cockshuttled between bandits in the brush and those representing the Carranza government" until "compelled to shut down."[59] In 1919 the property was a wreck.

It was not just during the Revolution and its aftermath when foreigners endured harsh treatment on the local level. William H. Mealy somehow managed to incur the wrath of the camarilla of Bernardo Reyes in Coahuila during the Porfiriato. He had borrowed more than 400,000 pesos from Banco de Londres, but after six years of constant harassment, he needed a further loan of 150,000 pesos. He was on the brink of disaster when he wrote Díaz for assistance in 1903.[60]

Land investors fell victim to bad management, partner squabbles, and lack of capital, all of which were exemplified by the difficulties of the Río Tamasapo Sugar Company, which purchased the 13,000-acre Hacienda Agua Buena in San Luis Potosí in 1903. The company invested US$1 million in a modern sugar refinery, a railroad, and other machinery. In 1909 H. B. Tanner, the president of the company, mortgaged the property for US$55,000 to Banco Hipotecario, evidently so that he, his brother, and his son could lease the neighboring sugar plantation, the Hacienda Tamasapo, planning to lease it to tenants who knew how to grow sugar and who would sell their production to the Río Tamaspo mill. In 1911 Tanner's brother sold his shares to a German, Luis Roever, who borrowed money from a German bank to purchase them. Rebel raids began in 1913, and as a result neither Tanner nor Roever was able to repay their loans and went into default. The Río Tamasapo board thereupon fired Tanner. Litigation ensued, complicated by the fact that Roever was a German citizen (this was during World War I). After some years, Tanner lost his investment.[61] Like

Bauchert, Urmston, Blocker, Mealy, and Giroux, Tanner had invested a fortune and lost it all. Unlike the others, he had mostly himself to blame.

The more modest foreign farmers and ranchers usually suffered the same obstacles and difficulties as the larger operations. Large or small, they required the same six requisites for success. Gideon Giroux, for example, bought three properties in 1909 for US$16,000 in Rayón, Ures, Sonora, consisting of 9,423 acres. He invested another US$15,000 in irrigation and fencing, and he planted half and left the rest for grazing. Giroux died in 1918, leaving the estate to his wife, who subsequently transferred it to her son in 1926. Apparently the family avoided agrarian conflict until they were devastated in 1937 when the government expropriated almost all the grazing land and all of the 279 irrigated acres, leaving the Giroux with 3,458 worthless acres because the expropriation also took their water rights.[62]

The smaller operators were particularly vulnerable to local political machinations. Gaston Morris, a farmer in Sinaloa, acquired 3,705 acres in the early 1920s, using a mortgage obtained in the United States to purchase the property. He failed because he refused to cooperate with other farmers in the region. Morris invested US$200,000 in improving the land and planted 1,000 to 2,000 acres of string beans, most of which went for export to the winter market in the United States. For eleven years he operated without incident. Then, in 1933 local farmers formed an agricultural association for the purpose of controlling winter vegetable production, designating Wells Fargo as its sales and marketing representative. Morris and some other farmers objected. They marketed their own crops, but they ended up having to pay a handling fee to Wells Fargo. Morris's objections quite likely led to his harassment by local agrarians. In 1933 the governor of Sinaloa ordered the expropriation of more than 3,200 acres, nearly Morris's entire farm.[63] Another foreign entrepreneur who ran afoul of local authorities was Joseph L. Fox, who went to Mexico in 1895 in order to improve his health. He first manufactured carriages in Irapuato, Guanajuato, then imported pianos and autos from the United States. His brother Edward joined him in 1905. At age forty-five he married a widow with one child in 1910 and had four more children. The Revolution forced him to move to Mexico City in 1914, where he stayed through the 1930s. He closed his carriage factory and started a tanning operation in 1915 and 1916, but had to close this as well. In 1915 at the height of the civil wars he purchased for 400,000 pesos the 10,000-acre Hacienda San Cristobal, a few miles south of León.

He avoided the agrarian reform by dividing up his land into small units in 1932. Unfortunately for him, in 1936 twenty of his two hundred and fifty peons asked for land for an ejido, despite the fact that fifteen hundred people (likely sharecroppers) depended on his farm for their livelihood. Those people were well fed, well clothed, housed, and had all the firewood they needed. Fox believed that the local political boss was behind this development. Foreigners continued to fall victim to local authorities in the form of agrarian committees during the 1920s.

The solutions to their problems were to sell or rent out their properties, evade the reform laws through dividing their lands into legal-sized units, or otherwise fight through the courts. C. K. Warren and Edna Warren Lackey owned two ranches in Galeana District, Chihuahua. Trying to salvage what they could, in the 1920s the Warrens leased their Ojitos and Palatada ranches to the Palomas Land and Cattle Company. But the Mexican Agrarian Committee tried to nullify the lease. Part of Palatada was involved in the proceedings for the restitution of the lands of the pueblo of Janos, one of the first villages to rise in Revolution in 1910.[64] The Warrens lost 50,000 acres and their water supply in 1921.[65] Undeterred by the reform, they then purchased Captain Urmston's ranch in 1924 for US$170,000. But by 1926 a badly frustrated C. K. Warren bemoaned that there was no law in Mexico with the local governments unable to protect foreigners and with livestock rustling rampant.[66] The US consul in Ciudad Juárez noted that outlaws had killed ten Americans since 1921 and that he personally could not go to Mexico because he feared for his life.[67] In 1926 the Warrens leased their ranch to Lee Davis, a cattleman from Amarillo, Texas.[68]

E. Rotan, the president of the First National Bank of Waco, Texas, was another unlucky investor in land, who eventually sold out. He purchased 452,000 acres in Durango in 1909 to raise cattle. The Revolution prevented him from taking any income from developing the property, and rather than producing income, he had to pay 12,500 pesos per year in taxes. He gave up trying in 1928, finding a group willing to buy the land for US$125,000, but he had to divide the land into eleven parcels to comply with the state law, which limited an individual's holdings to 50,000 acres. The president initially vetoed the division and sale, but subsequently approved.[69]

The revolutionaries, like the authorities during Díaz's time, were inconsistent. Charles P. Reiniger seemingly escaped the agrarian reform. He purchased 26,125 acres of excellent land along the Casas Grandes River eighty-five miles due west of El Paso, Texas, in 1914 from the Mormon Church, which he described as the "finest tract in God's green earth."[70] In Sonora, North American agricultural colonists also avoided expropriation through the 1930s: in 1936 there were a reported 117 American holdings in the Yaqui Valley of Sonora, 83 of which were 2.47 to 247 acres, and only 2 were more than 12,470 acres.[71]

RELIGIOUS SETTLEMENTS

There were two notable religion-based colonies in Mexico during the era, both of which were located in Chihuahua. The Mormons bought their first property in 1885. Early on, they experienced the conflicts between national and local authorities over foreign landownership. Initially, the Mormons received permission to colonize from both Díaz and his agent in Chihuahua, Governor Carlos Pacheco.[72] Their first encounter with local opposition came immediately, for they inadvertently settled on the wrong land, owned by the powerful Terrazas family.[73] They had bought the original tract from the Gómez del Campo family, another distinguished clan in Chihuahua and Mexico City.[74] Unfortunately for the Mormons, neither Díaz nor Pacheco had consulted with the local jefe político about the new colony and he, consequently, opposed it and ordered the Mormons out.[75] Their reception among local ranchers, farmers, and merchants, who deeply resented the Mormons' competition, success, and unwillingness to integrate into local society, was hostile. The settlers added to the resentment by paying higher wages to Mexicans than their neighbors.[76] The Mormons continued to buy more land, forming seven colonies in Chihuahua and two in Sonora by 1910 and establishing a number of soon flourishing stores and mills.[77] Contemporary accounts and historians disagree on the extent to which the colonists integrated into local society. Some have argued they remained culturally isolated. It is not clear whether they learned Spanish. Thomas Romney, one of the leaders of the colonies, maintained that relations with their Mexican neighbors were congenial.[78] Nonetheless, in the early stage of the Revolution rebels raided the Mormon colonies and forced them to flee. A number of the settlers returned after the fighting ended and reestablished their colonies.

The Mennonites were the second group. The Old Colony Mennonites, then living in Canada, had found government policies there increasingly incompatible with their ultra-conservative views that eschewed modern technologies, military service, and government interference in their community. In early 1921 they sent a group to scout the possibilities of their moving to Mexico.[79] Given the negative attitude toward foreigners prevalent at least among radicals in Mexico at the time and the pressures for agrarian reform, it is, perhaps, surprising that the Obregón government expended considerable effort to bring the Mennonites to Chihuahua. The colonists showed interest just as the Obregón administration adopted a new policy to encourage such settlements by paying some of their expenses and exempting them from some taxes.[80] The Mennonites negotiated the terms of their entry directly with Minister of Agriculture A. I. Villareal and President Obregón. The group purchased the Hacienda Santa Clara, near San Antonio de Arenales, in Chihuahua, owned by the Zuloaga family. There were initially fifty-five hundred settlers.

The Obregón government policy, as part of its overall goal to reconstruct the Mexican economy, was geared toward attracting agricultural expertise and investment. The administration clearly believed that one way to obtain both was the immigration of foreign farmers. The policy worked quite well in the case of the Mennonites, who poured millions of dollars into the land. They originated a burgeoning cheese industry and successful hog raising in Chihuahua. As their colony blossomed to twenty-three thousand during the 1930s, the Mennonites instigated a building boom and constructed their own infrastructure, some of it used by the community in general. The colonies also provided hundreds of jobs for Mexicans.

There were, however, ongoing areas of conflict. The Mennonites were in obvious violation of two important provisions of the Mexican Constitution of 1917 that forbade religious schools (Article 24) and religious institutions from owning land (Article 27). For the most part, the federal government ignored these issues. The pressures for land reform were not as easily circumvented, however. The government had actually forced Mexicans off the lands sold to the Mennonites in 1922. Moreover, it also subsequently removed squatters as well. Between 1930 and 1932 a dozen agrarian leaders who led efforts to expropriate Mennonite properties in the Bustillos Valley were assassinated, effectively ending agitation. The Mennonites expanded their holdings to Durango during the 1930s, where they again encountered agrarians seeking land. In 1935 Mexican squatters took over 6,500 acres and tried again in 1937, each time only to run into the opposition of Cárdenas and state authorities.[81]

98   FOREIGN LANDOWNERS

The federal government's permitting the Mennonites to purchase and maintain their lands with little interference in their internal affairs was, perhaps, the clearest example of Obregón and subsequent presidents' need to rebuild agriculture. The national administration was willing to ignore the sentiments of local agrarians and politicians. The Mennonites invested extensively in infrastructure and established a burgeoning cheese industry. The Mennonites' stimulation of the Chihuahuan economy was obviously important enough to have even ardent reformers like Cárdenas hold back from expropriating some of the region's best land.

LARGE OPERATIONS

The largest foreign landholdings were spectacular in size. They often had the resources and the six essentials for success, especially huge amounts of capital and the apparent willingness to invest for the long term. They also commonly had the advantage of connections to the highest ranks of government officials, including presidents, cabinet members, and state governors, although local politicians were not always quite so welcoming. Despite their many advantages, the giant operations were not often profitable.

The Hearst Estate

Babícora was an enormous hacienda owned by the Hearst family. The ranch was located 175 miles south of the US border in Temosachic, Guerrero, Chihuahua. To the north was the land of Luis Terrazas; to the south three villages—Santo Tomás, Matachic, and Ypomera—and the Madera Company; to the east the villages of Namiquipa and San Jerónimo; and to the west the new town Madera and the Madera Company. As it would turn out, the estate was located in the heart of the revolution of 1910. US Senator George Hearst bought the original holdings in two major installments in 1887 and 1897. He initially bought 900,000 acres of land for between twenty and forty centavos for each 2.47 acres (which equals one hectare). There were actually eleven different transactions that comprised the latifundia known as San José de Babícora.[82] The family reorganized the property in 1905, forming the Babícora Development Company. It then passed on to the senator's widow Phoebe, who subsequently transferred it to her son, William Randolph Hearst, in 1919.[83] The ranch had some success during the Porfiriato shipping cattle to the United States. In 1908 it had approximately seventy-five thousand head of cattle, two thousand horses, and six thousand sheep.[84] Apparently the ranch was well managed by a succession of Americans, though its general manager, Jack Follansbee, supposedly spent little time on the ranch, preferring New York City.[85] In addition to livestock, the estate grew corn, beans, oats, and potatoes. Hearst enjoyed quite good relations with government officials at all levels during the Díaz era.

When the Revolution broke out in 1910, some rebel leaders in western Chihuahua moved their families into the southeastern section of the Hearst estate. Barker actually became well acquainted with them. The ranch managers made no attempt to oust them. The new revolutionists appealed to Hearst employees to join the movement, but the recruiting effort, which Barker permitted, was unsuccessful. Not a single employee of Babícora joined the Revolution either then or subsequently, according to Barker.[86] The estate may have had as many as one hundred and twenty armed men to protect its livestock and other assets.[87] It nonetheless suffered depredations during the Revolution. Villa ordered the expropriation of Babícora in 1915.[88] In 1916 John Hays Hammond reported, "They have confiscated almost everything upon the Babícora ranch, as well as from their other properties."[89] The years 1920 and 1921 were tough on the hacienda with conditions "unsettled." The manager complained of cattle thefts and squatters.[90] In 1921 William R. Hearst traveled to Mexico and met with President Obregón, after which he changed the tone and substance of his newspapers' reporting about the Mexican head of state, making it far more favorable. There was a report that Hearst had obtained a US$205,000 contract to propagandize for the recognition of the Mexican regime by the United States.[91] In 1922 the US consul reported that Babícora was one of the few ranches that had escaped the Revolution with its herd intact. It was shipping two thousand head to Mexico City. The ranch had twenty-five thousand head at that time.[92]

Whatever the inclination of the national or state administrations, however, the neighboring communities, many of whom had fought long and hard for the Revolution, continued to exert enormous pressure for expropriating Babícora and transferring the lands to the neighboring pueblos. In 1922 Chihuahua in response to these pressures enacted a new Agrarian

Law, which limited holdings in the state to one hundred thousand acres. In 1923 new laws retroactively nullified the concession of the Valenzuela Surveying Company from which Hearst had purchased a large amount of his land. Despite the new law, the national government's Secretaría de Agraria ordered the Hearst estate to be left undisturbed. At that time, Obregón was positively disposed to Hearst, who was urging the US government to recognize the Obregón regime. Nonetheless, several neighboring towns petitioned for Babícora lands. In order to avoid conflict, the Babicora Development Company ceded those areas invaded by these pueblos.[93] The agitation for agrarian reform remained strong through 1923, but Chihuahuan officials seemed reluctant to incur the wrath of Hearst.[94] In early 1924 Obregón, replying to an earlier note from William Ferris, the hacienda manager, assured him of the executive's "kindly disposition" and that the government would treat Hearst fairly.[95] Nonetheless, in 1924 Santo Tomás was granted seventy-nine hundred acres from the Hacienda de Providencia on the Babicora Development Company property.[96] To defend his land, William Randolph Hearst again turned to his newspapers to attack the Mexican government.[97] In 1924 Hearst, on the advice of the US ambassador to Mexico, Charles Beecher Warren, hired Fernando González Roa as the estate's attorney.[98] González Roa was able to gain exemption for the estate from the proclamation nullifying the Valenzuela claim.[99] Ferris thought that the whole matter of the validity of Hearst's titles was settled. But it was to be only the beginning of the agrarian reform efforts.

With Fernando Orozco governor of Chihuahua during 1927 and 1928, Babícora seemed to have found an ally, who opposed attempts to confiscate the Hearst property.[100] Orozco had been a cattle buyer before he was governor and had conducted business with the ranch. He was committed strongly to restore the cattle industry in Chihuahua and saw the ranch as an important part of this strategy because it had one of the only large herds left in the state.[101] The pressure to expropriate the ranch was enormous, however. Consequently, the governor's office warned Babícora in early 1928 that it would have to comply with Article 27 of the Constitution or face expropriation.[102] The US ambassador to Mexico Dwight Morrow spoke with President Calles about Babícora's situation, but the president only confused matters because he blamed the problem on the state government, while the manager of the ranch attributed fault to Calles.[103] In March 1929 the national government ordered the state of Chihuahua to suspend all proceedings against the hacienda until the courts ruled.[104] With the advice of the new governor, Luis León, Hearst then adopted a new tactic and in October 1931 divided the hacienda into nine entities.[105] From 1938 to 1941 the estate received decrees of inefectabilidad, that is, it could not be expropriated for twenty-five years.[106] From 1917 to 1942, however, the estate lost 308,528 acres to donations, amplifications, and restitutions.[107] The most numerous petitions occurred from 1934 to 1938, the heart of the Cárdenas era. The pressures for expropriations grew intense during 1935 with Governor Rodrigo Quevedo, not an enthusiastic advocate of land reform, writing President Cardenas that the number of petitions would increase and that there was nothing he could do to stop them. He was attempting to get the company to cede additional lands for an agricultural colony.[108] By 1935 agrarians had occupied one hundred thousand additional acres, but there remained one million acres with about half of it excellent grassland.[109] Nevertheless, the onslaught continued. In 1935 the hacienda lost 10,048 acres to San Rafael de Manzanas;[110] San Gerónimo, Bachiniva, took 7,281;[111] another pueblo took 17,764.[112] The Hearsts fought back. In 1936 the people of neighboring San Rafael de Manzanas, Matachic, complained that the hacienda let its cattle invade their ejido, damaging their planting.[113] In 1938 the hacienda again experienced "illegal invasions of the henchmen of local politicians," who tried to seize 86,450 acres through the provisions of the law of *tierras ociosas*. The US consul claimed that legislators had relatives among the squatters.[114] In 1938 Babícora lost seventy thousand acres to four different villages.[115] With the governor of Chihuahua, Gustavo Talamantes, refusing to intervene, Cárdenas ordered the invasions to stop and sent in federal troops.[116] But the petitions and invasions continued, with no fewer than six hundred petitioners in 1939.[117] Rural police killed three squatters in July 1939. That same year Babícora lost 4,446 acres to El Agua de León.[118] Cárdenas ordered an end to all petitions against Babícora in 1939.[119] From 1943 to 1954, Hearst tried unsuccessfully to renew the decrees of inafectabilidad. Finally, in 1954, the federal government expropriated the remaining 649,328 acres.[120]

The Hearst estate, certainly by its managers' recollection, treated its workers quite well. According to James Barker, during the later Díaz era and the Revolution, the hacienda had many hundreds of Mexican residents; the ranch provided them with "living quarters, necessary domestic animals, schools for their children and reasonable credit at the hacienda stores, which sold the modest necessities at reasonable prices. They also drew rations."[121] Ferris claimed in a letter to Obregón in 1924 that the hacienda had fifteen hundred residents who farmed and tended to livestock. Houses for the workers were at that time being remodeled to have shower baths. The estate operated five schools and paid for the teachers. Ferris claimed, furthermore, that "for some years we have spent more than the business produced."[122]

The Hearst estate, perhaps the most obvious symbol of foreign landholding in all of Mexico, survived as a single entity for more than six decades. While there are few records of its operations available, there is evidence that it was a successful enterprise for most of these years. Nonetheless, for all its advantages—substantial capital, high-quality management, and extensive national political influence—it endured considerable difficulties. Local politics, particularly the pressures for land reform, continually created difficulties for Babícora and ultimately led to its dismantling.

Palomas Land and Cattle Company

The Palomas Land and Cattle Company had a similar history to that of the Hearst estate. It purchased the enormous tract of an estimated 2.5 million acres in 1907 for one million dollars.[123] With plenty of capital and connections, the company planned to construct a series of dams, cultivate 300,000 acres, and fence the property.[124] In 1909 it reportedly raised fifty thousand head of cattle.[125]

The company's downfall derived from its origins as part of the *terrenos baldios* (vacant lands) surveyed by Luis García Teruel in 1885. The title documentation was so uncertain that William C. Greene, the mining tycoon who operated in Cananea, Sonora, backed off his bid for the ranch.[126] In 1909, even before the outbreak of the Revolution, squatters invaded the area known as Laguna de las Palomas. Although a local court ruling soon forced out the invaders, the neighboring villagers would take advantage of the Revolution to continue their struggle.[127] During the 1920s, local pressure for redistribution of the hacienda's land overwhelmed the national government's reluctance to antagonize large US investors.

The small landholders and villagers of northwest Chihuahua had long-standing grievances against the giant estates in that region and led the Revolution in part to recover lands they claimed the surveying companies had stolen from them. The 1920s were a time when the Obregón and Calles regimes faced serious challenges from major rebellions in 1923 and 1926. The aggrieved villages were crucial potential allies. The same popular pressures that threatened Palomas were simultaneously instrumental in preventing the return of the Terrazas family properties or their sale to a foreign promoter.[128]

The Palomas Land and Cattle Company became one of the first estates to become a target of the land reform.[129] Squatters arrived in 1921 at the same time as the Secretaría de Agraria notified the company of its intention to expropriate its lands under the provisions of the Constitution of 1917.[130] Obregón evidently tried to stop the onslaught, but he was only able to slow it somewhat. First, manager Nelson Rhodes talked personally with the president, and then Palomas obtained an *amparo* from the courts that suspended any actions against its property.[131] By mid-June 1923, Obregón had stopped all movement for redistribution of the Palomas land.[132] But, in 1923 the national government again announced its intention to expropriate Palomas.[133] Federal and state officials, however, slowed the process. In 1923 a petition for Palomas lands was denied.[134] In 1924 the governor of Chihuahua overturned a grant made by the Comisión Local Agraria. The president of Palomas met with Chihuahuan governor Almeida and agreed to sell 87,433 acres to the federal government for redistribution to petitioners.[135] Another petition was denied in 1926.[136] That same year the federal government purchased an additional 16,991 acres for US$34,398. The company became a Mexican enterprise, the Compañía Palomas de Terrenos y Ganado, during the 1930s, apparently as part of the tactics to evade land reform. Another petition was denied in 1932.[137] Under President Cárdenas in 1936 the national government agreed to an indemnity for the property of four million pesos.[138] By 1938 the company, renamed the Compañía Ganadera de Chihuahua, was in liquidation. In 1938 and 1939 the Palomas lost another seventy thousand acres.[139] In early 1940 a series of legal maneuvers and negotiations with the federal government failed to resolve the conflict.[140]

SPECULATORS

The same formula for success applied to the various land speculators, who sought to take advantage of the unbounded optimism of those who sought their modest fortunes in Mexico. Because they were almost always short of working capital nearly all of the schemes failed miserably.

Land speculators were everywhere. The risks were great, for shady deals were commonplace and the likelihood of losing their own funds or the money of their investors was high. Both private landowners and government officials were more than ready to take advantage of foreigners. The Mexican government was complicit in these dealings, for it was quite willing to sell tracts of land with incomplete title documentation or poor quality soil or no access to water.[141]

Despite the high risk, the lure of fast money or a second chance was overwhelming in boom times. Mary Langley, for example, bought the San José ranch, a well-watered 26,000 acres seventy miles south of Ciudad Juárez on the Mexican Central railroad line in 1907 strictly as a speculative venture. But, as so many others, she was undercapitalized and could not meet the first payment of US$30,000 in 1909.[142]

The most common forms of speculation were colonization schemes, largely in the northern tier of the country. The national government supported these enterprises in the hope that they would attract reliable farmers who would introduce the latest crops and technology to Mexican agriculture.

The first extensive plans for colonization emerged during the 1880s with the simultaneous establishment of peace under presidents Manuel González and Porfirio Díaz, the construction of the two major north-south railroads, and the commissioning of surveying companies to prepare for the development of "unoccupied" government lands. Plans were quite diverse in their scope and origins. In 1884, for example, Díaz gave the go-ahead to a Belgian colony at San Francisco de Borja in Chihuahua for the specific purpose of introducing flax.[143] Two years later, E. Schnetz and Company bought a large tract in Galeana District in Chihuahua with the intention of placing families on 6,175-acre ranches.[144] The German Luis Huller obtained a concession in 1889 to survey and then colonize enormous tracts of land in Chihuahua.[145] Choctaw and Chickasaw Indians from the United States contemplated a colony in Chihuahua in 1898.[146] Thirty-four Boer families, in exile from South Africa after the war with the British, settled in Chihuahua in 1903.[147] Enrique Creel arranged for a loan that enabled the Boer contingent to purchase the property. In 1907 a Japanese group was reportedly looking for a site for a colony in Chihuahua.[148] All of these enterprises failed.

Most speculators operated with the idea of establishing a colony of small and medium-size farmers. One such agricultural colony development was the Sinaloa Land Company. In 1905 it purchased 1,586,975 acres at a cost of four million pesos. The company had no intention of farming the land, but rather sought to sell it off in small parcels. The land, however, needed irrigation and the company initially lacked a concession for water rights. The company proposed to obtain a concession drawing from the state's ten rivers, and it hired Joaquín Casasús, the científico fixer, to represent it. The company planned to build irrigation works and sell the water to the new farmer settlers.[149] W. L. Wright from St. Louis bought land south of Ciudad Juárez in 1909 for US$300,000 with the idea of spending US$200,000 to improve the property and then sell it off to colonists. Unfortunately for Wright, the Revolution broke out only a year later.[150]

Two of the most ambitious land schemes during the Porfiriato developed in Sonora in the Yaqui Valley. In 1890 Carlos Conant acquired a concession from the national government for 550,000 acres, organizing the Sonora and Sinaloa Irrigation Company. After ten years, marked by little success, the company went into the hands of a receiver in 1901 and was dissolved by the New Jersey courts in 1906.[151] Richardson Construction organized in 1904 to build a railroad from Guaymas, a port in Sonora, east through the Yaqui Valley, in order to develop the region into one of the richest agricultural areas in Mexico. It obtained 300,000 acres along the right of way.[152] Richardson then sold its railway concession to the Southern Pacific railroad in 1905, and the latter completed construction two years later. Richardson, meanwhile, retained its landholdings with the goal of building an irrigation network, selling the land, but keeping water rights, and then supplying water to the land it had sold for lucrative monthly fees. In 1906 the Richardson Construction Company bought an additional seven hundred thousand acres.[153] The prospects seemed bright, for the new property was rich, alluvial soil capable of growing a variety of crops, the new railroad provided excellent transportation to markets in the United States, and the local market (probably in the mining camps) was at the time booming as well.[154] The company successfully built irrigation for fifty thousand acres, which it sold mostly to small farmers. It also was establishing a town site. Unfortunately, the company had not earned any money as of May 1907. Over the next two years a bank in Newark, New Jersey, withdrew financing and in October 1911 cancelled the mortgage.[155]

Richardson, for several years, benefited greatly from support from the national government. Both Díaz and Madero approved a concession to

65 percent of the water of the Yaqui River.[156] Cooperation ended with the Revolution, when the company endured difficult times, which included uncooperative local officials, raids, and threats of expropriation. During the Revolution, the Yaqui Indians "came down into the valley to redeem from the whites lands which the Indians claimed for themselves."[157] The officers of the Richardson Company were in constant contact with the revolutionary governments at all levels to assure its protection. The Carranza government took away the company's concession in 1919, but Richardson regained it in 1922 by persuading the Obregón government that its interests and the government's interest in fostering small farmers were compatible. The two principals in the company, William E. Richardson and Herbert A. Sibbet, even went so far as to become Mexican citizens in 1925 in order to mitigate antiforeign sentiments against their operation.[158] Nonetheless, the Calles government purchased the stock and bonds of the company, by then named the Yaqui Delta Land and Development Company, in 1927 for US$1.4 million.[159]

LUMBER COMPANIES

With even more grandiose plans than the colonization companies, the lumber enterprises proved perhaps the most spectacular failures. They developed after 1900, when first the Chihuahua al Pacífico and then the Kansas City, Mexico, and Orient, the Río Grande, Sierra Madre, and Pacific, and the Mexico Northwestern railroads opened up the vast forests of western Chihuahua and Sonora. The most ambitious undertaking was the Sierra Madre Land and Lumber Company, the largest landholding in Chihuahua, which held more than 2.5 million acres. In 1907 the *Mexican Herald* claimed the SML&LC was the largest single lumber enterprise in the world.[160] William C. Greene, the copper-mining tycoon of Sonora, reportedly paid US$1.25 million for the property.[161] After he obtained a timber concession in 1904, Greene poured huge sums into saw mills, a pulp plant, a furniture factory, a lumberyard, and construction of a new wagon road from Temósachic to Ocampo.[162] Greene also established the town of Madera with a hotel, a hospital, school, and cottages for the American employees.[163] He then expanded by buying the National Lumber Company in Chihuahua City, which supplied timber for many of the mining operations in the state.¹⁶⁴ At its height, SML&L employed between thirteen and nineteen hundred people.¹⁶⁵ As with all of Greene's businesses, the company was undercapitalized and, consequently, did not survive the depression of 1907. Local merchants attached the mills, cottages, and other buildings in late 1907. The company shut down operations in mid-1908, paying its employees only 20 percent of what it owed them. Lenders foreclosed on the land in May 1909, and in July the company sold its property by court order to pay off creditors.

Although the depression of 1907 and his overextension ended Greene's dreams of an empire in timber, another foreign entrepreneur, F. S. Pearson, took over the operation, forming the Madera Company, Ltd.¹⁶⁶ Pearson, who also owned the Mexico Northwestern Railway, expanded the company's landholdings to more than three million acres and increased its production.¹⁶⁷

The Madera Company and its sister company, the Mexican Northwestern Railway, operated in an area of constant, heavy fighting during the Revolution and, consequently, endured many raids by various rebels. Madera was at times cut off from all communications because the combatants destroyed the railroad and telegraph lines.¹⁶⁸ The situation was so dangerous in August 1913 that the American employees and executives had to abandon the town.¹⁶⁹ The lumber operation reopened in early 1914, but quickly confronted a crisis when General Máximo Castillo demanded money to protect the company's property. The company refused to pay, but suffered dearly when Castillo killed several railroad employees. Troubles deepened in May 1915 when the Madera Company's workers went on strike to lower commissary prices. They claimed that their wages of between 1.50 and 3.00 pesos a day were not sufficient for their sustenance. The company had been paying in currency issued by the army led by Pancho Villa, but that currency's value had declined sharply and workers suffered as a result.¹⁷⁰ The increase in violence forced the company to order all Madera Company foreign employees to leave the area in July 1915.¹⁷¹ In the early fall of 1915 Roy Hoard, the manager of the Madera operations who had maintained excellent relations with Villa up until then, faced the general as the latter retreated from his defeats at the hands of Obregón. Villa held Hoard for a harrowing couple of days before releasing him.¹⁷²

In 1917 the Mexican government discovered that the original timber concession of the railroad was never "protocolized (and thus invalid)," thereby threatening the ruin of both the lumber company and the railroad. Working through Hoard's friends, former governors Enríquez and León, and General Rodrigo Quevedo, the companies eventually confirmed their titles.[173] Then, in order to avoid difficulties with local agrarians, the companies sold off sections of their holdings to influential Mexicans, such as Generals Enríquez, Quevedo, and Maximiliano Márquez.

During the 1920s the company was vulnerable under the provisions of the Constitution of 1917, but Hoard established important friendships with President Calles and the members of the Almeida family, who were powers in Chihuahuan politics during the 1920s, that apparently insulated it against agrarian reforms.[174] Neither Calles nor the Almeidas were sympathetic to land redistribution.

Both the railroad and lumber enterprises continued, but after the Great Depression struck in 1930 the combined enterprises barely broke even, with the latter far more profitable than the former. In 1933 the SML&LC reached an accord with the Mexican government by which in return for recognition of its remaining holdings it ceded 1.25 million acres to the nation.[175] That deal provided only temporary respite, for in 1937 the national government embargoed all the property of the Mexican Northwestern because of unpaid taxes on its preferred stock.[176] After a number of years of tough negotiations, in 1945 Hoard sold the railroad and timber companies to Eloy Vallina, one of the country's most important bankers.[177] The Mexican Northwestern had sunk more than twenty-five million dollars into its operations during the course of thirty-five years with no return.

Because timberland was mostly undeveloped and many sections of the land were subject to disputed ownership claims, the foreign lumber companies were targets for agrarian reform. The vast holdings of the Cargill Lumber Company, for example, were among the most controversial in Mexico because the tract contained land whose ownership local villages disputed. Julio and José Limantour had obtained the 543,000 acres from the federal government in 1888, setting off the Tomochi rebellion and subsequent massacre in 1892. The Limantours, who did not develop the land, sold the tract to the Cargill Lumber Company in 1906. After losing parts of the land to expropriation in the 1930s,[178] the company's property was in the hands of the national government by 1940.[179] The International Land and Lumber Company, with 360,620 acres, also was expropriated in the 1930s.[180] The Durango Land and Timber Company (Compañía Maderera de Durango), owned by a partnership of Americans and Mexicans, fared no better, losing 90,000 acres to expropriation in October 1938, victims of the governor of Durango, who sought the timber for himself.[181] Few of the foreign-owned lumber companies ever moved beyond speculations. The enormous investments required in milling equipment and transportation stymied development. Despite often-favorable treatment from the Díaz and revolutionary regimes, considerable capital, and expert management relations, even the Sierra Madre and Madera companies ultimately failed.

CONCLUSIONS

Given the geography and climate, often requiring enormous investments in irrigation and fencing, the uncertainties of the market, and difficult transportation, Mexican farming and ranching were risky. Even with the six essential factors, foreign landowners failed. Of course, most lacked many of these requirements, especially sufficient financial backing and amenable relations with the various levels of government and elites. The Díaz regime saw foreign investment as the most appropriate method to modernize agriculture. The revolutionaries after 1920 regarded foreigners as the pillars of the desperately needed agricultural reconstruction. But in neither case, nor during the heaviest fighting between 1910 and 1920, did the national government privilege or prejudice foreigners. Foreign landowners, moreover, rarely operated any differently than their Mexican counterparts. And it was likely that they provided higher pay and better working conditions.

The Díaz regime freed up millions of acres of so-called vacant lands for private purchase, hoping to attract foreigners to farm, particularly to produce export commodities. These policies were only minimally successful and had, perhaps, unanticipated consequences. First, large foreign operations, such as Hearst, Palomas, and the Mormon and Mennonite colonies (considering them each as whole entities, rather than many smaller concerns), often created resentment among Mexican elite landowners and smaller Mexican farms because they competed for both export and domestic markets. The Mormons, for example, captured much of the market for supplying mining camps near their colonies, which would have otherwise resulted in opportunities for local Mexican farmers. Second, because the national and state governments sometimes insisted that the foreign companies provide certain amenities, such as schools or medical care, they were more attractive to workers. Labor was scarce in the north, so the need to compete for a workforce was quite costly for Mexican hacendados, which also bred ill feelings among local elites. Third, the big foreign landowners employed their own private police and either bribed or employed local authorities, thereby creating another influence in local politics to rival that of the local elite. The Revolution further complicated the situation, for during the 1920s and 1930s, with the old landowning elite weakened or destroyed, local agrarian organizations joined the competition with their demands for land redistribution.

During the two decades after 1920, the revolutionary regime thus confronted the desperate need to rebuild from the war damages incurred and then the equally pressing need to recover from the Great Depression. It had to encourage farming, reconstruct agriculture, maintain relations with foreign investors, and limit the autonomy of local pressure groups, such as agrarian organizations and political camarillas. The revolutionary regime, like its predecessor, played one group off another.

The search for balance—the refurbishment of the elite-foreign enterprise system after 1920—explains the seeming inconsistencies of the regime's agrarian policies. For example, in the early 1920s Obregón approved the return of the confiscated properties of the Terrazas-Creel family and their sale to an American. Local pressure arose from agrarian groups to force the governor to veto the deal. A. J. McQuatters, the prospective buyer, was a speculator who wanted to divide the land into small parcels and sell them to immigrant colonists. But such colonization schemes were shaky at best. At about the same time, Obregón approved the entry of the Mennonites, who purchased an enormous hacienda that had many claims against it by neighboring villages, from an old elite family. This sale the government protected, using force when necessary. The Mennonites, unlike McQuatters, had the resources to develop the land and did so successfully.

There was neither favoritism nor bias against foreign landowners. Their treatment was no better or no worse than that of Mexican landowners. Díaz privileged wealthy hacendados no matter what their nationality. The revolutionaries harassed or left alone landowners depending on local circumstances. The revolutionary regime doled out land as a form of political patronage, putting itself in the middle of the reform process. But since it was not strong enough, at least during the 1920s and 1930s, to impose its will on local elite landowners or land-seeking villages, nor could it develop the economy without foreign investors, it had to reconstitute a version of the elite-foreign enterprise system.

It was not strong enough to take on Hearst, in the most obvious case, until the 1950s. As local agrarians exerted pressure, the government gave in a little at a time, not prepared to risk alienating either the agrarians or the Hearsts. So cautious was the national government that the less influential Palomas Land and Cattle Company deferred expropriation until the 1940s. Foreigners surely owned a huge amount of land in Mexico from 1880 to 1940, but the elite-foreign enterprise system did not give away Mexico under either Díaz or the Revolution. It was not easy for foreigners to make money. The landowners that generated profits did so only after investing enormous sums of capital in irrigation, fencing, seed, transportation, and breeding. Palomas and Hearst took decades to build their herds to fifty to seventy-five thousand in 1910. There is no evidence that they remitted huge dividends. It is not likely they ever earned back their investments. Nor is there any documentation that their employees were badly paid or mistreated. These patterns are quite evident in the history of one estate for which we have a more complete set of records.

FIVE

The Corralitos Company

The history of the Corralitos Company, a US corporation, operating an enormous ranch and several mines in northwestern Chihuahua, Mexico, very close to the US border, is an important case study of foreign-owned business in Mexico during the eras of dictator Porfirio Díaz (1877–1911), the Revolution (1910–20), and the revolutionary reconstruction (1920–40). Despite a number of crucial advantages in conducting its business, such as ample capital and considerable support from Mexican national authorities, the company experienced only a handful of profitable years in a half-century. I maintain that although it is but one case study, when we consider it with the examples presented in Chapter 4, the history of the Corralitos Company provides a clear indication that many, if not most, foreigners in business in Mexico encountered continuous, substantial obstacles and that very few foreign entrepreneurs or enterprises consistently earned profits from their Mexican ventures over the long term during the period from the 1880s through the 1940s. Its history is also illustrative of the workings of the elite-foreign enterprise system.

Success for foreign-owned mining and ranching enterprises in Mexico required all of the following six circumstances: sufficient capital to purchase necessary equipment and pay for daily operations; competent management; a steady market for minerals or agricultural commodities; accessible transportation; a reliable workforce; and the maintenance of good working relations with local, state, and national authorities. Corralitos was fortunate in that it had all of these essentials, but it nonetheless failed, although both its mining and ranching operations were profitable sporadically.

In exploring the factors that determined success or failure for foreigners in Mexico, the histories of the Corralitos Land and Cattle Company and its sister firm, the Candelaria Mining Company, provide us with examples of the difficulties in the complex Mexican business environment from 1880 until 1940.[1] The Corralitos/Candelaria enterprise began in the early 1880s with the sale of a vast tract of land and mines in Galeana District in northwestern Chihuahua to a group of New York entrepreneurs headed by Edwin D. Morgan, a prominent banker.[2] The investors were willing and able to invest large amounts of capital in breeding stock and irrigation for the ranch and in the most up-to-date equipment for the mines. The management team led initially by Britton Davis, then George A. Laird, the mine manager, and E. C. Houghton, the ranch manager, were experienced and knowledgeable. The markets for cattle and silver were strong until the depression of 1907. Proximity to the US border and the construction of the Mexican Northwestern Railroad after 1900 assured access to convenient transportation. Local ranchers provided a generally reliable workforce. In addition, the owners were extraordinarily well connected in the United States, and their stature allowed them access to the highest officials in the government of Mexico from Porfirio Díaz to the revolutionary general Pancho Villa to the revolutionary reconstruction president Alvaro Obregón (1920–24). Nonetheless, despite seeming to have all of the conditions for success in place, the vast undertakings ultimately failed. In the end, it was just too difficult to conduct business in the uncertain conditions of Porfirian, revolutionary, and reconstruction Mexico.

Candelaria Angel and Mariano Aguirre discovered the mines at San Pedro de Corralitos in the municipality of Nuevo Casas Grandes, state of Chihuahua, seventy-five miles south of the US border, in 1839. Local hacendado José María Zuloaga acquired the mines shortly thereafter. The Zuloaga family maintained the property for many years. In 1884 George Zempleman, representing Edwin D. Morgan, purchased twenty-one mines.[3] The founder's grandson, also named Edwin D. Morgan, set up the Candelaria Mining Company at first as a subsidiary to the Corralitos Company, which owned the Corralitos ranch, and then as a separate entity in 1895. Later, in 1902 the directors, in order to comply with Mexican laws prohibiting foreign ownership within the twenty-league zone of the US border, set up the Compañía de San Pedro, S.A., to operate the mines. Finally, in 1909 Candelaria reorganized and incorporated in New Jersey.[4]

The early years were a struggle. Supplies were difficult to obtain and consequently expensive.[5] After some years of unprofitable results, Candelaria prospered from 1900 to 1908, as the mines produced more than US$3 million with an average return of US$700,000 a year.[6] In 1905 Candelaria was the primary producer of silver in Chihuahua. In 1907 the company, then the second-ranked producer of silver in the state, operated fourteen mines in San Pedro and another six mines under the name of its subsidiary, the Aventurera Mining Company.[7] But, in keeping with the boom-and-bust pattern of Mexican mining, Candelaria experienced severe difficulties in the economic depression of 1907 because of the sharp drop in mineral prices. Both it and Aventurera closed their operations in March 1908 and did not resume until 1909 and then only on a reduced scale.[8] From July 1908 until October 1909 the Candelaria expended just over one million pesos (a peso = US$0.50), while taking in only 220,000 pesos from ores shipped.[9] George Laird, the mine manager, complained of the "frustrations" in operating Candelaria, including high smelter rates, taxes, the lack of funds and ever-increasing capital needs.[10]

The outbreak of the Revolution in 1910 almost immediately affected Candelaria. Rebels destroyed the railroad, which prevented the company from obtaining coal that it used to power its equipment. As a result, it had to close down its pumps at the end of December 1910. Rebels also looted the company's supplies. Disruptions continued despite the victory of the opposition to Díaz, led by Francisco I. Madero, in May 1911, because opposition to Madero arose in western Chihuahua among his former supporters.[11] Conditions deteriorated in fall 1911 to the extent that the manager of Candelaria, George A. Laird, halted mining. General José Ínes Salazar, of the federal army, looted Candelaria. Laird left a caretaking staff and went to the United States.[12] Through the end of the Madero presidency (March 1913), the dictatorship of General Victoriano Huerta (1913–14), which sought to restore Díaz's policies, and the civil war between the forces of Venustiano Carranza and Pancho Villa (1914–15), former followers of

Madero who led moderate and more radical factions, respectively, Candelaria was unable to resume operations. Combatants raided and looted the company. In October 1915, for example, passing troops turned everything topsy-turvy at Candelaria and depleted the drug store.[13] The abandoned mines flooded beyond repair.[14] In December 1917 government troops "systematically demolished" the Candelaria property.[15] Candelaria was insolvent and in receivership by 1917.[16] An inspection in 1921 estimated that it would cost US$300,000 to repair the damage.[17] In 1927 the Candelaria Company formally suspended operations, never to resume.

Not atypical of all mine operators, both native and foreign, in Mexico throughout the period 1880 to 1940, the Candelaria Company was at the mercy of climate and geology. Mines were, furthermore, quite vulnerable to the ravages of armed conflict because neglect or scavenging commonly led to flooding or cave-ins. Even with all of the conditions seemingly favorable, Candelaria was profitable in only eight years of nearly fifty years of foreign ownership. This was hardly a record of exploitation.

CORRALITOS

For more than two decades, the Corralitos ranch proved a disappointment to its investors. Nonetheless, as a whole, for many years, it remained a promising property. Colonel William Greene, the owner of the Cananea Copper Company in Sonora, offered US$1,350,000 for the ranch and mines in 1906.[18] At the time the company had US$900,000 in debt and had returned nothing to its investors in years.[19] A. W. Ivins, who represented Mormon interests in the region, inquired about a possible purchase of Corralitos the following year.[20] Despite its excellent location, fertile, well-watered land, and seemingly endless capital, the property only began to flourish in 1910. By that time Corralitos was an 850,000-acre property that grazed forty thousand "high-grade Durham cattle," twelve hundred horses, and one hundred eighty mules. The operation yielded net profits in 1910 of approximately US$100,000.[21] But 1910 was the first year that interest was paid on the company's bonds and the first year it paid any dividend on its stock. Even then, preferred stockholders, who were due 6 percent, received only 2 percent.[22] Corralitos president Morgan (the founder's grandson) estimated the value of the property in 1910 at US$2 million.[23]

Prosperity was short-lived, for the outbreak of the Revolution in 1910 brought immediate difficulties. By 1919 depredations added up to US$660,000, according to the estimates of the ranch general manager, E. C. Houghton.[24] The ranch escaped the worst until early 1913, when Houghton reported that "wholesale stealing . . . has caused us no end of trouble."[25] They could not keep any supplies on hand, for as soon as word got out provisions had arrived on the ranch, a band of revolutionists arrived and took them.[26] Despite the difficulties, the ranch earned a profit in 1913.[27]

In 1914 Corralitos acquired a subsidiary ranch on the US side of the border and transferred six thousand head of cattle, most of them breeding stock.[28] In September 1914 a small garrison of Constitutionalist soldiers occupied the ranch, whose management had fled across the border. Bandits occupied another section in the northwest. E. D. Morgan's inspection found little damage to the property. Surprisingly, Morgan was quite pleased with the farming operations.[29] But by March 1915 conditions had deteriorated, as Mexico descended into political chaos. Morgan, with much livestock shifted to New Mexico, focused on farming, planting a thousand acres in alfalfa and another thousand in corn and beans. There was still no physical damage to buildings or wells.[30]

The greatest damage occurred in the years 1915 to 1917. In 1915 the company pushed to transfer all its cattle across the border. Houghton had to meet with Pancho Villa, who made his headquarters in Chihuahua, in order to gain approval to export the cattle. When they met in the general's private railroad car in Juárez, Villa demanded a payment of eight dollars per head in advance by the next day. The alternative, Villa asserted, would be expropriation of all the cattle. Houghton consulted next with the Constitutionalist consul who warned Houghton that Villa's defeat was eminent and that Corralitos would never receive a penny in compensation for any funds paid to Villa. Houghton also reported the rumors of Constitutionalist expropriations of cattle from the neighboring Palomas Land and Cattle Company ranch, also foreign-owned. Then, in the week of October 3, one thousand head of cattle, several horses, and a considerable quantity of corn were taken from the Corralitos range. Houghton reported, "A great number of wounded cattle have been encountered on the range, and some dead ones, proving that cattle have been shot down and destroyed."[31] Eventually Corralitos paid Villa and transferred five thousand head.[32]

March 1916 brought disaster. Villa in retreat stopped at the Corralitos, terrorizing the Mexican workers, horribly killing several members of one tenant family, and taking whatever movable supplies that remained.[33] Nonetheless, by June 1916 the mess made by the villistas was cleaned up. The alfalfa crop was still in the field and other farmland was ready to plant. US troops from the Pershing Expedition that were chasing Villa after his raid on Columbus, New Mexico, used one sector of the ranch, Tres Alamos, as a major encampment.[34]

The company struggled to salvage what it could. From the time the management left in 1917, scared off by the ramifications of the US invasion, various rebels stole fifteen hundred cattle, two to three hundred horses and mules, three hundred hogs, and a considerable quantity of supplies, hardware, and machinery. Combatants destroyed all of the fences, corrals, and windmills. In an effort to prevent further losses, the company transferred cattle from Corralitos to property in New Mexico. Between the transfers and the thefts, the ranch's herd declined in size from 12,274 to 8,165 during 1917.[35] Rebel depredations continued. The Mexican government was unable to establish order.[36] As if the damage were not enough, in September 1917 the first rumors arose that the government would expropriate the company's land.[37] Houghton recommended that the company lease its farmland to "reliable people on shares." By sharecropping the land, he hoped to prevent any claims of abandonment of the property, while bringing in a modest income.[38] But Houghton could not get to the ranch to arrange to lease out its land.[39]

Although the worst of the fighting was over, the troubles for the ranch continued. Houghton reported a great deal of vandalism at Corralitos in early 1919.[40] In 1920 the company began to rebuild, repairing fencing, but a potential threat arose when squatters occupied Tres Alamos, an area near the Corralitos River, in order to obtain water. Houghton suggested that the company purchase a half interest in the water rights held by the abandoned Mormon colony to ensure the company's water supply. There was also a "great deal of petty stealing and other disagreeable features to contend with."[41]

After the passage of the Law of Unused Lands in mid-1920 squatters invaded Corralitos. They occupied twenty thousand acres along the banks of the river.[42] Another group later settled an area known as Casa de Janos, taking over a dam, canals, tanks, and homes built by the company.

A third band established itself in Arroyo Seco. The company, in order to strengthen its claim on the land, brought back some of its cattle herd from New Mexico. In response, the squatters burned the pasture, trying to force the company to remove the cattle.[43] By March 1921, there were approximately one to three hundred squatters on five thousand acres of the ranch's best land. The squatters built irrigation ditches from the Corralitos River, depriving the rest of the ranch of much-needed water.[44] In early 1921 there was some discussion of bankruptcy, though the company had only a US$4,000 monthly payroll. It had no mortgage and many salable assets.[45] E. C. Houghton was among a group attacked in October 1921 on the road through Dublán, a neighboring settlement. One person died and two were wounded.[46] This was only one of a number of violent incidents in the region. Houghton complained to the US consul that "Americans get no protection in the neighborhood of Casas Grandes. . . . The property of the Corralitos Company is treated as common property. . . . Our land has been squatted upon and we have been denied the use of it; wood and hay are cut and hauled away at will."[47]

In a meeting with Governor Ignacio Enríquez in early 1922, Houghton claimed that the time had come "when the Government of Mexico had made it impossible for large landowners to continue in business; and that they had destroyed the Corralitos property as a cattle breeding enterprise; also that they had destroyed the farming . . . by allowing squatters to take water." He maintained that the invasion of the squatters and the passage of the new agrarian law had "made it almost, if not quite, impossible" to sell any part of the ranch.[48] At this point the company was unable to pay its current expenses.[49] Shearson Hammill and Company lent the company US$12,600 to sustain it for the succeeding quarter.

A great shock came when the interim governor of Chihuahua José Acosta Rivera ordered the restoration of sixty-four *sitios de ganado mayor* (each sitio de ganado mayor = 1,755 hectares or 4,335 acres) to the ejidos (common lands) of Casas Grandes in early 1923.[50] Houghton protested frantically. President Obregón at first declined to interfere with what he categorized as state business.[51] He claimed that the proceedings adhered to the law and that the government would deal with the legitimate claims of the village of Casas Grandes for land it had lost.[52] In June Obregón in correspondence with Governor Enríquez suggested that they work out a deal.[53] The company then entered into prolonged negotiations with the Local Agrarian

Commission, the National Agrarian Commission, the governor, and the president. Obregón maintained that the resolution of the matter should be "moral and equitable."[54]

After it became clearer that the company's holdings were in jeopardy, the Corralitos management tried a number of times to lease or sell its property. In 1922 the company attempted to sell its herd to E. K. Warren or Randolph Hearst, both owners of large ranches in the area.[55] The same year the company negotiated with J. B. Moling of Kansas City for the sale of the ranch for US$1.5 million.[56] In November 1923 Houghton negotiated a deal whereby the Livestock and Agricultural Loan Company of New Mexico leased all of Corralitos's land in Chihuahua, except the Ramos pasture, for one year. The following year, the company negotiated with the Newman Investment Company for sale of 450,000 acres for US$275,000. The directors, however, did not accept the offer.[57] In a last-ditch effort, in 1926 the company began negotiations to sell the property to the Mexican government. Corralitos proposed a price of six dollars for each of the first 100,000 acres and a half dollar for 337,000 acres.[58] Ultimately, President Plutarco Elías Calles (1924–28) turned down the deal because the Mexican economy was not strong enough to permit such an investment.[59]

From then on the ranch came apart piece by piece. In 1927 the National Agrarian Commission expropriated Corralitos lands for ejidos. That same year, two US citizens, John Steinkampf and Harry Smith, obtained small parts of the ranch through a Mexican intermediary, Francisco Irigoyen, who bought sixty-two thousand acres just northwest of Casas Grandes and the Mormon colony at Colonia Dublán. They held the land until the administration of President Lázaro Cárdenas expropriated the parcel in 1937 and 1938 and distributed it to locals. According to the *Periódico Oficial del Estado de Chihuahua*, in 1929 the state government liquidated Corralitos for payment of taxes.[60] The judicial process continued, however. The government embargoed fifty thousand acres of the ranch again for nonpayment of taxes in 1931.[61] The ranch lost five thousand acres to the town of Janos in 1933.[62] The company claimed losses of US$102,252 because of the expropriation of forty-eight thousand acres 1934 and 1936 in Janos and Nuevo Casas Grandes.[63] The Colonía Hidalgo won thirty-five thousand acres from Corralitos in 1937.[64] In 1941 Rodrigo Quevedo, a former governor of Chihuahua and reputedly one of Mexico's preeminent drug lords, and William W. "Billy" Wallace bought what remained of the hacienda for US$100,000.[65]

Despite having the necessary elements for success for mining and ranching enterprises in Mexico—sufficient capital to purchase necessary equipment and pay for daily operations, competent management, a steady market for minerals or agricultural commodities, accessible transportation, a reliable workforce, and the maintenance of good working relations with local, state, and national authorities—Corralitos failed. Let us now examine more closely the components to try to understand better how Corralitos, and perhaps business in general, succeeded or failed during the three eras under study.

CAPITAL

The wealthy board of directors of the Corralitos Company was willing to expend substantial funds so long as prospects were sound. When conditions had improved markedly after the mid-1890s, the Corralitos board had committed substantial funds. In 1898, for example, it bailed out the mining operation with an infusion of US$300,000.[66] This, however, proved an excellent investment because the mines boomed during the next decade. Because of flooding in 1908, the company expended another approximately US$400,000, installing some of the most modern and expensive equipment.[67] To the board, having produced US$3 million in ores since 1900, the mines seemed well worth the investment. The Corralitos Company also invested heavily in the ranch in 1904. This included the subdivision of the property into many farms and ranches and the construction of 464 miles of barbed-wire fence.[68] E. D. Morgan claimed that between 1900 and 1910, the company invested US$150,000 per year in farm equipment and improved cattle.[69] After ten years of damage between 1910 and 1920, however, the management was wary of expending any additional funds after it borrowed funds to maintain the ranch in 1922. New legislation threatened the very basis of private property in Mexico, and local politics in Chihuahua were too uncertain to assure the company's interests. The onslaught of squatter invasions on the Corralitos property inserted too high a degree of uncertainty into the operation. Once the board of directors ended its capital commitment, the enterprise was doomed.

MANAGEMENT

The Corralitos board of directors from the beginning had the foresight to employ experienced, highly competent management. The mining company hired Britton Davis, a graduate of the US Military Academy, to run the operation in 1886.[70] His colleague Morris Parker described Davis as a man "of excellent physique, had an outstanding personality, and spoke fluent Spanish. He was fairly conversant with cattle and a qualified Indian fighter—all in all a man capable of conducting and protecting . . . [Corralitos'] interests."[71] He was unable to make the company profitable, however. George A. Laird, a capable mining supervisor, succeeded Davis and managed Candelaria during its most productive period. Under Laird were two highly qualified miners, D. Bruce Smith, the superintendent, a veteran of Mexican mining, and Morris B. Parker.[72] From the reports he issued to his employers, it is clear that E. C. Houghton, the ranch manager, was a highly skilled administrator who had vision and expertise and who cleaned up the operation after he took over. Houghton supervised the enormous investments in the ranch in 1904. He also presided over the operation's most profitable years, although he was unable to prevent its ruin during the Revolution.

Again, as was the case with the availability of capital, it was not the lack of skilled or persistent management that doomed the Corralitos enterprise.

MARKET

The market for cattle was generally good throughout the years from 1880 to 1910. The Revolution, of course, disrupted transportation and demand. Even more important, cattle were crucial targets for competing rebel armies, which sold off livestock to raise funds for arms. Corralitos was seemingly unable to make money regardless of the shifting cattle market until 1910. After the 1880s the demand for Mexican cattle from the United States increased greatly. Between 1881 and 1892 Mexico exported an average of 367,000 pesos worth of cattle per year.[73] Corralitos apparently benefited from a short-lived boom in the 1890s when new tariffs for cattle imported into the United States allowed it to ship ten thousand head in 1896. As a result, it had little stock on its ranges except for yearlings.[74] But cattle sales did not create profits.

By 1900 the cattle industry had become a crucial element of Mexico's economy. From 1906 to 1909, the United States imported 150,000 head of Mexican cattle.[75] In 1911 the demand was such that cattle were selling at US$29.50 a head.[76] Corralitos experienced its most profitable years in 1910 and 1911. The Revolution, however, nearly destroyed cattle raising by depleting herds. To make matters worse, whatever the demand across the border, export taxes levied by the revolutionary factions and unreliable transportation, made it difficult and expensive to ship livestock. In the aftermath of the Revolution market demand was high, but the supply of cattle was insufficient to meet it. Through the 1920s the supply of cattle was too low to satisfy even the domestic market. The ten years of civil war had decreased the number of cattle in Mexico from more than 5 million head to 1.75 million, a cut of approximately 67 percent.[77] The Mexican national government heavily taxed cattle exports in order to assure that ranchers satisfied domestic needs before they could export.[78] Both foreign and native cattle ranchers, however, were at the same time under siege by agrarian reform laws and were unable to increase their herds. In 1930 the United States enacted the Smoot-Hawley tariff, which added to the already heavy burden of taxation on Mexican cattle exports.[79] Nonetheless, the US market grew. Cattle exports increased from 14,354 to 179,367 from 1924 to 1929. The Great Depression of the 1930s put an end to this boom.[80] The recovery of cattle exports, however, came much too late for Corralitos.

TRANSPORTATION

The availability of reasonably priced transportation was crucial to the profitability of both the mining and ranching operations. The mines flourished only after the railroad reached western Chihuahua, providing cheap transport of ore to the smelters in El Paso, Texas, and Torreón. In 1897 and 1898 the Río Grande, Sierra Madre, y Pacífico railroad was built to Casas Grandes and Corralitos, linking the mines of San Pedro to the company's mineral-processing plant in El Paso.[81] A decade later, the company built two railroad spurs to the Mexican Northwestern line, which had taken over the RG, SM, & P.[82] The Ferrocarril Noroeste de México constructed a line from Juárez to Terrazas in 1909.[83] The Candelaria/Corralitos operations accounted for 95 percent of all ores and 50 percent of all cattle transported by the RG, SM, & P.[84] As we can see from the chronology, the boom times for both Candelaria and Corralitos coincided with the construction of the railroad. Both the mining and ranching operations stagnated until then. Nonetheless, when the depression struck in late 1907, the Candelaria management, faced with low ore prices, complained to the federal government about high freight rates on the Río Grande, Sierra Madre y, Pacífico line in 1909.[85] During the Revolution, railroad transportation was sporadic.

WORKFORCE

The labor supply, like in much of northern Mexico, was "none too plentiful."[86] By 1904 the mining complex at San Pedro Corralitos had 1,850 Mexican residents, 400 of whom worked at the mines or mineral-processing plants.[87] At its peak production, Candelaria's four camps with twenty mines had a population of approximately 5,000 and the number of laborers reached 1,000.[88] Although the workforce varied, it averaged around 700.[89] This included a large number of boys ages thirteen to fifteen. The latter were helpers for the most part, but they also worked in the narrow veins of the mines.[90] Evidently, the majority of the skilled miners were small ranchers or sharecroppers from the district, who combined farming and mining.[91] According to Morris Parker, the turnover of workers was 200 to 300 percent annually, which meant that the company payroll included two to three thousand names. When the local labor supply was scarce, the company established an agency in Zacatecas, a mining center further south, from which it imported miners and their families at its expense. Candelaria offered wages at nearly double the rate in Zacatecas.[92] The company tried to attract and keep its labor providing schools, a doctor at no cost, and a pension for those too old or sick to work.[93] Candelaria also met its labor needs by employing about one hundred Chinese workers.[94] The most pressing labor shortages for both the mines and the ranch occurred in 1909,[95] when hand labor was expensive and hard to get.[96] The mines employed American foremen, shift bosses, and timekeepers. It used contractors to work on shafts, drifts, and raises.[97]

The only reports critical of Candelaria's treatment of its workers appeared in the El Paso newspapers in 1910. The manager of the company, George Laird, however, maintained that the "camp was running so smoothly that the officials cannot appreciate it."[98]

The Corralitos Company apparently employed a mix of tenants and workers. In 1911 it had at least seven Mexican tenants who farmed.[99] For example, in 1916, the Casas Grandes farm was sharecropped by an "old Mexican employee"; the company was to receive half the crop.[100] According to Houghton, the company treated its sharecroppers in the standard way in Chihuahua at the time. They received land, seed, work animals, farm implements and tools, firewood, money, and other objects that would enable them to survive until the harvest. The manager believed that the workers "always received the legitimate product of their labors."[101]

The Revolution, of course, brought complications. In 1914, for example, the company faced a dilemma. If the ranch stopped paying its present occupants, Houghton feared they would avenge their treatment by destroying the recent physical improvements to the property. He recommended that the company continue its farming operations and continue to pay its tenants, even if it lost crops, so that it would protect its investment.[102]

Corralitos was quite fortunate in its labor supply, for the combination of local, skilled labor and imported unskilled workers was sufficient to keep the operation functioning through 1914. Thereafter, the Revolution siphoned away the labor force and limited mobility.

POLITICAL RELATIONS

The ranch's relations with national, state, and local authorities were crucial to its survival and dictated its eventual demise. Its managers tried their best to obtain and maintain good political relations. The difficulties were enormous and endless, even during the Porfiriato, when the national regime was generally favorably disposed toward foreign investment. In a number of instances Corralitos management found themselves with seeming support from the national government, or state governments, but the locals were unwilling to cooperate. During the Díaz era, though the dictator was cooperative, municipal and district authorities were at odds with the company and objected strongly to its autonomy from their jurisdiction.

Relations with local authorities went well in the early years, for the ranch (including the mines) had its own local government and the superintendent acted as the jefe político.[103] However, local politicians, unlike some of their state- and national-level colleagues, resented the company's autonomy.

Authorities in Casas Grandes complained that the Corralitos-Candelaria complex was outside their jurisdiction. Jefe político Francisco Matéus of Casas Grandes regularly protested the lack of cooperation of Britton Davis, who managed the mining operations. In 1904, for example, Davis had prevented a census in San Pedro. Moreover, he employed his own private guards, who would not allow municipal authorities to enter.[104] In order to placate the locals, the Corralitos Company resorted to the age-old method. Morris Parker reminisced that during his stay at Candelaria from 1898 to 1901, the local *comisario* (municipal government official), his assistants, and the local judge were on the company payroll, although they were all state employees.[105] George Laird, the manager of the ranch, reported in 1910 that the two companies paid the jefe político of the district a salary of US$100 per month. The companies also paid for local services, such as water.[106] To ensure the support of the national government the company employed Luis Mendez, a much-used intermediary for foreign enterprises, as its lawyer in Mexico City.[107] The company also hired as its attorney in Chihuahua Manuel Prieto, who had excellent connections among the local oligarchy, to negotiate water rights and taxes.[108]

The Revolution exacerbated the tensions with local authorities, who were impotent or unwilling to defend the ranch. Houghton maintained in 1913 that the civil authorities "have put us to all the trouble possible."[109] To prevent further problems, he and two other employees visited General José Ines Salazar and agreed to pay him US$7,500 for protection. No sooner had they received their receipt for this transaction than another band of "Mexican cut-throats" robbed them.[110] In early 1914 Houghton reported "cattle being branded and killed in all surrounding towns. No law, no order, no one to appeal to, no defense possible."[111] Later in the summer of 1914 E. D. Morgan (the founder's grandson) paid for and received an appointment with Pancho Villa. Morgan did not come away from the meeting with any definitive arrangement, but he was nonetheless hopeful.[112] Later Villa raided the ranch and murdered a number of its employees. In 1919 Houghton reported, "The local authorities either have no power or are afraid to act, and for my part, I am sure I don't know of anything that could be done even if they desire to do so."[113]

The most persistent problems for Corralitos involved titles and boundaries. One of the initial crises E. C. Houghton encountered after becoming general manager in 1895 was that the boundary line of the property was "in dispute, it being unmarked and undefined."[114] Morgan (the younger) complained that putting the land titles in order was "one of the most tedious and difficult of the works that I have had before me." Many of the titles were not even in the company's name. Morgan straightened out the mess using the "advice of the very best lawyers in the country."[115] A most pressing legal problem arose in 1911 involving the protection of its water rights, particularly in the Janos River.[116] The eastern boundary of the ranch was long disputed by the adjoining neighbors. Morgan hired a Mexican engineer of "best repute and highest standing in Chihuahua" whose findings were accepted by all the involved parties. Morgan anticipated some land exchanges that would easily end the dispute.[117] Disputes over boundaries and water rights were relatively commonplace occurrences in Mexico at the time; unclear titles and rights haunted foreign and Mexican investors alike.

The Corralitos Company overcame another important legal obstacle in 1902, when the directors, in order to comply with Mexican laws prohibiting foreign ownership within the twenty-league zone of the border, set up the Compañía de Ramos, S.A., to operate the ranch. It employed "a Mexico City straw" to own the property.[118]

The Revolution, of course, vastly complicated the legal situation. Moreover, state and local authorities often exerted more control over Corralitos's fate than they had under Díaz. Laws passed in 1917 made it necessary for Corralitos to confirm its water rights and to pay taxes to validate its claims.[119] At the same time the pueblo of Janos petitioned the Local Agrarian Commission (the locally based, revolutionary agency responsible for land reform) for restitution of ejidos, consisting of thirty-five thousand acres.[120] The company was willing to sell the land in question to the settlers or the federal government, but would not cede its ownership rights.[121] Again the company employed old tried-and-true methods, bribing the governor of Chihuahua to keep the peons from squatting on its lands, but the agrarians invaded the property anyway.[122]

Management met with authorities frequently, but local political considerations overwhelmed the ranch in the long term. For example, Houghton met with the governor of Chihuahua in early 1921. The governor "put his cards on the table," informing Houghton that he had no choice but to enforce the Idle Land Law. He had tried to impose the least burden possible on landowners, but he could not legally instruct jefes políticos not to accept land denunciations (claims for land allegedly stolen from the villages under the Díaz regime). The governor agreed to protect the company's interests so far as was in his power by "giving us the protection of the law and the authorities." He advised that the company should allow the squatters to plant idle lands and then at the expiration of their leases to claim the lands. The governor also thought it was likely that the government would expropriate the land, if it appeared "very valuable to the people."[123] An exasperated Houghton claimed in November 1921 that "protests to officials, both municipal and state, [were] bringing us no relief."[124]

The company was not shy in going to Mexico City for redress. Houghton protested the squatter invasions of 1920 to all levels of the Mexican government from the municipality to the president.[125] In early 1921 Houghton once again turned to a high-priced, influential agent to look after the company's interest, hiring Licenciado Manuel Prieto at fifty dollars a month.[126] E. D. Morgan (the grandson) met with Secretary of Agriculture Villarreal in February 1921. The secretary claimed that "it was not the intention of the government to injure people who had done as much as we had for the property and especially foreigners."[127] He then met with President Obregón, who maintained that "it was not at all the intention of the government to pauperize the well-to-do holders to further pauperize the poor."[128] Houghton met with Obregón in late December 1921. Obregón stated that he favored the Agrarian Law and distribution of small plots. He would not and could not go over the head of Governor Enríquez without consulting with him in the matter and would not go against him "unless he found that the Governor or the Agrarian Commission had exceeded their authority." The president added that he thought that the Corralitos matter "was one that could be easily arranged."[129] Houghton then met with Governor Enríquez and the head of the Agrarian Commission Gustavo Talamantes in mid-January in Ciudad Chihuahua. Talamantes maintained that the only people occupying Corralitos at the time were those put in temporary possession under the Agrarian Law of June 23, 1921. He denied that the squatters had taken away lumber and hay or that they had deprived the ranch of water to which it was entitled. The governor claimed he had ordered the squatters to stop building canals.[130]

Governor Enríquez foretold the ranch's doom when he declared, "It is an utter impossibility for the Government to remove these people; they have started to make homes and to cultivate the land, and at the end of the period set forth by the Idle Land Law, it will be necessary to apportion and donate lands to them." He was willing and did send a detachment of rurales (rural police) to prevent the squatters from siphoning off water and stealing timber and hay. The rurales would be under his orders not those of the municipality.[131] To settle the matter the government would purchase 100,000 to 150,000 acres across the southern part of the valley. An engineer was shortly to survey. The governor agreed to pay US$8.25 an acre for the prime land and US$5 for the grazing land. (Presumably the state government would then turn over the land to local people with legitimate claims.) Houghton was skeptical that the governor would keep his word.[132]

In May 1922 Chihuahua adopted a state land-reform law that limited individual holdings to one thousand hectares of irrigable land, two thousand hectares of semi-irrigable land, four thousand hectares of land dependent on rain, and forty thousand hectares of grazing land. Corralitos had three months, until September 1922, to present plans to divide its property.[133] Corralitos went to court to prevent the loss of its land. In March 1923, the governor "marked" a huge chunk of the ranch for expropriation.[134] Within weeks the ejidos of Janos took over land and established homes, workshops, and a school.[135] By 1926 Corralitos was willing to sell to the government, but President Plutarco Elías Calles refused because of adverse economic conditions.[136] To make matters worse, the company's Mexican advisor Manuel Prieto cautioned that the Corralitos was vulnerable with regard to its titles. Not one of the titles from the original purchase was in possession of the company.

In August 1922 the board of directors agreed that Corralitos would ignore the Agrarian Act adopted by the state of Chihuahua because to do otherwise would mean that the company would forfeit its rights to protest to the US government.[137] In September 1922 the US Department of State reported to the company that "the authorities of Chihuahua are not averse to entering into private negotiations with interested American property owners, with the view of arriving at satisfactory arrangements."[138] But after five years of seemingly futile efforts to sell the property, in 1927 Corralitos succumbed to the inexorable force of agrarian reform. It was thereafter merely a matter of time. The dismantling process took perhaps a decade. The company eventually recouped a small amount from the Mexican-American Claims Commission.[139]

Corralitos was caught in the middle of regional and national politics. Chihuahuan political leaders who were, ironically, generally strong advocates of the rights of private property, had no choice but to placate the local agrarian movement by redistributing land from the large estates because their hold over the region was quite tenuous. Pancho Villa, headquartered in Durango just a short ride from Hidalgo de Parral, the mining center in southern Chihuahua, loomed as a threat. Villa had been bought off temporarily by the national regime in 1920, but his presence as the former champion of land reform and his enduring popularity in Chihuahua underlined the need of local authorities to obtain the favor of local agrarians in the regions that had once given Villa support. The people in the Casas Grandes-Janos region were among the first to rise in revolution in 1910. As a result, Corralitos was likely to be an important target.

Although its investors were well connected in the United States and its management regularly had access to high-ranking Mexican government officials, Corralitos was vulnerable in part because it may have been less influential than the other foreign landowners in the area, most notably William Randolph Hearst, the newspaper publisher, whose Babícora estate extended over a million acres. Powerful people owned Corralitos, but none as influential as newspaper tycoon Hearst.

If there was any foreign enterprise that should have succeeded in Mexico from the 1880s through the 1930s, it was Corralitos. It was one of the very few foreign operations in Mexico that possessed each of the elements requisite for sustained profitability: capital, management, market, transportation, labor force, and political connections. Nonetheless, although both the mines and ranch experienced short periods of prosperity, the company was unable to sustain itself over the long term and ultimately failed. Despite all its advantages, Corralitos had only one period of sustained growth that lasted from 1898 until 1907 for the Candelaria mining operations and perhaps from 1910 to 1913 for the ranch. The businesses were simply too risky, too dependent on unpredictable geology or weather to prosper for any prolonged period even when political circumstances were stable. Good relations with government, which were by no means assured either during the Díaz era or later, did not assure profitability. Clearly, Mexico was not quite the haven nor the endless source of profits for foreigners during the Díaz dictatorship that some historians have claimed.

Although their record of profitability prior to 1910 was mixed, it may be that the mines and the ranch would have experienced enhanced prosperity, if not for the Revolution. The violence and destruction between 1915 and

1917, however, effectively ended any hopes that the huge previous investments would yield results without even larger commitments. The revolutionary agrarian reform of the 1920s doomed the agricultural enterprise. But the fact that the enterprises experienced less than a decade of profitability out of forty years in business might lead us to conclude that the good years were only temporary, the Revolution notwithstanding.

Because of the scarcity of documentation (to date), our conclusions regarding the universality of the Corralitos Company's experience are limited. We do not have a standard for success or failure in terms of profitability over time for either domestic or foreign-owned business in Mexico. We do not know what percentage of foreign mining or ranching businesses succeeded or failed. Nor do we have more than a very sketchy sense of the overall success or failure rates for all such operations, Mexican or foreign, with which to compare Corralitos. One comparable cattle ranch, the estates of Luis Terrazas in Chihuahua, generated between five hundred thousand and one million dollars in revenue from cattle exports between 1883 and 1889, roughly the same annual yield as Corralitos in its best year in 1910.[140] But it took twenty-five years of investment for Corralitos to reach the level of the Terrazas. We have no records to indicate whether the Terrazas maintained the level of income of the 1880s thereafter. (Though I suspect they did.)

CONCLUSION

It seems reasonable to come to a number of conclusions. First, Mexico was not as favorable a location for foreign business during the Díaz era as some historians maintain. Because success for foreigners depended on several crucial elements being in place and most foreign enterprises did not have these, it was highly unlikely that foreign entrepreneurs could succeed in Mexico from the 1880s through the 1930s. Even those businesspeople who had the necessary conditions in place were unable to consistently and continually prosper over the long term. Corralitos's ranching operation was only profitable after thirty years of investment and struggle. Second, the Revolution did not impact the company in quite the way the current historiography might indicate. It was not damaged because it was operated and owned by foreigners. Revolutionary armies of all factions sought supplies and funds. It did not matter what the source was, Mexican or American.

Railroad transportation was taken from everyone, not just foreigners. Third, the experience of Corralitos during the 1920s and 1930s indicates that the balancing act between the national regime, foreigners, and local elites continued, albeit complicated considerably by the demands of agrarians for land redistribution. The elite-foreign enterprise system continued to operate, seeking a new equilibrium.

SIX

Foreign Mining Entrepreneurs

Mining was the engine that drove the Mexican economy from the earliest years of the Spanish colonial era through the Díaz dictatorship, the Revolution, and the postrevolution. It was, aside from the railroads, far and away the largest recipient of foreign investment.[1] By 1910 foreigners dominated the mining sector, with the *Engineering and Mining Journal* estimating that foreigners controlled 90 percent of the operating property: Americans with 75 percent, and Europeans with 15 percent.[2] Despite the vast sums foreigners invested, they did not operate unfettered, for they, too, were subject to the checks and balances of the elite-foreign enterprise system. And although mining was the most lucrative sector of the economy, earning profits was by no means guaranteed. In order to obtain success, foreign-owned mining enterprises in Mexico, just like agricultural operations, required all of the following six circumstances: sufficient capital to purchase necessary equipment and pay for daily operations; competent management; a steady market for minerals; accessible transportation; a reliable workforce; and the maintenance of good working relations with local, state, and national authorities. And like in agriculture, most companies and individuals involved in mining lacked at least one and usually more of these required components. In fact, the preponderance of operators barely managed to scratch out a living.

Nonetheless, a considerable number of companies were at least for a time profitable and some earned great riches. The profitable enterprises always required enormous capital investment. The American Smelter and Refining Company earned tens of millions of dollars in Mexico, but it invested vast sums.

Because mining was at its best risky, few mining companies extracted substantial wealth for extended periods. Many enterprises, moreover, reinvested their profits and did not distribute dividends to stockholders. As one historian put it, there were many "skyrockets," which flared brilliantly, only to crash rather suddenly.[3] It was clear by 1910 that the trend was toward larger enterprises and the Revolution brought about further concentration. As the *Engineering and Mining Journal* explained, "low grade ore was at the small profit phase of the industry and requires great capital," resulting in bigger companies.[4]

Because mining was Mexico's most important economic sector, foreign domination has been the subject of considerable assessment and controversy. Some Mexican revolutionaries and historians later accused the foreign-owned multinational mining companies of exploiting the nation, sending out of the country vast profits, and treating their workers badly. When we look more closely, the historical record reveals a more complicated picture.

All of the six requirements were hard to acquire. Capital, the single most important factor in mining because the cost of equipment and technology was so high, was scarce or unavailable, especially for marginal operators. As with many export commodities, mineral markets were uncertain with recurrent booms and busts. The United States, the major market for Mexican ores and the main source of potential capital investment, suffered major economic downturns in each decade from the 1870s through to the period of the Mexican Revolution and into the 1930s. Transportation was expensive until after the second wave of railroad construction that began in 1900. During the Revolution, transportation was erratic and prone to stoppages because of infrastructure destruction and the assumption of control of the railroad lines by military forces. Relations with local authorities and elites were not a given with many conflicts over mine titles and resentment about relatively high wages paid by the outsiders. Competent management was not always easy to attract to isolated, often dangerous areas. Much of foreign mining activity was "speculative and poorly planned," and the failures far outnumbered the successful ventures.[5] A report of a state committee in 1886 calculated that "so numerous were the failures of foreign mining ventures that outside capitalists no longer wanted to invest. Poor management and faulty organization were largely responsible."[6] By 1890 in Sonora there was a "virtual state of panic . . . because of the bankruptcy of companies due to imprudence and sheer stupidity."[7] Poor or even mediocre management insured that profits were unlikely. To make matters worse, foreign companies struggled to acquire a reliable labor force. Especially in the north, mine workers were mobile. Many miners saw the shafts as only part-time work, returning to their villages and farms for harvest. Absenteeism was rampant. Despite the relatively high pay and acceptable working conditions, mining remained dangerous and arduous.

Unlike in the case of foreign landowners, the documentation about the mining sector is extensive with numbers of corporate annual reports and prospectuses, professional journals, personal memoirs, and government reports. Nonetheless, the evidentiary basis for my assertions is predominantly anecdotal. For example, there is no reliable comparative data that illustrates whether foreigners were more or less successful than Mexicans in business during any of the three periods under study.

A BRIEF HISTORY

The history of mining in Mexico from 1854 to 1940 divides roughly into four periods.[8] During the first era from 1854 to 1890, there were a few brave, perhaps foolish, Mexican and foreign adventurers who ignored civil wars and political uncertainties. High transportation costs, political disorder, and uncertain markets hampered their development. Conditions improved dramatically after Díaz took the reins of power in 1876 and railroad construction began in the early 1880s. One of the earliest and best-known Americans was Alexander Shepherd, who in 1880 set up operations in Batopilas, Chihuahua, in the isolated sierras of western Chihuahua. But successes were rare and profits virtually nonexistent. The second era took place after the completion of the north-south railroad lines, the Mexican Central and the Mexican National, in the mid-1880s and the passage of the McKinley Tariff in the United States in 1890, which eased the way for US and European investors to plunge into mineral production and smelting. Depression in the 1890s delayed full development, but the new century brought a great boom. Investors from the United States, Great Britain, and France poured huge sums into Mexican mining. The Díaz administration welcomed the foreigners, though local elites did not always treat them kindly. The third era, the Revolution from 1910 to 1920, brought the mining industry tough times, for many companies suspended operations for substantial periods because they were stymied by the violence, lack of transportation, loss of workers to revolutionary armies, and extortion (sometimes masked as taxes). The Great War in Europe created considerable demand for minerals, however. In the most destructive years from 1913 to 1917, the Revolution caused widespread abandonment of smaller properties. Foreign managers and workers fled the country. Highly capitalized ASARCO led the way toward consolidating the industry by actively expanding its mine holdings. As the violence was lessening in 1917, the promulgation of a new constitution created uncertainty as to the future of the industry.

A report written in 1916 by a consortium of forty-five US companies outlined experiences of eleven of the companies: during the period from the outbreak of the Revolution until late in 1912, operations were normal, although some areas endured disturbances earlier in 1912. All shut down from 1913 through 1916, with scattered, limited exceptions, most notably early in 1915.[9] The miners complained of widespread ore theft and lack of government assistance in preventing the thievery. There was a hint of recovery in 1916, but a typhus epidemic, threatening decrees, the recurrence of banditry, and the inability of the government to assure safety for mining personnel stymied any reconstruction. In 1916 no government could protect the American companies.[10] Transportation was difficult at best, and the railroads were in "deplorable" condition.[11] The companies claimed to have invested more than US$125 million, employing 62,216 workers with a yearly payroll of more than US$18 million,[12] and estimated their losses at US$7,246,031, excluding lost profits.[13] The report further claimed that "the general evidence before us makes it clear that that . . . steps have been taken, whether deliberately or ignorantly, to frustrate the resumption of business activity and to jeopardize the safety and existence of industrial undertakings for which American citizens are responsible."[14] The mining companies complained of increased taxes on mining property and "arbitrary and unlawful threats of confiscation if operation of mines is suspended for more than 60 days continuously or 90 days intermittently in any one year."[15] The fourth era, the postwar from 1920 to 1940, brought both a monumental battle over the ownership of subsoil rights and the emergence of a powerful labor union movement that obtained crucial support from the revolutionary national government and many state governments.

Despite the odds against their success, contemporaneous advertisements to the contrary, foreigners flocked to Mexico in search of their personal pots of gold at the end of the rainbow. To many dreamers, Mexico was the land of opportunity. From the wealthiest, sophisticated investors to the most scraggly prospectors, they sang the praises of the possibilities. No hardship or calamity cooled their ardor. They seemed to wear blinders as they plunged ahead. J. D. Hubbard, for example, wrote to the stockholders of the Chicago Exploration Company in 1909 that their current purchase was "the best mining opportunity that has ever been presented" to the company. He was enthusiastic despite the fact that it had been nearly impossible to find suitable mines for purchase at reasonable prices for the previous four years.[16] Nothing seemed to daunt these miner-entrepreneurs. One wrote to the *Engineering and Mining Journal* in December 1912 that he "was in Durango yesterday. . . . I met a mining man from Chalchuites. . . . He reported that seven days ago they looted his town, burned all the stores, robbed him of his money and clothes, and threatened to shoot him. He intends to try it again as now is the time to get bargains in mining property."[17]

There were several types of foreign mining entrepreneurs in Mexico. Innumerable promoters and speculators tromped all over the country. They purchased "promising" properties, usually from Mexicans, and then tried, often unsuccessfully, to raise the necessary capital to exploit their mines. The local sellers had commonly mined for decades, digging the easy-to-reach veins and perhaps scratching out profits or even hitting an occasional bonanza. Some of the mines dated to colonial times. As often as not, these mining men were looking for quick profits, and they commonly found themselves the victims of shady sellers. A second category comprised miners who had come as workers or low-level supervisors who sought to strike it rich on their own. They had a hard road indeed, for they had no connections and little capital. A third group was made up of engineers or experienced supervisors or managers who went to Mexico in the employ of large companies and either moonlighted with their own mines or went out independently. Large mining companies were the fourth category. For my purposes I will divide them into small and large operators.

SMALL OPERATORS

Speculators, promoters, ne'er-do-wells, prospectors, and engineers, the latter two categories including both moonlighters and full-time independent operators, poured into Mexico, booms and busts notwithstanding, from the 1880s through 1940. Many foreign miners lived by their wits. During the 1880s, for example, ore buyers swarmed over Mexico in search of high-grade ore at cheap prices. These hustlers often cheated the sellers by deducting for moisture, inaccurately weighing and sampling, and offering cash discounts. They often diluted samples with worthless crushed rock. One observer called the business a "jungle-like environment."[18] Fifty years later, one observer noted another promoter named Parodi, whom he described as "an Italian miner of rather questionable reputation in these parts who for some years has been living off the interest he has been able to excite in several suckers who have bitten at the bait he has offered."[19]

As the *Engineering and Mining Journal* described it, "Rich, undeveloped mines that were discovered by poor Mexicans were so numerous that it is regarded by Americans and other foreign speculators not worthwhile to do any prospecting on their own account. They find it cheaper to buy the claims of natives."[20]

Some miners thought they were too smart to be swindled. Mining engineer John Leroy Drug arrived in Suaqui Grande, Sonora, in 1922. His strategy was to avoid any deals with

> the professional high-grader known in this country as *gambusino*. Instead I engaged as a guide an old reliable native who was recommended as thoroughly reliable and who had ridden this range for the last forty years. I found that old Manuel knew the location of nearly every old mine, prospect, and outcrop in this district. . . . The result was that with Manuel's knowledge of the district we looked at more than a hundred properties, which resulted in our acquiring four of the best holdings. At the same time we avoided the tricks of the professional prospect shower.

Drug may have been fortunate in his choice of Mexican associates, but "hundreds of these professional prospect showers make their living at this game. In some instances when a newcomer bargains with some of them to see their prospects he is paying for a chance to see various properties that have been examined and turned down by a score of other individuals." It was "indeed difficult for the newcomer to distinguish between the reliable and the unreliable native miner."[21]

To say that the newcomers did not always display the best judgment is, perhaps, an understatement. Even the savviest of the miners sometimes made costly mistakes. Guillermo Beckman, one of the more successful promoters in Chihuahua during the Porfiriato, revealed to a friend in 1908, "I sold my half interest in that mine [La Palmilla] to Pedro Alvarado for one hundred pesos, and I thought that at the time I was getting the best of the bargain." Soon thereafter La Palmilla went into bonanza and yielded Alvarado untold wealth.[22]

Alf Enkeball typified the small-scale independent operator. He wrote from Sonora in 1926:

> My prospect is in the Durazno Mountains. I am working at it as best I can and manage to get out gold enough to keep up the taxes and buy a little grub once in a while, but the best I can do is just to keep the wolf from the door. . . . It is impossible for me to get ahead enough to buy tools and equipment needed. If I could find someone who would come to Mexico and work with me and equip the prospect with a small plant, a nice, steady income could be had, which would add greatly to the pleasure of this interesting life in Mexico.[23]

Enkeball seemed oblivious to the manifold difficulties that the implementation of the new constitution and new laws presented.

The dilemmas that confronted small foreign entrepreneurs were manifold, as described by E. J. Bumsted in a letter to the *Engineering and Mining Journal* in 1929:

> The lone mine manager, in an isolated place, sometimes without any protection whatever and always employing a semi-hostile people . . . must not antagonize the rebels but at the same time must stand well with the government. He must account to the government for all explosives purchased, but upon demand he dare not refuse the rebels what they ask. If this becomes known his supply is cut off and he may be accused of aiding the rebels—a serious charge.

In the fall of 1928 Bumsted had contracted to set up a mining operation in Nayarit, seventy miles south of Tepic. When he arrived in Guadalajara from the United States, he received warnings against traveling to the mine, then in rebel-held territory. His first order of business after arriving at the mine was to arrange a meeting with the local rebel commander, Lorenzo Arriola. Arriola agreed to leave him in peace and allow him unhindered travel. Soon, however, the local authorities changed. The new rebel leader Guadalupe Flores demanded money and raided the mine when it was not forthcoming. Although Bumsted ultimately paid Flores 20,000 pesos, the mine subsequently endured repeated raids.[24] Without connections and with limited resources, located in an isolated region, Bumsted had little chance to succeed.

The Revolution accentuated the importance of the relations with local authorities and emphasized the inconsistencies of law enforcement in Mexico, which made it difficult for businesses to prosper. An anonymous letter written to the *Engineering and Mining Journal* in 1920 related one of many illustrative tales. While operating a mining property in Chihuahua, carrancista soldiers occupied the letter writer's camp, ostensibly to protect it. Instead they stole his mining supplies. He protested to the proper authorities in Chihuahua, and they ordered the major in charge to return ten stolen cases of dynamite. The major, however, demanded fifty pesos to return the dynamite, which the writer agreed to pay, but only when the dynamite was returned. A few days later, the major came back without the dynamite, explaining that the thieves had sold the contraband to a Spaniard in Sonora who too operated a small mine. Unfortunately, the Spaniard had already used the dynamite. The major had ordered his soldiers to arrest the Spaniard, whom he offered to bring to the writer, and, if the latter desired, the major would have the Spaniard shot. When the writer inquired why the Spaniard was to be held to blame, the major reasoned that since it had been the Spaniard who had used the dynamite, he was guilty and should be shot.[25] The rules for conducting business in war-torn Mexico were uncertain at best. Neither foreigner had sufficient connections or resources to avoid thievery or extortion.

Perhaps the greatest threat to foreign entrepreneurs with or without connections was prolonged litigation over titles, boundaries, and transactions. There were cases in which the legal wrangling endured for decades. Bill McGinty (probably a nom de plume), a prospector in western Durango, wrote to the *Engineering and Mining Journal* in 1915, reporting on the drawn-out litigation over the "Candle-Harry" mine, illustrating the extent of the potential difficulties. According to McGinty, the mine "has been quarreled over for so many years that the litigayshun has become quite a pastime an' a post-graduate course for lawyers of all kinds, includin' plain lawyers, shysters, imminent counsel, diplomats, Secretaries av State, Mexican licenciados, provishn'l presidents, inventors av internayshn'l law, . . . and other criminals."[26]

One of the most notorious instances was the dispute over the Las Maravillas mine in Naica, Chihuahua, that went on from 1903 through 1926, when the Supreme Court ruled. The claimants spent ten million pesos in legal expenses. The heirs of Santiago Stoppelli sued the Compañía Minera de Naica, S.A., for the return of the Maravillas Mine and the profits generated by the mine plus interest. The object of the litigation was the American Metals Co., Ltd., which through the Compañía Minera de Peñoles, S.A., of Mapimi, Durango, owned 40 percent of the stock of the Compañía Minera de Naica. The stakes were high, for the mines were extremely rich although they endured many production stoppages during the Revolution.

Santiago Stopelli had discovered and claimed the Maravillas mine in 1896. Stopelli then entered into an arrangement with Saturnino González that allegedly transferred his rights to the mine in return for five hundred pesos and twenty-five of the hundred shares outstanding of the Compañia Minera de Naica, S.A. Stopelli's heirs claimed that he never actually sold the mine, but rather permitted the company to work it. They also claimed that he had received no monies for the use of the mine and had paid for the shares in the company. The company further maintained that Stopelli allowed his shares to "be vacated" in 1899. He died in 1903.

The heirs first brought suit in 1905, and the Naica company settled for 30,000 pesos. When the mine proved quite profitable, however, one of Stopelli's heirs brought suit again, this time claiming that the Maravilla property was in fact owned by the family and not by the Naica company. The Supreme Court of Mexico eventually upheld a lower-court ruling in favor of the Stopelli family. The intrigue went beyond the courts, for there were rumors that two powerful Mexican politicians, Roque Estrada, a ranking official in the War Department, and late General Benjamin Hill, formerly secretary of war under President Alvaro Obregón, had interests in the

Stopelli claim, perhaps assuring the heirs' ultimate victory in the courts.[27] The Stopelli won out, likely because they had more powerful allies.

Taking on influential locals was a costly undertaking. In a dispute over the Dolores mines in Santa Eulalia, Chihuahua, J. P. Hutchinson came into conflict with Jesús Aguirre Nevarez and General Juan Hernández. Hutchinson in partnership with two other notable American entrepreneurs, Charles M. Schwab and Augustus Heinz, had purchased the mines in 1907 from the widows Escobar who had been in dispute with Nevarez over the mines since 1893. Local potentates Luis Terrazas and Enrique Creel, reportedly relations of the Escobars, tried to intervene on their behalf, but Hernández, the military zone commander, was an ally of President Díaz. In 1907, armed with a court order, General Hernández seized the property.[28] Caught between powerful rival elite members, Hutchinson lost out.

Local authorities could make life miserable for foreign investors, no matter who they were. Henry Tabor, a prominent Colorado politician, purchased a mine in Jesús María, Chihuahua, in 1883. It took nearly a decade and three "settlements" before he escaped from litigation with a powerful local family over its title.[29] Influence in Mexico City did not always help. The San Carlos Copper Company, which had invested US$2 million and employed fifteen hundred people, sought the help of President Díaz in 1902 in order to "avoid constant difficulties it had encountered." Although the company had sought to win over the locals by paying the police and building schools and the state governor had worked "decisively and energetically" on behalf of the operation, in late 1902 the locals were asking for more medical facilities. Faced with additional, huge investments in equipment and transportation, the company turned to Díaz to rescue it from the demands of state authorities.[30]

The threat of litigation was a common tactic to extract additional funds from unwary foreigners. W. A. Pritchard, representing an English company, bought the majority of shares in the Santa María de Guadalupe y Anexas in Zacatecas, only to find that partners Señores Artigas and Conde engaged in legal maneuvers that forced him to buy the remaining shares at an "excessive" price.[31] He complained to Porfirio Díaz without result.

Another important group of foreign entrepreneurs originally came to Mexico to manage the daily operations of US-based and -financed mining companies and then sometimes branched out, moonlighting with their own mines and then establishing their own companies. Those who achieved success generally established working relations with local elites. Among the most prominent were the Long brothers of Hidalgo de Parral, the largest mining region in the state of Chihuahua. James I. Long arrived in Santa Bárbara, a mining camp adjacent to Hidalgo de Parral, in 1887.[32] His brother R. J. Long followed him in 1891.[33] James managed the Hidalgo Mining Company and was president of the Palmilla Mining Company and general manager of the Alvarado Consolidated Mines Company.[34]

Pittsburgh investors organized the Hidalgo Mining Company in 1884, buying mines in Minas Nuevas, a section southwest of Hidalgo de Parral.[35] The company earned US$116,000 in 1891.[36] According to the *Mexican Herald*, the company continued to obtain "good results" from its five mines in 1896.[37] By 1901 the company had purchased seventeen mines, built two ore-processing mills, and employed between four and five hundred men.[38] The Hidalgo Company suffered a severe setback in 1901, when a fire destroyed one of the mills.[39] The company recovered quickly and soon was in excellent condition, "producing the best ore in the camp."[40]

The company also constructed a narrow-gauge railroad, the Parral & Durango Railroad, to take advantage of the 160,000 acres of heavy timberlands it owned in the Sierra Madres. This line earned small profits from 1900 to 1905, when its net earnings were US$110,000.[41] It also built a sawmill, and its lumber operations generated another US$27,600 in profits during the same years.[42] By 1903, Long reportedly represented firms that did almost 50 percent of the mining business in Parral, while employing fifteen hundred men.[43] Reportedly his mines were well run.[44]

In addition to the properties James Long administered for Pittsburgh capitalists, he had his own interests as well.[45] Beginning in 1901, he was the manager and attorney for the Durango Cattle Company, which leased land from the Parral & Durango Railroad.[46] He also bought and sold mines.[47] The Hidalgo Mining Company sold out its seventeen mines and the Parral and Durango Railroad, with its 160,000 acres, to an Anglo-French syndicate in 1906. The new firm, the Parral Railway and Mining Company, with Long managing the railroad, was to invest US$5 million.[48]

Although both its mines and railroad were profitable at the time the company was sold, the boom did not last. Like all Chihuahuan mining operations, the depression of 1907 hit the Hidalgo Company hard. In late 1908 it suspended operations. Because its mines produced low-grade ores, when the market price for minerals declined the company could not operate profitably.⁴⁹ Management was optimistic about its prospects, however, for they had plans to invest further in the operation by building an experimental plant for the cyanide process in Minas Nuevas.⁵⁰ Nonetheless, in 1909 the Hidalgo Mining Company sold all its properties, including the railroad, to a syndicate, headed by A. J. McQuatters, for US$1.5 million.⁵¹ It is likely that the company sold out because a number of major shareholders were pending estates.⁵² By 1910 Hidalgo was again the largest producer in Parral, and the enterprise was crucial to the resurgence of the region.⁵³

During the Mexican Revolution James I. Long continued to manage the Alvarado Mining and Milling Company, and it was the only company operating in Parral after most foreigners had sent their families across the border in early 1912.⁵⁴ In mid-1913 Alvarado Mining and Milling brought out of Mexico US$600,000 of gold and silver to prevent confiscation by the Mexican revolutionaries.⁵⁵ McQuatters, the president of Alvarado Mining & Milling, was the first American to return to Chihuahua in 1916.⁵⁶

Neither Long nor McQuatters escaped the Revolution unscathed, however. McQuatters found the company's property and mill badly damaged and the stores looted, allegedly by the Constitutionalists.⁵⁷ But the indefatigable McQuatters reopened Alvarado after nearly four years in 1920 with plans to increase its capacity, using a new stock offering to finance the expansion.⁵⁸ Hidalgo and Alvarado sold out to ASARCO in 1922.

These modest operators ran the gamut from total failures to considerable success. Our most successful case, James I. Long, was an exception, in that his companies benefited from infusions of capital and his sound and powerful local connections. The governor of Chihuahua, Enrique C. Creel, for instance, personally set the amount of taxes Long was to pay.⁵⁹

LARGE OPERATORS

Although mining was risky at best, ASARCO was not the only mining company that profited in Mexico. So long as the mining operations had the six elements required, it was possible to earn enormous sums. The list of sometimes fantastically profitable enterprises was long. All of the most profitable enterprises, however, invested substantial capital to purchase the properties, buy equipment, and pay its labor force.

French investors, for example, operated a number of money-making mineral companies in Baja California, San Luis Potosí, the state of Mexico, and Michoacán. The latter case, involving the Compañia Las Dos Estrellas, S.A., provides an excellent example of the necessity of having all the six factors present. French engineer Francisco J. Fournier was a visionary miner, who after he found a promising formation in the area along the border of the states of Michoacán and Mexico in the early 1890s, struggled to convince others to invest.[60] He ultimately raised 200,000 pesos by selling off other holdings. In 1898 Fournier established the Compañia Las Dos Estrellas, S.A., with 300,000 pesos in capital. Surviving another setback during the economic downturn in 1901–2 the operation hit bonanza in 1902 and continued to earn fantastic profits through 1911, reaching its peak of 12 million pesos in 1911 and totaling 35 million pesos during the decade. The company suspended operations in 1912 because it was unable to maintain its workforce during the Revolution.[61]

Fournier was especially adept at forging influential connections. He hired Lic. José Luis Requena, the well-known intermediary, who represented several other foreign mining interests, to assist the enterprise in Mexico City, and he included on his board of directors additional important figures, including Guillermo Landa y Escandón.[62]

The history of the El Potosí Mining Company in Santa Eulalia, Chihuahua, a producer of zinc, provides us with a good case of how mining companies endured their ups and downs because of the markets and the relationships with local authorities. A notably unsuccessful business before the Revolution, El Potosí sold out to the Howe Sound Company during the civil wars. Howe Sound invested considerable capital in the operation in the 1920s. The 1930s began hopefully. Its annual report that year commented that "the amazing fact of the change of administrations [from Ing. Andrés Ortiz to Col. Roberto Fierro] was that no loans or advances were called for."[63] But challenges remained, for the report also related that a new tax of 1 percent on gross income placed a "terrific burden on some firms, impossible on others which—operating at losses—had insufficient cash or credit to meet the call."[64] Another threat arose from the resurgent labor union, the CROM, and the new labor law that was favorable to workers. The union's primary demand was to replace the old contract system with a daily wage, which the company predicted would raise its costs considerably.[65] The new taxes and increased labor demands came at a time when six consecutive years of declining metal prices led to a precipitous decline in revenues. The company was in such straits that it had to take drastic actions, letting one unit default on its taxes, not renewing its lease on another, and relinquishing a concession in Zacatecas.[66] In 1932 the company sought and received permission from the government to lay off 250 workers and to cut wages and hours for its remaining workers.[67]

At least on the surface, the local authorities continued to be cooperative in 1932. The annual report that year maintained that "the local officials of your Companies have continued to maintain friendly, but not too intimate relations with both federal and state executive authorities."[68] Three El Potosí employees were elected to municipal officials in Aquiles Serdán (formerly Santa Eulalia) in 1933.[69]

In 1934 the tide turned against El Potosí with the various levels of government allying with the miners' union to increase pressure on the company to improve wages and working conditions. Its annual report claimed that "our relations with state authorities have not been as pleasant as formerly due to the fact that this management has refused to accept without discussion various exorbitant and unjust demands made upon your companies."[70] When the company continued to resist labor demands, the governor of Chihuahua revoked its concession. The Supreme Court, however, overturned the governor's decision. Nonetheless, the state legislature rewrote the law and canceled the concession again.[71] Then the state went even further, demanding back taxes from the company in the total of 500,000 pesos. The company countered by obtaining a stay.

The local union struck for a day in 1935 before the Department of Labor ordered its members back to work.[72] That same year local authorities proved uncooperative in trying to curb the notable increase in ore thefts.[73] By 1936 contacts with local officials were reduced to the "lowest possible minimum," and labor conditions had reached rock bottom: "Every sector of industry was threatened and harassed by the labor organizations which included many impossible demands in their preemptive petitions to their employers."[74] Market forces then intervened again when, at the end of the decade and into the early 1940s, the zinc industry went into depression. El Potosí shortened the workweek, lowered wages, and limited production.[75]

El Potosí despite its considerable capitalization, persistence, and skill could not turn a profit from the late Porfiriato through to 1940 because it lacked three crucial criteria: a steady market for its products, good relations with government, and a secure workforce.

Mexican miners often got the better of the foreigners. In many cases they exploited the easiest veins and then sold out to foreigners because they lacked the capital and, perhaps, technical expertise to mine deeper. At the mines at La Trinidad in isolated Sahuaripa, Sonora, the Mexican owner Matías Alsúa had taken considerable profits from the mines, regarded as "the most valuable of any in Sonora," through the 1880s, and then he sold out to an English syndicate for US$1.5 million, at the time the largest mining sale in northern Mexico. The foreigners invested heavily in deeper tunnels and better processing equipment, and they built a new wagon road to the Sonora Railway. Even with the support of local authorities, the project failed, for the English went bankrupt, abandoned the mines, and left behind an enormous debt.[76] Before it went under, the company had endured a strike of its labor force in 1889 over the issue of it paying wages in scrip.

Of the high-profile entrepreneurs who operated in Mexico, three in particular stand out for their flamboyance and controversial records. They are all quite good examples of how the elite-foreign enterprise system worked, how foreign investors struggled, and how historians may have misjudged their activities and impact. Alexander Shepherd, William C. Greene, and Robert S. Towne were larger-than-life figures, who in the years from 1880 to 1916 had enormous aspirations that they only partially fulfilled. They invested millions of dollars, employed thousands of workers, generated virtually no profits for their stockholders, and ultimately failed, their enterprises bankrupted or sold to larger companies. All died in disrepute after various periods in the limelight. Historians have used Shepherd and Greene especially as examples of foreigners exploiting Mexicans, reaping huge profits, mistreating their employees, and operating beyond the law. But the historical evidence is more mixed. Each of them, for example, eschewed profit remittances (dividends) to their stockholders in order to reinvest in their companies. This policy provided for expanding employment and acquiring better equipment. Furthermore, there is ample evidence that they treated their workers at least as well as any other domestic or foreign company.

The cases of Shepherd and Greene are particularly controversial. One historian has labeled Shepherd a tyrant, an embezzler, and a madman.[77] To many, Greene, the "copper skyrocket," was a speculator and a charlatan; he lasted less than a decade, his empire collapsing like a house of cards in the depression of 1908.

ALEXANDER SHEPHERD

Alexander Shepherd's mining operations in Batopilas, Chihuahua, were based on his driving personality and vision, strict control of his workforce, and close relationships with local, state, and national authorities, particularly the Terrazas family and Porfirio Díaz. What the enterprise lacked was a steady source of capital, a consistent market for silver, and low-cost transportation.

John Mason Hart has harshly assessed Shepherd's operations in Batopilas:

> First, he sought to reorganize and centralize political control over the mining areas of the Copper Canyon complex by having the president approve large land grants and appoint sympathetic individuals as the "governing officers" to replace freely elected pueblo leaders. Second, he worked to achieve direct control over public works projects, such as roads and aqueducts, in order to further the development and industrialization of the mines. And, third, he moved to achieve racial segregation at Batopilas by enlarging the residential quarters in the Hacienda San Miguel and thereby maintaining the separation of Americans from mestizos and Native Americans across the river in town.[78]

Taken in context, however, Shepherd's actions may not have been as sinister as Hart claims. There is little doubt that Shepherd sought to manage local politics, but his actions were quite in keeping with the machinations of the elite-foreign enterprise system.

He, like Mexican elites, tried to control or at least influence local authorities. They had learned the hard lesson that they had to maintain control or at least exert considerable political influence in order to protect their economic holdings. Furthermore, Díaz, as he grew stronger over the years, replaced many local elected leaders with his appointees, thus this was not a phenomenon particular to Batopilas. Since the Batopilas Company was the largest employer in the region, it was more than likely that any official, appointed or elected, would have some connection to it. It is hard to find fault with Shepherd's efforts to improve transportation in and out of Batopilas. The area was quite isolated, and moving ores to market was very costly. Lastly, Shepherd was by no means alone in separating foreigners from Mexican workers. Undoubtedly race was part of the reasoning, but class was a factor as well. Managers never lived in close proximity to workers. Hart has chosen to proffer a highly negative interpretation for the commonplace.

From another viewpoint, Shepherd had displayed enormous persistence and resourcefulness, raising capital, refurbishing old mines, discovering new veins, and installing modern equipment for processing the ore. "He found the region wild and peopled with ignorant peasants," spouted one observer, "he left it well developed and with schools, hospitals, and all other evidences of efficient leadership."[79] In this analysis the boss was paternalistic, but he wielded his powers with a light hand.[80]

The Batopilas Mining Company, founded in 1880, was the oldest and one of the largest mining operations in Chihuahua during the Díaz era. Shepherd arrived in Chihuahua in 1879 and bought the Batopilas mines from a syndicate associated with Wells, Fargo, and Company. He rapidly expanded the enterprise, obtaining in 1886 a favorable concession from the Mexican government. The mines did not yield quick profits. During the first seven years the annual production averaged only about 600,000 pesos. Shepherd had spent more than 2 million pesos just in the first two years.[81] In 1887 Shepherd consolidated several other mining companies in the area, forming a giant corporation. By 1888 he had reportedly invested US$5 million and employed between three and six hundred people, depending on the season. By 1892 Shepherd employed more than a thousand. Batopilas grew from three hundred to five thousand inhabitants during the same time. Despite the enormous difficulties and expense of transportation, very high interest rates on borrowed capital, and massive expenditures on capital improvements, through most of its first two decades the company earned small profits that Shepherd reinvested in the operations. By 1900, however, the company had fallen on hard times. Shepherd died in 1902. His son Grant took over the business, and it continued as an important silver producer although employment dropped to a low of 132 in 1905. A short recovery followed with three profitable years from 1905 through 1907; the company declared dividends for the first time in twenty years. In 1909 Shepherd sold out to British investors. The company earned profits in 1913 and 1914, but thereafter the Revolution disrupted operations. The mines reopened in 1919, but by 1925, with no new veins, it shut down.

The Batopilas Company had to struggle with the six requirements for success. Consequently, over the years it did not produce a windfall for its stockholders. The boss had considerable difficulties in raising capital. After the initial US$2 million investment, in 1887 his newly reorganized company tried to float a bond issue for US$1 million, but only sold half this amount, receiving US$200,000. He was forced to invest almost all his own money in the company and delayed paying dividends to stockholders indefinitely.[82] By David Pletcher's estimates Shepherd spent millions on new plants and equipment, such as two US$500,000 ore-processing mills, a million-dollar dam, and a narrow-gauge railroad. Hart claims that in actuality the mines yielded enormous profits, which Shepherd stole in order to maintain a lavish lifestyle for himself and his family.[83]

Transportation was problematic. It was 236 miles from the mines to the Mexican Central Railroad. Later the construction of the Chihuahua al Pacífico Railroad cut the distance by 25 percent. Freight took twenty-four to twenty-eight days to Chihuahua City. Half the distance was traversable only by mule trains, which were very costly in part because they required private guards to protect them from bandits.[84] It was difficult to generate profits in an operation that sank so much money into getting its ores to market.

Maintaining a workforce in the isolated Batopilas region was a continuous challenge. Shepherd's treatment of his workers has become the subject of controversy. The most obvious sources of labor, the local Tarahumara people, were reluctant to toil in the unhealthful, dangerous conditions that prevailed in the mines and smelters. Yaqui Indians from Sonora, whom authorities had impressed or who had fled from the authorities during their rebellion, were another source. John Mason Hart claims that working conditions at Batopilas were terrible. The Yaquis, whose labor contracts were sold to Batopilas in 1880, reputedly died because of lung infections that resulted from the dampness and filth of the mineshafts.[85] Pletcher, to the contrary, maintains that Shepherd "treated his foreign and native workers fairly, according to the standard of the times." He also claimed that wages in the Batopilas District had risen from less than one peso to two or three pesos because of the company. Wages were comparable to other mining regions. In addition, the Batopilas Company provided employees with medical care, a free hospital, and free prescription medicine. Like William C. Greene and other foreign companies, it paid its American employees higher wages than its Mexican workers. Hart makes much, too, of the payment of miners in scrip redeemable at the company stores, arguing that this was exploitative and amounted to debt peonage. This claim does not take into consideration the difficulties in obtaining currency and the isolation of the Batopilas camp, which limited retail options for the workers.

According to Pletcher, Shepherd held his Mexican employees in high regard (so long as they were properly directed), and they in turn regarded him as their *patrón grande*.[86] Pletcher describes the attempt at union organizing in Batopilas as rather benign with simple reason prevailing to end the effort, while Hart maintains that the boss called in federal troops and crushed the movement.

Shepherd's relations with Porfirio Díaz and the Terrazas-Creel family were a pillar of his enterprise. His initial interaction with the local elite was when he purchased 122,500 acres around Batopilas from the Valenzuela family, which had in partnership with other elite families obtained the tract through their surveying company. The Valenzuelas later sued him over mine titles, but he settled the case in 1884. He then became close with President Díaz, who was the godfather of at least one of Shepherd's children. Díaz granted his approval of labor contracts for Yaqui Indians who had been captured by the federal army in Sonora, where the Yaquis had rebelled against the loss of their ancestral lands.[87] More important, Díaz in fact made no objection to Shepherd's autonomy. Enrique C. Creel, another firm ally, assured the cooperation of state authorities. Shepherd and the local jefe político had complicated relations because Shepherd clearly operated outside the latter's authority. But they cooperated to keep order and prevent pilferage.[88]

Although Shepherd was reportedly one of the two foreigners Díaz trusted, the entrepreneur did not escape from crucial limitations imposed by the government.[89] The 1886 concession that gave the company the right to exploit abandoned mines over a large extent of land and exempted it from import duties on equipment and most federal taxes also provided that the company become Mexican and set a minimum level of employment. Shepherd agreed as well to smelt 75 percent of his ore in Mexico and not in any way to involve a foreign government in financing his business.[90]

Shepherd maintained his autonomy partly by employing a force of seventy well-armed men to protect the operation and to escort the bullion on the long, dangerous trips to the port of Mazatlán or the mint in Chihuahua City.[91] Hart presents this a sinister aspect of Shepherd's business, but Shepherd was not the only entrepreneur to maintain his own small army. The Hearst estate in northwestern Chihuahua had eighty armed cowboys in its employ in the 1910s.[92]

Given the longevity of the Batopilas operation, it was only minimally profitable. From 1880 to 1887 the Shepherd companies paid out US$1 million in dividends. For the next fifteen years, there were no other such payouts. After he died, however, under the leadership of his sons and others, the company earned US$1.7 million from 1902 to 1910. In addition, it paid off all its old loans by 1906. In 1907 it declared its first dividend, US$55,870. It earned profits again in 1913 and 1914, but then never again did so.[93]

The Batopilas Company provides us with an illustrative example that even with advantages there was no certainty that foreigners would earn profits in the risky mining industry or that they exploited either Mexico or its people. Like many of the robber barons of the late nineteenth century, Alexander Shepherd was difficult to categorize as either visionary or villain.

WILLIAM C. GREENE

William C. Greene's empire did not last nearly as long as that of Alexander Shepherd, but his impact was far greater. One biographer called him "swashbuckling."[94] Speculator, propagandist, promoter, Greene became one of the symbols of exploitative foreigner and Yankee imperialism because of the strike at his Cananea camp in 1906, which resulted in a melee between an invading force of Arizona Rangers, Mexican federal troops, and the strikers.

In 1898, William C. Greene, an Arizona rancher, purchased an option for the Cobre Grande group of mines from the widow of a former governor and member of one of the most powerful elite families of Sonora, General Ignacio Pesqueira, for 47,000 pesos. He began with a wing and a prayer with two American partners. The original plan was to sell off the mines, which they accomplished. But the buyer did not produce enough to make the deal worthwhile to Greene, so he took back the mines.[95] He then founded the Cananea Consolidated Copper Company, S.A., in 1899 in Cananea, Sonora, forty miles from Naco, Arizona. His concession included

35,000 acres. The company paid 25,000 pesos per year for the right to hold its claims. The mines produced low-grade ore that was costly to process. It required enormous capital investment in high-technology equipment. He convinced one of the members of the Standard Oil group, Thomas W. Lawson, to finance his vision. Lawson quickly reneged, but Greene found new backers and then issued stock in his company on Wall Street. However, he had to fight off Lawson and his allies, who sought to take over the mines. While Greene spent most of his time winning and losing great fortunes in New York, his company expanded rapidly. It bought millions of dollars worth of mines and 486,000 acres of timberland. The Mexican government granted a formal concession in 1904. The copper deposits, as it turned out, were enormous! The tycoon built up an entire community at Cananea with housing, stores, and a hospital.

The mining companies generated low profits. Greene Consolidated had declared dividends of more than US$2 million between 1900 and 1902, but likely only because he used the proceeds from stock sales to pay them.[96]

Greene was not satisfied with Cananea Consolidated and in his heyday sought to vertically integrate his mining operations by investing in land for livestock and timber to supply his mines. He purchased 344,000 acres in the Cananea Mountains for US$300,000 from an American and another tract of 137,000 acres for US$51,000 from a local family.[97] He began to build a railroad, the Cananea, Yaqui River, and Pacific Railway, from Cananea to Naco, Arizona.[98] Then he embarked upon his most ambitious scheme, the Greene Gold-Silver Company, incorporated in 1902, which was to buy up old abandoned silver and gold mines across about three million acres in Sonora and Chihuahua.[99] For example, he purchased the Santa Eduviges Mine in 1906 for US$326,000.[100] Most of his purchases required enormous expenditures in plants and roads. His third project was the Sierra Madre Land and Lumber Company, for which he obtained a huge timber concession. In order to be able to ship the company's lumber to the Greene Gold-Silver mines, he purchased the Río Grande, Sierra Madre, and Pacific Railroad.

The end came quickly, however. The strike of mine workers in June 1906 started the fall. Greene lost control of Greene Consolidated Copper in early 1907.[101] A variety of lawsuits were filed against Greene's companies for not paying their bills.[102] J. P. Morgan and Company called in Greene's notes and tried to take over the Sierra Madre Land and Lumber Company.[103]

paying the salaries of mayors or police, or by buying property from local elites. The Revolution ultimately brought substantial change to the relations between the national government and foreign mining companies because of the return of subsoil rights to the nation and the implementation of rules that required miners to operate their properties or lose their concessions. Finally, there is little credible evidence that foreigners mistreated their Mexican workers. More often than not, the presence of foreign-run mining operations raised the wages of the surrounding regions, both in the mines and the fields. Particularly in the north there was competition for workers.

There is little doubt that the impact of foreign mining companies in Mexico will continue to be the subject of considerable controversy, especially in the case of the multinational enterprises such as ASARCO, but it is clear from the examples we have discussed that historians can make a strong argument that they did not generate excessive profits nor did they exploit either the nation or its workers.

SEVEN

The American Smelting and Refining Company in Mexico, 1890–1940

The American Smelting and Refining Company (ASARCO) was the largest mining and smelting company in Mexico from 1900 to 1940.[1] As an enormous, multinational corporation, run by a powerful US family, the Guggenheims, it, like the major railroad lines, had a crucial role in the system of triangular relations between the national government, state and local elites, and foreign companies that formed the backbone of Mexican politics and economics from the mid-nineteenth through the mid-twentieth century.

In order to obtain success, foreign-owned mining enterprises in Mexico during the dictatorship of Porfirio Díaz, the Revolution, and postrevolutionary era required all of the following six elements: sufficient capital to purchase necessary equipment and pay for daily operations; competent management; a steady market for minerals or agricultural commodities; accessible transportation; a reliable workforce; and the maintenance of good working relations with local, state, and national authorities. Most companies and individuals that conducted business in this most important sector, which foreigners dominated, lacked at least one and usually more of these conditions. ASARCO was exceptional in that it had all of the required elements in abundance. Unlike other foreign enterprises, which, for the most part, experienced little success in Mexico, ASARCO was vastly profitable.

The following chapter explores the place of the large multination corporation in the Díaz system and how its situation changed during and after the Revolution. In terms of its relations with various levels of Mexican government and elites, ASARCO, like other foreign companies and individuals, sometimes experienced rougher handling by local or state authorities. However, ASARCO stood out in that it obtained unparalleled access to the halls of power in Mexico City throughout the era and in that, despite occasional setbacks due to the exigencies of civil war, the corporation remained profitable and expanded substantially during the Revolution and the period of revolutionary reconstruction. It is also important to note that although the company extracted enormous profits from its Mexican operations, almost continuously from 1900 to 1940, it also invested huge sums. I would therefore argue that the multinational company did not exploit Mexico by digging out easy, unwarranted profits. The company took great risks that paid off. The most important transformation that affected the company in the revolutionary and postrevolutionary years was the intrusion of strong, activist labor unions into the relationship between it and the Mexican government.

HISTORY

Meyer Guggenheim had built an empire of silver and lead in the United States, beginning in 1881. His company, M. Guggenheim, entered Mexican smelting in order to assure its profitability after the McKinley Tariff of 1890 raised the cost of imported Mexican unprocessed ores. The construction of the two major Mexican railroads, the Mexican Central and the Mexican National, each completed in the 1880s, was crucial, for they provided cheap transportation for bulk shipments of ores, initially directly to export markets and later to smelters located in both Mexico and abroad, and they supplied inexpensive transportation for imported mining machinery. The Guggenheims moved quickly. By the end of 1891, they had explored the possibilities in Mexico, negotiated a wide-ranging concession for mining and smelting, and set up a new enterprise, La Gran Fundición Nacional

Mexicana (the Grand National Mexican Smelting Company) in Monterrey. The company subsequently leased a number of mines in northern Mexico and established ore-purchasing agencies in the states of Hidalgo and San Luis Potosí. By 1893 they had invested US$3 million to put in operation two silver-lead smelters.[2] Two years later the Guggenheims completed a new copper and lead smelter in Aguascalientes. In the next three years their subsidiaries bought up fifty-five mines in the region of the smelter, coming to control more than half the ore production in the state of Aguascalientes.[3] The Guggenheims had only just started.

In a process that began in the late 1890s the Guggenheims won control of the US "smelters' trust," the American Smelting and Refining Company. Initially through ASARCO's subsidiary, Guggenheim Exploration, the corporation began a twenty-five-year buying spree in Mexico. In its first five years, ASARCO and its associated companies purchased and modernized scores of mining operations, built and bought a number of feeder railroad lines, and then reorganized them more functionally.

In 1902 alone Guggenex expended US$25 million in acquiring mines in northern Mexico.[4] Indicative of the willingness of the Guggenheims to lay out large sums to buy productive mines was their purchase of the Velardeña Mining and Smelting Company, completed in 1904, which required an outlay of US$7 million.[5]

In 1905 Guggenheim Exploration transferred its holdings and several additional acquired mining operations to the American Smelters Securities Company (ASSCO), another ASARCO subsidiary. ASSCO operated until 1923 when it dissolved, transferring its assets to the Compañia Minera Asarco, S.A., a Mexican company.

From 1905 until the overthrow of Porfirio Díaz in 1911, ASARCO confronted three potential challenges: the Monetary Reform Law of 1905, which established Mexico on the gold standard; the Mining Law of 1905; and the depression of 1907–9. The Monetary Reform Law ended the windfall profits that had accrued to silver producers because government mints had purchased silver at high prices. The Mining Law, however, lowered taxes on silver production to compensate for the provisions of the Monetary Reform Law. New technology, in the form of the cyanide process for extracting silver ore, lowered the cost of production, allowing the company to maintain profitability. As a consequence, the new regulations did not adversely affect ASARCO.[6]

Having weathered the Díaz government's efforts to regulate the mining industry, ASARCO confronted the successive challenges of a major economic downturn in 1907 and the outbreak of rebellion in late 1910. The depression cut the company's earnings and caused it to decrease production, and employment.[7] ASARCO took advantage of the downturn to buy up promising properties owned by failing companies. In 1909 the company began a new US$25 million investment program in Mexico, including the National Metallurgical Company in 1910.[8]

The initial rebellion against Porfirio Díaz, led by Francisco I. Madero, broke out in November 1910 and resulted in the dictator's exile in May 1911; it was fought primarily in Chihuahua and Durango where ASARCO had invested heavily. Under the national governments headed by Madero (1911–13) and General Victoriano Huerta (1913–14), who overthrew and murdered Madero, ASARCO, for the most part, continued its operations. In 1911 rebels raided mining camps and disrupted railroad transportation. It became difficult to obtain supplies for the camps and coal for the smelters. The company, however, continued to buy up mining properties and to generate impressive profits.[9] The following year the company absorbed losses from new raids by a group of rebels opposed to Madero, led by Pascual Orozco, a former ally of Madero. Nonetheless, ASARCO achieved record profits.[10] The civil war that erupted after Huerta took power, however, badly disrupted transportation and jeopardized the company's employees in many areas. Heavy fighting caused ASARCO to close down many of its operations, and as a consequence, its earnings suffered.[11] The company closed its smelters at Monterrey, Matehuala, and Velardeña.[12] Rebel forces looted the Chihuahua smelter in July, causing ASARCO to evacuate the families of its American employees.[13]

Although ASARCO tried its best to maintain its operations from 1910 to 1920, circumstances were often not favorable. After the two US invasions, the occupation of Veracruz and Tampico in 1914, and the Pershing Expedition in 1916, for example, the company deemed the situation too dangerous for its foreign personnel and closed its mines and smelters.[14] At times there was no transportation because the warring factions appropriated the railroads. On other occasions, coal, needed to fuel both railroads and smelters, was unavailable. According to R. F. Manahan, who compiled a valuable history of ASARCO in Mexico, "Insofar as circumstances permitted, every feasible effort was made to operate the mines; but conditions changed so frequently, particularly in the northern region, that operations were, generally speaking, sporadic."[15]

Difficulties continued through 1914 and 1915 because the company was caught in the middle between the rival factions led by Venustiano Carranza (Constitutionalists) and Pancho Villa (villistas), respectively. In mid-April 1914, the company suspended all its operations in Mexico, ordering its American employees to leave Mexico in the wake of the US invasion and occupation of the Mexican Gulf ports of Tampico and Veracruz.[16] In spite of the civil war, there had been little damage to its plants through the end of 1914.[17] ASARCO again closed its smelters, except its Chihuahua plant, in May 1915.

The worst period was between 1915 and 1916, when the government disintegrated and warring factions wore a bloody path through the center of the nation. The Santa Bárbara Unit did not produce milling ore from late 1915 through the end of 1919.[18] The scarcity of railroad cars during this period caused ASARCO to purchase its own locomotives and freight haulers.[19]

The US invasion of Mexico in 1916 created a very dangerous situation for ASARCO, for the company not only had to contend with the warring armies of Villa and Carranza, but anti-American sentiment as well. In March 1916 the company again evacuated its American employees.[20] By the end of the year, it operated none of its smelters in Mexico. Nonetheless, the mining division continued to purchase properties at bargain prices. By the end of the summer of 1916, most of the ASARCO smelters were back on line; once again, it was making money and even raised wages.[21]

During the next four years, ASARCO gradually resumed operations. There were ongoing obstacles. Pancho Villa, although defeated everywhere else, still hampered production with his guerrilla activities in Chihuahua.[22] More threatening was the new Constitution of 1917, Articles 27 and 123 of which threatened the rights of foreign property owners. The Constitution nationalized subsoil rights, including, of course, minerals. It also contained a number of provisions for labor, including the eight-hour day, six-day week, limitations on overtime, equal pay for equal work, regional minimum wages, employer obligations to provide housing, schools, and health care, workmen's compensation, and the right to strike. In 1918 ASARCO reorganized as a Mexican corporation, becoming the Compañia Minera de Asarco, S.A., in order to comply with recent Mexican laws. Many units were still not on line in 1918, and the company estimated its total losses at US$1.5 million.[23] Villa and the Constitution notwithstanding, Chihuahua experienced a mining boom in 1919.[24]

For ASARCO the 1920s were to be a decade of great challenges and enormous expansion. In 1920 Alvaro Obregón, the leading Constitutionalist general, overthrew Carranza and won election as president. His new government negotiated a settlement with Pancho Villa, thus establishing a measure of peace in Mexico for the first time in a decade. The first difficulties arising from the Constitution of 1917 were unresolved and troubling. The Constitution's assertion of the nation's ownership of all resources below jeopardized all of the company's mining properties. Particularly vulnerable to government takeover were those properties the company had left undeveloped. The second set of threats to the company involved the newly energetic labor unions, invigorated by other provisions of the Constitution regarding labor. In addition, some of the problems, such as the shortages of railroad cars because the government diverted them to military operations and shortages of coal, were left over from the civil wars.[25] Furthermore, ASARCO executives continued to complain about high railroad rates and high taxes.[26]

Through the end of the 1920s ASARCO continued to invest large sums in equipment and new operations, in particular coal mining in Coahuila and in silver-lead properties in Santa Eulalia and Hidalgo de Parral in Chihuahua.[27] The smelter in Avalos, Chihuahua, just outside Chihuahua City, became the largest lead smelter in the world.[28] In 1924, for example, ASARCO announced construction projects in Mexico costing US$10 million.[29] By the end of the decade, however, labor militancy intensified, while simultaneously the market for silver plummeted.[30]

During the 1930s ASARCO experienced growing labor militancy, as well as increased pressure from the government for the company to provide minimum wages and schools and housing for its workers. As the decade progressed, especially after Lázaro Cárdenas and his prolabor administration took office in 1934, strikes increased and workers' demands became more extensive and insistent. With the onset of the Great Depression in full force in 1930, ASARCO reduced the workweek in response to the fall in mineral prices.[31]

ASARCO, THE MEXICAN ELITE, AND GOVERNMENT AT VARIOUS LEVELS

In a letter to Porfirio Díaz in 1908, Daniel Guggenheim, president of ASARCO, admitted that "these vast mining and smelting operations were begun under the solicitation and the most favorable supervision, regulations and laws of Mexico on behalf of my family.... The laws and the administration of the laws regulating and affecting our business ... were everything which I could desire."[32] The Guggenheims enjoyed full access to the dictator from 1891 until the Revolution forced him out in 1911. The family, furthermore, took exceptional measures to construct ties to various levels of officials in Mexico City and the provinces, especially in the north, the location of most of ASARCO's mines.

When the Guggenheims looked to Mexico in 1890 they discussed the possibilities with a prominent mining entrepreneur in Monterrey, Joseph A. Robertson, who had widespread links to important families in northern Mexico. They then associated with Edgar Newhouse, who accompanied Daniel Guggenheim to Mexico and used his influential contacts to further the Guggenheims' interests. He quickly arranged for two crucial members of Díaz's ruling circle, Emeterio de la Garza and General Bernardo Reyes to act as intermediaries with Porfirio Díaz. The president met with them and approved their concession to establish their business in Mexico.[33]

The most common relationship the Guggenheims and their companies enjoyed with the Mexican elite was in the purchase or lease of the elite's property by the Americans. In 1896, for example, Consolidated Kansas City, later part of ASARCO, leased three sets of mining claims in Santa Eulalia, Chihuahua, from Pedro R. Prieto, Manuel Gameros, and Federico Muller, all prominent citizens of the state.[34] In 1896 and 1899 the Guggenheims purchased mining property from Martín and Pedro Elissague in Santa Bárbara. In 1899 they obtained the Tecolotes from Pedro and Francisco Erquicia for 700,000 pesos.[35] In 1903 the Guggenheims bought several mines in Jibosa (near Jiménez) Chihuahua for 200,000 pesos.[36] In 1923 ASARCO leased Las Plomosas from the heirs of Manuel Gameros.[37]

Before 1910 the Guggenheims enjoyed access to the highest echelons, including Don Porfirio himself. General Bernardo Reyes, the political boss of Nuevo León, and a close ally of Díaz, granted the Guggenheims their concession for smelters in Monterrey in 1891. The only hitch arose when

Jose Y. Limantour, the finance minister, held up a tax exemption for the export of silver bullion.[38]

Nonetheless, close relations with the dictator did not mean that ASARCO avoided the need to maintain excellent rapport with state and local authorities as well. Furthermore, local conditions were not always optimal either during the Díaz era or the Revolution. The blessings of the central government did not always carry much weight in the provinces. Chihuahua was a crucial case in point. Prior to 1910, the company had to pay steeply to operate. Confronted with the overwhelming political power of the Terrazas family, which controlled state politics and whose economic empire was perhaps the most formidable in Mexico, the Guggenheims reluctantly, but gracefully, gave in. After 1900 there was heavy demand for a smelter in Chihuahua City. The Terrazas family had invested in mining and smelting for decades, but was unwilling to risk the huge capital required to build a smelter. After Enrique Creel, the family's second-in-command, became governor in 1904, he pressured the Guggenheims to construct a smelter near Chihuahua City, threatening to build a competing smelter if the Americans refused. At the same time, the Guggenheims attempted to purchase the Maderos' Compañía Metalúrgica Mexicana, which operated a smelter in Torreón, the only Mexican-owned smelter in the country. However, despite prolonged negotiations, the deal with the Maderos did not work out. Consequently, ASARCO built the requested smelter near Chihuahua City. The cost was high, for ASARCO had to purchase the state concession for a smelter from the Terrazas, and Luis Terrazas, the head of the family, sold the company a parcel of his land for the smelter. Juan Terrazas, Luis's son, obtained the concession to operate the company store at the site.[39]

There were instances when local elites resisted the Guggenheims' plans. A group in the state legislature of Aguascalientes, against the expressed wishes of the governor, opposed the Guggenheims' application, already approved at the national level, for a concession to construct a smelter in 1894 and delayed it for some time. The Guggenheims appealed to Díaz, who dispatched Emeterio de la Garza, who in cooperation with Governor Alejandro Vázquez del Mercado, negotiated with the legislators for approval.[40] Shortly thereafter, the Guggenheims had to obtain land to build the smelter. This, too, required the intervention of de la Garza and Governor Vázquez del Mercado. Finally, a dispute with a neighboring landowner held up construction of a railroad spur for a year because he claimed that the smelter and line would ruin his property. President Díaz ordered the expropriation of the land.[41]

On occasion ASARCO cooperated with local authorities for the common good. In 1909 Dr. Charles E. Husk, the physician in the company-built and -maintained hospital, worked with the municipal government in Santa Bárbara, Chihuahua, to stamp out a serious epidemic of smallpox.[42]

During the wars that ravaged Mexico from 1911 to 1920, ASARCO's local executives negotiated constantly with whatever military forces threatened its facilities. The company paid when necessary in the form of loans or taxes. There were kidnappings for ransom. Its executives complained endlessly about the disruptions, the lack of transport and coal, and the capriciousness of the different policies of the various factions. The company continued to reach arrangements with regional and local political bosses after 1920, but, in addition, had to contend with national leaders under enormous pressures to improve working conditions. The company's great advantage was the government's desperate need for reconstructing the Mexican economy. Since mining was the nation's most important industry, ASARCO had considerable leverage in its negotiations with government officials at all levels. With tens of thousands of employees, ASARCO was one of the foundations of the nation's economic recovery.

ASARCO executives were well aware of the importance of relations with the government. Coincident with the outbreak of the Revolution in the fall of 1910, Henry R. Wagner, who headed the company's Mexican operations, moved its headquarters from Aguascalientes to Mexico City, reasoning that "as a great part of our business was carried on with the government and especially with the railroads, I felt that we should be near enough to them to be able to get quick action."[43]

Wagner made a considerable effort to make connections with the victorious Maderos in 1911. He had considerable reason for worry, since the Maderos's smelter operation was a direct competitor of ASARCO, and a few years before, the family and the company had unsuccessfully negotiated the sale of the former's smelter. Felix Summerfeld, an old friend, later a notorious villista gunrunner, arranged for Wagner to meet Francisco Madero. The ASARCO executive was unable to obtain even the vaguest assurances of protection from the revolutionary. On the advice of Summerfeld, he was to see Francisco's brother Gustavo, who "was the brains of the affair."⁴⁴ Wagner succeeded in making arrangements through Gustavo for access to railroad transportation and for adjustments in export taxes.⁴⁵

From 1911 to 1915, the peripatetic Wagner negotiated personally or indirectly with a who's who of revolutionary leaders. In August 1912 he paid 8,000 pesos to Pascual Orozco to allow ASARCO's bullion to pass through Ciudad Juárez. Wagner delivered the funds to the defeated Orozco across the border in El Paso, despite the fact that the general was in no position to enforce the deal, in order to demonstrate to all the revolutionaries that "we would make our word good . . . whoever they were."⁴⁶

According to Wagner, ASARCO was willing to go to considerable lengths to gain Madero's favor. When the new president promised to raise peons' wages to a peso a day, ASARCO increased the wages of common laborers to a peso a day at the Aguascalientes plant, doing so "in the belief that we ought to do what we could to help the new administration."⁴⁷ Wagner met with Villa personally in December 1913, when the general threatened to take over and to operate the Chihuahua smelter unless ASARCO restarted it. Villa wanted ASARCO to process ores he had confiscated from other mining companies. Wagner through difficult negotiations agreed to reopen the smelter, and Villa did not insist the company smelt the confiscated ores.⁴⁸

In the midst of the civil wars, there was not always agreement between the national government and the regional bosses. In early 1914, for example, the "Mexican administration" advised Villa to return one million pesos stolen from ASARCO.⁴⁹ It was not uncommon for rebels to extort funds in the form of taxes, loans, or kidnapped employees, or simply rob facilities of supplies, livestock, and equipment. In 1914, Pancho Villa allowed the company to operate, but he held thirty employees for ransom of 35,000 pesos.⁵⁰ According to another report, however, in 1914, while the carrancistas took all the railroad rolling stock, Villa, with whom the company had excellent relations, allowed ASARCO transportation.⁵¹ Wagner found out the hard way that field officers did not always obey their superiors. Even Villa could not always control his subordinates. One villista general held a considerable amount of ASARCO's bullion in 1913, despite Villa's orders to return it to the US company. Eventually Wagner secured the bullion with a "reasonable" ransom.⁵²

In at least one instance, ASARCO lost possession of its facilities. In 1915 Pancho Villa demanded that ASARCO reopen its Chihuahua smelter and tributary mines or he would operate them with his own forces. The company protested that the lack of transportation hampered its operations (although it was willing to restart its smelter in order to alleviate the widespread unemployment in the state). Villa took over the smelter and confiscated silver and lead ore that ASARCO was unwilling to process because it lacked technical staff.⁵³

Perhaps the best example of ASARCO having to pay off leaders of the warring factions took place in 1919. In January Pancho Villa, who remained in the field against Carranza, raided Santa Eulalia. Villa told ASARCO's local managers that he would destroy the company's Chihuahua smelter and its Parral mines, unless ASARCO paid a large sum. The military zone commander General Jesús A. Castro sent two hundred troops to Santa Eulalia and placed a permanent garrison at the smelter. Nonetheless, Villa occupied Parral in April. Villa's agent, Colonel Baltasar Piñones, informed ASARCO that the company was to pay 50,000 pesos to prevent his sacking the city. He held the staff of the Veta Grande Unit for ransom. The managers only had 3,000 pesos in cash, which they turned over to Piñones, promising to pay the balance. A few days later Luz Corral de Villa, Pancho's wife, picked up the remaining 47,000 pesos (and was kind enough to leave a receipt that Marucci found in the archives).⁵⁴ There was a report in mid-1920 that officials of ASARCO had "tendered an elaborate dinner" for Villa and Luz Corral in Santa Bárbara at which "cordiality and good-feeling abounded."⁵⁵

Although the postrevolutionary era brought continued challenges, the company maintained a generally positive relationship with the national governments of Adolfo de la Huerta (1920), Alvaro Obregón (1920–24), and Plutarco Elías Calles (1924–28 and behind the scenes, 1928–34). Difficulties in obtaining sufficient railroad transport and coal continued. In 1920 ASARCO protested to Calles, then the minister of war, that it could not continue to operate if he gave all the railroad cars to the military. It also desperately needed coal to run its smelters. The government had confiscated the coal ASARCO had sent to Chihuahua. To make matters worse, there was a shortage of dynamite in Chihuahua as well.⁵⁶

The company continually lobbied for lower railroad rates and reduced taxes, both on imported supplies and equipment and on exported minerals. In 1921 ASARCO demanded that the government make its imported equipment and supplies and its exports of gold, lead, and zinc exempt from taxes.⁵⁷ Several months thereafter, the company reached agreement with the Department of Transportation whereby the National Railways would provide better service at lower rates.⁵⁸ In 1922 ASARCO reached another agreement whereby it obtained a favorable reduction in haulage rates from the Santa Rosita coal fields, in return for its spending larger amounts on bettering conditions for its workers.⁵⁹ In 1924 ASARCO again protested the increase in railroad rates in conjunction with the Cámara Nacional de Comercio and the Chihuahua Cámara de Comercio.⁶⁰

Government cooperation was particularly important in ASARCO's dealings with the resurgent mining worker unions. Often presidents acted favorably to the company. In July 1920 the president Adolfo de la Huerta settled a widespread strike against ASARCO that idled six thousand workers.⁶¹

At the local level, as during the Díaz era, cooperation was not guaranteed and if forthcoming was not inexpensive. During the large strike in Chihuahua in 1923, the governor, Ignacio Enríquez, was supposedly disposed toward the strikers rather than the company, but the national government dispatched two hundred soldiers to protect the ASARCO smelter. Enríquez solicited a loan for 300,000 pesos to be used to defray the expenses of the *defenses socials,* or municipal guards, which formed the basis of his support in the state. ASARCO refused. Federal troops thereupon withdrew from Parral.⁶² (This was at the time of the rebellion led by Adolfo de la Huerta against Obregón, when generals Manuel Chao and Nicolas Fernández were active rebels in southern Chihuahua.)

The situation in San Luis Potosí in 1924 typified the complexity of ASARCO's relations with the different levels of government. Governor Aurelio Manrique Jr. took office as governor in 1924. His policy was to encourage the organization of unions and to support them to obtain higher wages in part through the rulings of the local Board of Conciliation and Arbitration. ASARCO had recently purchased an unfinished smelter in the state capital. The company hoped to finish the smelter and furnish ore from its locally owned mines. On completion the smelter was to create five thousand jobs. The company, however, stopped construction in February 1924 because of strikes against its mines in Matehuala and Charcas. Governor Manrique, who had initially backed the strikers, withdrew his support under pressure from local businesspeople and the central government. The strikes quickly failed. Both the central government and Calles, who visited

San Luis Potosí in April, gave assurances of support to the company. There was a new strike threat at the local ASARCO mine in June. The company then announced its plan to close the mine under strike. The national government again pressured Manrique to withdraw his support of the union. In some instances the federal authorities were willing to push industries to the point of government takeover, but in the case of ASARCO the stakes were too high and risky.[63]

The company was not afraid to take on the Mexican government at any level. In 1926 ASARCO carried out its threat to close operations when the Supreme Court ruled unfavorably on labor issues.[64] In 1932 the state of Chihuahua ended its litigation against ASARCO in its effort to nullify contracts written in 1905 and 1909 about payments of taxes.[65]

During the 1920s the federal government definitively took command of relations with the mining sector. New laws prohibited the states and municipalities from imposing taxes on metal production, profits from mining, or capital invested in mineral extraction, with the exception of a small tax on ore processing. The states were to receive a part of federal tax revenues from mining. In 1924 the government instituted income taxes.[66]

At times the federal government seemed to favor the mining giant. During the 1935 strike, two hundred soldiers guarded ASARCO facilities.[67] In 1939 the government intervened to end several strikes against the company.[68] Even in Chihuahua, the state government seemed at times to cooperate. Governor Talamantes mediated a strike in the state in 1939.[69]

Cárdenas brought more militancy and deeper government involvement on behalf of workers. The profitable foreign enterprises were a logical target. But apparently even Cárdenas had a price. In 1939 ASARCO lent the Mexican government US$7.5 million to be repaid by deducting taxes.[70]

A CASE STUDY OF HOW BUSINESS WAS DONE[71]

M. Guggenheim Sons "quietly acquired" in 1902 and 1903 a mining operation known as the Bonanza y Anexas. Acting for Guggenheim Exploration, its two representatives, R. C. Gemmell and J. M. Ortiz, acquired sixteen claims over four hundred acres about four miles from Mazapil in the northeastern part of the state of Zacatecas. The mines were located on the Hacienda de Bonanza, a large ranch. The owner, Manuel Rodríguez Orozco, in 1900 had obtained a concession from the state of Zacatecas to build a smelter on the property. In 1902 he agreed to sell the mines, ranch, water rights, and appurtenances to ASARCO, but he kept half the slag dumps. Licenciado Emeterio de la Garza, a member of president Díaz's inner circle, represented the Guggenheims in the transaction. The Guggenheims later transferred the Bonanza group to ASSCO in 1907 and then to the Compañía Minera Asarco, S.A., in 1923.

During the most tumultuous years of the Mexican revolution, 1913 to 1916, Bonanza suspended work, but ASSCO allowed contractors to mine on a royalty basis. From 1913 to 1921, the mines produced only eighty-three tons per month, whereas in the twelve or so years previous they yielded twelve hundred tons per month. "Because of the small scale of the operations and the contract system of production, the Bonanza unit did not suffer very serious losses, perhaps" US$5,000 during the civil wars. The company in 1920 and 1921 repaired the tramway, installed new equipment, and then actively explored and developed the mines for six years. But in 1928 ASSCO determined that the mines were no longer feasible for direct operation, removed the tramway and equipment, and subsequently leased the mines to independents.

In the meantime, the company confronted the repercussions of the new revolutionary laws. In order to circumvent the restrictions the Mexican Constitution of 1917 imposed on landownership by foreigners, ASARCO set up a "silent partnership," R. E. Mora y Compañía, S. en C., to hold the 12,330 acres of ranch land. By 1930, however, the agrarian reform had expropriated one-third of the land and given it to a local community, the Congregación de Cuauhtemoc formed on the hacienda. The government did not pay (as of 1947) the bonds ASARCO received as indemnity for the expropriation. In 1935 the state authorities decreed the expropriation of ASARCO's water rights (water was and is the most valuable commodity in Mexico), but the Supreme Court of Justice overturned the decree.

Here on a relatively small scale, we have an example of the strategies ASARCO and its various subsidiaries followed. The formula was to purchase promising properties, invest large sums, and smooth the way with various levels of government authorities. ASARCO, however, did not go unscathed in the rough and tumble of the Revolution and its aftermath, but by employing its enormous capital and a measure of flexibility and persistence, it continued to be profitable.

EXPANSION IN THE FACE OF UNCERTAINTY

What was extraordinary about the history of ASARCO in Mexico was how its executives transformed the wreckage of the Revolution, especially the fierce civil wars between 1913 and 1920, to the company's enormous advantage. With its huge financial resources ASARCO went on a buying spree of Mexican mines and smelters. In 1910 ASARCO acquired the National Metallurgical Company (Matehuala, Cobriza) and through that company the Tiro General Mine (San Luis Potosí) and the Potosí Central Railroad. Between 1910 and 1912, it obtained a number of properties in the Pachuca region of the state of Hidalgo. In 1913 the company bought the famed Velardeña mine for US$350,000. From 1915 to 1920 it purchased nearly all the productive mines in Veta Grande. In 1917 it acquired the Compañia de las Minas de Cobre de Magistral. From 1917 to 1920 it expanded its mine holding in Hidalgo de Parral, Chihuahua, one of the country's oldest and most productive mining centers.[72]

From 1919 to 1922 ASARCO and the other major smelters scrambled to acquire mines. They formed or expanded their exploration departments and bought new properties, concentrating mainly on those near railroads or population centers.[73]

The pace of acquisitions picked up as President Alvaro Obregón established a semblance of peace in 1920 after he overthrew Venustiano Carranza (1917–20). ASARCO bought the Mexican Northern Mining and Railway Company (Parral Consolidated, Alvarado Mining and Milling in Parral, Parral and Durango Railroad Company) and the Towne Mines, Inc. (Compañía Metalúrgica Mexicana, Montezuma Lead Co., Somberete Mining Co., Mexican Lead Co.), Las Plomasas, La Alfareña (Santa Bárbara, Chihuahua), Los Lamentos (northeast Chihuahua), and La Taviche (Oaxaca) in 1923 for at least US$3.1 million.[74]

ASARCO's ambition was enormous. The company began development in the Sierra Mojada region of Coahuila, making sixty-seven claims in 1921.[75] It also bought distressed properties in other districts in the state.[76] The company spent large sums in Rosita to develop coal mines.[77] In 1924 ASARCO took over the Veta Grande and turned Villa Escobedo, "a crumbled mass of adobe huts ... abandoned" into a burgeoning camp with fifteen hundred employees.[78] It built new plants in Parral and Santa Eulalia, investing millions.[79] The investment continued apace through 1929.[80] The company expanded further during the 1930s, despite the Great Depression, acquiring major holdings in Cuarto Cienegas, Coahuila, Santa Bárbara, Chihuahua, and Catorce, SLP.

LABOR RELATIONS

As was the case with both Alexander Shepherd's Batopilas Company and William C. Greene's Cananea operations, the evidence about ASARCO's treatment of its workers indicates that the giant corporation acted no better or worse than the then-current practices in Mexico and may have, in fact, paid better and provided better working and living conditions. ASARCO negotiated hard and only reluctantly raised wages. The last years of the Díaz regime allowed workers considerably more leeway in attempting to obtain higher wages and working conditions. Thus, the first labor agitations occurred with a one-day protest in mid-1907.[81] The triumph of the Madero rebellion provided further opportunities for organized workers. Miners went on strike for higher wages at Velardeña in 1911, and strikes quickly spread throughout Chihuahua.[82]

During the years 1911 to 1920 the company proved adept at adapting its labor policies to the needs of the moment. The company calculated a delicate balance between worker demands and its status as a major employer in times of economic hardship. Its Matehuala smelter successfully continued to operate through difficult circumstances, paying its workers in 1918 more than it had in 1910. This was despite the fact that there was no likelihood of provoking strikes, partly because there were thousands of unemployed miners in the district, but also because the company heavily subsidized corn, keeping the price at below half of what the market charged. Workers were not about to give up this guaranteed, cheap supply of food.[83]

When the civil wars of the Revolution ended, ASARCO confronted a new set of challenges in the form of labor unions, which became increasingly militant during the 1920s, seeking better wages and working conditions. In July 1920 the corporation endured its first postrevolutionary strike at its smelters in Aguascalientes, Matehuala, and Velardeña. In response ASARCO raised wages: unskilled labor received 40 percent, while others got 25 percent.[84] The company steadfastly refused to recognize the union, even when it faced increased pressure from the government.[85] In September two thousand workers at Tecolotes in Santa Bárbara struck for a month, winning a raise of twenty-five centavos for unskilled workers.[86] The year of labor unrest ended in October when a coal miners' strike closed all the ASARCO smelters.[87]

In addition to higher wages, the mining unions struck often to prevent reductions in the workforce and disciplinary firings. The downturn in metal prices in 1921 caused ASARCO to reduce its labor force, discontinue work at its mines, and ultimately close its smelters.[88] In response to the passage of Chihuahua's radical labor law and in an effort to prevent the proliferation of strikes at the newly reopened Avalos smelter in Chihuahua in the spring of 1923, ASARCO instituted a profit-sharing program with its employees.[89] Nonetheless, workers struck at the Chihuahua smelter in 1923, demanding higher wages and rehiring of four workers the company had fired for organizing activities. The situation was tense enough for the government to send two hundred soldiers to protect the smelter. The company settled the strike after a few days.[90] The average pay for the workers was 2.50 pesos per day, twice the minimum wage.[91]

ASARCO continued to use its position as a major employer throughout the country as a negotiating tool. The national government and some state governments at times sided with the company in order to maintain employment. In February 1924, ASARCO suspended work at the construction site of its new smelter in San Luis Potosí because of strikes at its mines in Matehuala and Charcas. As a result, the governor of the state, Aurelio Manrique Jr., withdrew his support of the strike, and it ended soon thereafter. After assurances proffered by both Manrique and President Calles, the company resumed construction. In June another strike broke out at another mine in the area, eliciting a threat from the company to close the mine. Again the strikers backed down. It was clear that the unions and the governor could not obtain support from the Calles administration if they risked mine and smelter shutdowns at a time of economic uncertainty.[92]

The Great Depression and its accompanying drop in the prices of mineral ore caused widespread layoffs. The Santa Eulalia and Santo Domingo units were the first to request permission from the local labor board (*Junta de Conciliación y Arbitraje*) to reduce the workweek to three days.[93] Eventually, after some heated negotiations, the company reduced the workweek by one day (Thursday).[94] Two years later, ASARCO petitioned to close Santa Eulalia with its eight hundred employees.[95] In July 1934 the Sindicato de

Obreros y Empleados de la Región Carbonífera struck ASARCO's Carboniferas de Sabinas, where the wages were the highest in the country. The workers returned after two weeks.[96]

ASARCO generally did not fear strikes or unrest because there were many unemployed workers. In San Luis Potosí the company subsidized corn prices, selling to its workers at 35 to 70 percent discounts.[97] It avoided wage increases at Matehuala, paying its workers at the same rate as in 1910: one peso a day for unskilled surface workers, 1.50–2.00 pesos for ordinary face workers, and 2.00–7.00 pesos for skilled workers, depending on their trade. The company was innovative in its resistance to union and government pressure. In 1934 the company filed suit in federal court to prevent enforcement of a higher minimum wage in Chihuahua, the first such suit ever brought in Mexico.[98] With the advent of the administration of Lázaro Cárdenas in 1934, pressure on the company increased. ASARCO confronted a series of important strikes and generally was willing to accede to reasonable demands. Although the unions and company agreed to a pact in 1934 that set the wage scale at comparatively high rates and provided free housing and health and recreational facilities not found in Mexican-owned industry, 1935 was a tumultuous year.[99] In January 1935 there was a five-hour strike at the Avalos smelter, when two thousand workers protested the company's refusal to raise the minimum wage from 1.5 to 3.0 pesos per day; the company compromised at 2.75.[100] In August there was another walkout of twelve hundred miners in Santa Eulalia, Santa Bárbara, and Parral, led by the Síndicato Industrial del Trabajadores, Mineros, Metlúrgicos y Similares.[101] Strikers' demands included a 20 percent wage increase, payment for the duration of the strike, and firing of the personnel manager.[102] ASARCO granted wage increases to underground workers at Parral and Santa Bárbara from 0.75 to 3.10–3.60 pesos per day.[103] At Avalos ASARCO settled a month-long strike in December by paying the workers 80 percent of their pay for the strike period.[104] In 1936 ASARCO suffered a series of setbacks. Cárdenas ordered the company to build model homes for miners in Parral. The Mexican Supreme Court upheld the ruling of the minister of education that the company construct schools at its Santa Bárbara facility.[105] In 1936 two thousand employees struck the ASARCO smelter in San Luis Potosí. Again the company compensated the workers for their time during the strike, this time at 70 percent of their wages. It also raised the minimum wage between 3 and 10 percent.[106] The metallurgical workers union in 1937 walked off work for an hour on each shift at each smelter to demonstrate for their demand for a standardized collective national contract.[107] The same year ASARCO ended labor conflict at Aquiles Serdán by raising the minimum wage to 3.60 and 4.00 pesos for surface and underground miners and by donating 5,000 pesos to build a recreational hall.[108] In February 1938, workers at the Monterrey smelter struck over the discharge of 266 of 450 employees.[109] A similar action occurred when the company laid off sixty at the Chihuahua smelter.[110] The union and ASARCO were at odds over wages and conditions, and the company fired sixty troublemakers. The union ordered the workers back to work. ASARCO suspended operations.[111] Five thousand coal miners belonging to the Sindicato de Trabajadores Mineras, Metalúrgicos y Sindicatos went out on strike at ASARCO's Santa Rosita facility in late August 1938.[112] Later in the year ASARCO workers went out at Real del Monte and its Monterrey smelter.[113] In early 1939 the national miners' union demanded a payment of 750,000 pesos for workers at Aquiles Serdán because the company had violated the collective contract.[114] Chihuahua smelter workers went on strike for nearly a year in 1938 and 1939 to protest the layoffs of 450 employees, winning a raise, but the company won more control over the number of workers.[115] There was another brief strike at Avalos and other facilities in 1939 as well.[116] At the beginning of 1940 the national union demanded higher wages at Avalos, Santa Bárbara, Parral, San Luis Potosí, and Coahuila.[117]

According to the US intelligence reports, by 1941 labor was very strongly organized and difficult to negotiate with under any circumstances.[118] By 1937 ASARCO employed nineteen thousand people in Mexico with an annual payroll of forty million pesos. The cumulative effect of union actions was quite evident for the cost per person, which had been 3 pesos in 1931, had risen to 5.65 pesos in 1937.[119] (See Table 7.1.) Thus, during the depths of an economic depression, ASARCO's workers' wages rose by 88 percent. This indicates that the miners' unions were very strong, that ASARCO was profitable and able to afford the increases in labor costs, and that ASARCO did not exploit its workers during this period. ASARCO clearly had determined that by acceding to some union demands it would not only assure its reliable workforce but also achieve a favorable relationship with governments at all levels.

TABLE 7.1 Average Wage Cost at ASARCO, 1931–1937

Year	Pesos
1931	3.00
1932	n.a.
1934	3.35
1935	3.87
1936	4.87
1937	5.65

Source: James B. Steward, American Consul-General, to Secretary of State, Feb. 21, 1938, 812.504/1713, USNARG 59.

PROFITABILITY

ASARCO was probably the most successful foreign enterprise in Mexico during the period from 1900 to 1940. With the exceptions of 1908, 1909, 1910, 1914, and 1921 the company netted more than one million dollars in profits each year. From 1907 to 1924, the years for which we have reasonable statistics (from the *Annual Reports*), the company's net profits totaled more than US$35 million. (See Table 7.2.) Compared with other mining operations, this was an enviable record. However, when we evaluate these profits in relation to capital investment, we see that ASARCO had to invest enormous amounts to make these profits. In two instances—in 1902 with US$25 million in new mines, and in 1924 with US$10 million in new construction—ASARCO invested amounts equal to its profits for the time. As we well know, mining was a high-risk enterprise. ASARCO was successful because it had the capital and willingness to undertake risk.

TABLE 7.2 Estimated Profits at ASARCO, 1900–1925

Year	Profits (in US dollars)
1900	*
1901	*
1902	*
1903	*
1904	*
1905	*
1906	*
1907	1,250,000 (= 1.8 million pesos)
1908	500,000
1909	500,000
1910	700,000
1911	2,000,186
1912	3,114,104
1913	1,185,153
1914	935,192
1915	1,984,977
1916	2,725,222
1917	4,069,242
1918	2,686,239
1919	1,816,869
1920	2,242,199
1921	710,802
1922	2,458,695
1923	3,465,579
1924	3,081,425
1925	Not broken out

* No profits

Source: For the period 1907–1925, see Horace D. Marucci, "The American Smelting and Refining Company in Mexico, 1900–1925" (PhD diss., Rutgers University, 1995), pp. 264, 525.

CONCLUSION

The American Smelting and Refining Company was unusual in Mexican business history because it had all of the components for success. Its executives, led by the Guggenheim family, strategically used its enormous available capital to overcome the innumerable obstacles to conducting business in Mexico's difficult economic environment. The company used its capital to purchase government cooperation, employ the latest technologies, hire the best people, assure transportation, obtain scarce supplies and equipment, pay off union officials and employees, and ride out market downturns. The Guggenheims had enough money, courage, persistence, and ambition to succeed where few others did.

Despite the enormous amounts of capital ASARCO invested and the considerable profits it extracted, the company never was beyond the control of the Mexican government. Although adept and connected, the company still had to pay in some ways even more than the smaller operations. It had to build a smelter that it did not want in Chihuahua. The Guggenheims could not budge Díaz from his new mining law in 1910. The giant corporation could not escape revolutionary taxes. Nor could it avoid the consequences of the Constitution of 1917. It was far and away the most successful foreign enterprise in Mexico from 1880 to 1940, but it had to play by Mexican rules.

EIGHT

Conclusion

The object of *Pesos and Politics* has been to revise the current history of business in Mexico by using several case studies of Mexican family-owned and foreign-owned businesses. It argues that the succeeding Mexican regimes from the 1870s through 1940 constructed a flexible, elite-foreign enterprise system that featured a changing set of checks and balances between the five to seven competing groups that vied for political influence and economic power at various levels of government and community. This study refutes two widely held views of the role of foreign enterprise in Porfirian and revolutionary Mexico, first arguing against the notion that Mexicans were not in control of their own economy, and second countering the claim that foreign businesspeople exploited Mexico at any point during the eighty or so years under study. It asserts that few foreign companies or individuals made any money in Mexico. Those who succeeded invested enormous sums of capital to yield their profits. In the greater view it is an argument that foreign corporations and individuals were not to blame for Mexico's underdevelopment. Underlying the discussion of business and politics is also a claim for continuity. While the Revolution most certainly was a cataclysmic event for the economy, at the same time there were many aspects of it that remained basically the same. The agricultural and mining sectors maintained their dominant places, foreigners kept their crucial role, the government continued its function as an intermediary, and elites contested among themselves as always. That is not to say, however, that the economy remained static.

MEXICANS IN CONTROL

Mexico was not an easy place to conduct business during its first hundred and twenty years after independence. Endless warfare, lack of political consensus, expensive and unreliable transportation and communications, minimal domestic capital, and an absence of a consistent, stable set of regulations and laws were formidable obstacles to entrepreneurship. For three decades the dictatorship of Porfirio Díaz eliminated some of these economic obstructions. The regime chose to solve the problem of capital shortage by attracting foreign investment. The successor revolutionary regimes, despite their often-heated radical rhetoric against foreign companies, adopted a similar strategy. From the 1880s through 1940 funds from abroad arrived in spurts into Mexico, concentrating on railroads, mining, and agriculture.[1] In their strategies both Porfirian and revolutionary regimes were scrupulously careful not to allow foreigners to obtain too much influence. Mexicans controlled their own economy. The clearest examples were in Díaz and Limantour's brilliant strategy to fend off the incursions of the great US railroad tycoons while at the same time maintaining an environment attractive to investors through the railroad consolidation from 1902 to 1911, the post-1920 regime's handling of the giant American Smelting and Refining Company, permitting it to expand and invest enormous sums, but at the same time containing it, and, of course, the expropriation of the foreign-owned petroleum corporations in 1938.

Control over the economy was not, however, necessarily centralized. Neither the Díaz dictatorship nor the postrevolutionary regime ever reached the status of the "Leviathan" state, at least through 1940.[2] The ballyhooed advent of the official party in 1929 did not by any means immediately end the fragmentation of politics. As a result, the national government might not scrutinize or interfere with a foreign company, but it would have to adhere to the dictates of the municipalities or states. It was nearly impossible to go unscathed. Even mighty ASARCO had to pay in Chihuahua to the Terrazas. The continuous negotiations and renegotiations at various levels were expensive and time consuming, but while this elicited loud complaints, it rarely deterred foreigners from investing. Whatever the case, Mexicans held sway over the conditions of business, even if there was not always a coherent or well-thought-out policy; Mexicans made and oversaw the implementation of the rules and regulations.

Of course, I cannot argue that foreigners, especially those with huge stakes in Mexico, did not have influence. Daniel Guggenheim had complete access to Porfirio Díaz. William Randolph Hearst, the newspaper tycoon, assuredly influenced President Obregón to protect his Babícora ranch, at least temporarily. But regardless of foreigners' political or economic clout, they were only one consideration in the process of policymaking. Díaz and his postrevolutionary successors juggled with many interest groups. Both pre- and revolutionary leaders played the contestants against each other, and this did not always work to the advantage of foreign investors. Foreigners were, most assuredly, not at the heart of Mexican economic policy or government actions. Domestic political considerations were always at the center of government actions and leaders' strategies.

NO EXPLOITATION

Exploitation could have existed in at least two forms. First, foreigners could have extracted enormous profits without any domestic linkages to the economy, in the form of wages, rents, and goods and services purchased locally. The notorious exploiters were supposedly the mining companies, which allegedly "stole" nonrenewable resources with little return to the host country. We have viewed considerable evidence that foreigners generally did not reap enormous profits. Even the American Smelting and Refining Company, which was profitable, did not earn a particularly high return on investment, certainly to the extent to which we could brand it exploitative. Moreover, the mining companies in particular, but also the agricultural operations, invested huge amounts of capital into their enterprises. Foreigners often took over mines that had been abandoned for decades or that previous Mexican owners lacked the funds to get to all but the easiest veins. Tunneling, water control, transportation, and equipment were expensive.

With the exception of the Madero family, entrepreneurial Mexicans with access to capital were notably reluctant to invest in the high-risk industry. Even the Terrazas, for the most part, steered clear. Mexico's most important industry, thus, could not have functioned without foreign capital. Similarly, foreigners improved vast tracts of undeveloped land, particularly to grow export commodities. They expended enormous sums on irrigation, fencing, better livestock breeds, and equipment.

Backward and forward linkages were, to be sure, minimal except in terms of rents and wages. Foreigners bought their equipment and supplies abroad; they simply were not available in Mexico, for the most part, although there were local firms, such as the Terrazas's Compañía Industrial Mexicana, that obtained mining machinery contracts. However, foreigners expended large sums buying and renting mining and agricultural properties. This money had to at least trickle down into the economy as a whole. Obviously, salaries and wages provided the most important linkages.

This leads us to the second potential form of exploitation. Foreigners could have employed their workers paying meager wages and providing inexpensive, unsafe, unsanitary conditions. For the most part, however, while no workers during the era from 1880 to 1940 anywhere in the world were well paid or even justly paid, and few enjoyed anything other than barely acceptable labor environments, foreigners in Mexico paid at least the going rate for the region where they were established. They adhered to the pattern discovered by Friedrich Katz that labor in the northern tier earned higher wages and experienced better benefits and conditions, while those in the center earned little better than subsistence wages, and those in the south endured the harshest situation, in some parts of that region near slavery. In the north, because of the competitive market for skilled labor in the mines, foreigners ruffled the feathers of local elites by paying higher wages than the prevailing rates. I have encountered no evidence that foreigners paid less than the local going rate for wages in any region. Aside from the undocumented accusation of John Mason Hart about Batopilas of slavelike conditions, there is no indication that foreigners exploited workers to any greater extent than other capitalists of the period.

CONCLUSION 185

CONSISTENCY IN THE TREATMENT OF FOREIGNERS

In effect I maintain that all businesspeople had roughly similar experiences. Foreign landowners faced the same problems as Mexican landholders of similar status. During the Porfiriato, the owners of large estates with family and political connections received favorable, if not privileged, treatment from governments at all levels. Mexicans and foreigners alike obtained tax breaks, access to cheap land, and protection from the authorities. They also had similar relationships with local villages, which supplied temporary workers and contested land boundaries. Despite the notorious cases of William Benton and Rosalie Evans, both murdered by revolutionaries during the military stage of the Revolution, foreign landowners with large holdings were treated no better and no worse than Mexicans with large estates. Native Mexicans like the Terrazas extended family, in fact, endured far harsher treatment. Everyone from the largest to the smallest landholder suffered the raids and confiscations perpetrated by the rival armies. During the presidency of Obregón, there was some easing of the pressures against foreign landholders because his administration did not want to alienate the United States, which had withheld diplomatic recognition of his government. We need only to look at the cases of the Hearst estate on one hand and the Terrazas estate on the other to understand the complexities of the implementation of land reform. The Hearsts, though they kept the bulk of their enormous ranch through the early 1950s, endured a steady erosion of its size through expropriations. After Villa expropriated the Terrazas's lands in 1913, the Mexican government purchased the Terrazas estate in the early 1920s and allowed family members to reacquire some of the best lands a few years later. The Terrazas extended family emerged after decades as among the largest cattle ranchers in the country. Hearst was gone for good.

PRE-REVOLUTION AND REVOLUTIONARY REGIMES

I have argued that there was not very much difference, if any, between the way the Díaz regime and the revolutionary governments treated foreigners. Their policies were similar in that they both maintained the elite-foreign enterprise system of balancing the various competing groups and interests. They both sought to encourage foreign investment as the most efficient means to develop the nation's economy. The most obvious changes occurred during the years of heaviest fighting when funds, supplies, and ordnance were scarcest. But it was certainly not just the foreigners who suffered. The people in the countryside endured forced loans, forced military service, and extortion, perhaps to a greater extent than the foreign businesspeople, miners, and ranchers. The fighting, of course, caused damage to everyone's holdings and disrupted the whole economy.

While the implications of my conclusions are for another project, asserting that Mexicans controlled their own economy from the 1850s through the 1940s and that the nation did not kowtow to or favor foreigners forces us to take a harder look at Mexican economic development and politics. If Mexico was less developed than it should have been (not necessarily a given) and foreigners were not ostensibly at blame for this situation, then what accounted for the nation's unfortunate circumstances?

Notes

Chapter 1

1. There is considerable disagreement among historians as to when the Revolution ended, with some claiming 1920, 1929, 1940, or 1946. For my purposes, 1920 is a useful date because it marks the end of the most intensive warfare and the beginning of economic reconstruction under Alvaro Obregón, which continued through to the end of the presidency of Lázaro Cárdenas. I label the period from 1920 to 1940 "revolutionary reconstruction" because the phrase underlines the delicate balance between rebuilding the economy and instituting the sometimes radical reforms mandated by the Constitution of 1917 and victorious agrarians and workers.

2. Peter Evans, in his *Dependent Development: The Alliance of Multinational, State, and Local Capital in Brazil* (Princeton, NJ: Princeton University Press, 1979), found a similar phenomenon, which he called the "triple alliance" in Brazil. See also Mark Wasserman, "Foreign Investment in Mexico, 1876–1911: A Case Study of the Role of Regional Elites," *The Americas* 36 (July 1979): 2–21.

3. There are excellent studies of other parts of the Mexican economy. See, for example, Jeffrey L. Bortz and Stephen Haber, eds., *The Mexican Economy, 1870–1930: Essays on the Economic History of Institutions, Revolution, and Growth* (Stanford, CA: Stanford University Press, 2002); Stephen H. Haber, *Industry and Development: The Industrialization of Mexico, 1890–1940* (Stanford, CA: Stanford University Press, 1989); Noel Maurer, *The Power and the Money: The Mexican Financial System, 1876–1932* (Stanford, CA: Stanford University Press, 2002); Mario Cerutti and Carlos Marichal, eds., *La banca regional en México (1870–1910)* (Mexico City: El Colegio de México and El Fondo de Cultura Económica, 2003); Mario Cerutti, *Burguesía y capitalismo en Monterrey, 1850–1910* (Mexico City: Claves Latinoamericanas, 1983.) See also Sandra Kuntz Ficker, "La historiografía económica reciente sobre el México decimonónico," *Mexican Studies/Estudios Mexicanos* 21:2 (summer 2005): 461–92; and María Eugenía Romero Ibarra, "Panorama general del desarrollo de la historia empresarial en México," *Historia Mexicana* 3:207 (Jan.–Mar. 2003): 831–72.

4. Carlos Marichal and Mario Cerutti, eds., *Historia de las grandes empresas en México, 1850–1930* (Mexico City: Universidad Autónoma de Monterrey/Fondo de

Cultura Económica, 1997); María del Carmen Collado, *La burguesía mexicana: El emporio Braniff y su participación política, 1865–1920* (Mexico City: Siglo Veintiuno Editores, 1987).

5. For an overview of the period 1821 to 1911, see Mark Wasserman, *Everyday Life and Politics in Nineteenth-Century Mexico: Men, Women, and War* (Albuquerque: University of New Mexico Press, 2000); and Daniel Cosió Villegas, ed., *Historia moderna de México*, 10 vols. (Mexico City: Editorial Hermes, 1964–71).

6. For the history of the twenty years after 1920, see Jean Meyer, *Historia de la revolución mexicana, periodo 1924–28: Estado y sociedad con Calles* (Mexico City: El Colegio de México, 1977); Enrique Krauze, *Historia de la revolución mexicana, periodo 1924–1928: La reconstrucción económica* (Mexico City: El Colegio de México, 1977); Lorenzo Meyer, *Historia de la revolución mexicana, periodo 1928–1934: Los inicios de la institucionalización. La política del maximato* (Mexico City: El Colegio de México, 1978); Lorenzo Meyer, *Historia de la revolución mexicana, 1928–1934: El conflict social y los gobiernos del maximato* (Mexico City: El Colegio de México, 1978); Luis González, *Historia de la revolución mexicana, 1934–1940: Los días del presidente Cárdenas* (Mexico City: El Colegio de México, 1981); Alicia Hernández Chávez, *Historia de la revolución mexicana, 1934–1940: La mecánica cardenista* (Mexico City: El Colegio de México, 1979); Luis González, *Historia de la revolución mexicana, 1934–1940: Los artífices del cardenismo* (Mexico City: El Colegio de México, 1979).

7. Peter H. Smith, *Labyrinths of Power: Political Recruitment in Twentieth-Century Mexico* (Princeton, NJ: Princeton University Press, 1979); Roderic A. Camp, *Entrepreneurs and Politics in Twentieth-Century Mexico* (New York: Oxford University Press, 1989); Roderic A. Camp, *Mexico's Leaders: Their Education and Recruitment* (Tucson: University of Arizona Press, 1980).

8. Mark Wasserman, "Strategies for Survival of the Porfirian Elite in Revolutionary Mexico: Chihuahua During the 1920s," *Hispanic American Historical Review* 67:1 (Feb. 1987): 87–107.

9. Jurgen Buchenau, *The Last Caudillo: Alvaro Obregón and the Mexican Revolution* (New York: Wiley-Blackwell, 2011); Jurgen Buchenau, *Plutarco Elías Calles and the Mexican Revolution* (Lanham, MD: Rowman and Littlefield, 2007); Roger D. Hansen, *The Politics of Mexican Development* (Baltimore, MD: Johns Hopkins University Press, 1971).

10. Smith, *Labyrinths*.

11. Mark Wasserman, *Persistent Oligarchs: Elites and Politics in Chihuahua, Mexico, 1910–1940* (Durham, NC: Duke University Press, 1993).

12. Ramón Eduardo Ruíz, *The Great Rebellion, Mexico 1905–1924* (New York: W. W. Norton, 1980), pp. 377–81; Dudley Ankerson, *Agrarian Warlord: Saturnino Cedillo and the Mexican Revolution in San Luis Potosí* (DeKalb: Northern Illinois University Press, 1984), pp. 85–86.

13. Ankerson, *Agrarian Warlord*, p. 85. Obregón from the time he resigned as war minister in 1917 until he took over as president in 1920 acquired a virtual monopoly on the sale of Sonora-grown chickpeas to the United States, as well as several other

businesses. See also Nora Hamilton, *The Limits of State Autonomy: Post-Revolutionary Mexico* (Princeton, NJ: Princeton University Press, 1982), pp. 84–90.

14. A letter from an unnamed "prominent English businessman" to Consul General Philip Hanna, Dec. 1917. Hanna to Secretary of State, Dec. 24, 1917, USNARG 59, 812.00/21636. Cited in Dudley Ankerson, p. 86.

15. See Stephen Haber, Armando Razo, and Noel Maurer, *The Politics of Property Rights: Political Instability, Credible Commitments, and Economic Growth in Mexico, 1876–1929* (Cambridge: Cambridge University Press, 2003), for a somewhat different interpretation that excludes politics from the analysis.

16. Wasserman, *Persistent Oligarchs*; Allen Wells, *Yucatán's Gilded Age: Haciendas, Henequen, and International Harvester, 1860–1915* (Albuquerque: University of New Mexico Press, 1985); Mario Cerutti, *Burguesía y capitalismo en Monterrey, 1850–1910* (Mexico City: Claves Latinoamericanas, 1983); Alex M. Saragoza, *The Monterrey Elite and the Mexican State, 1880–1940* (Austin: University of Texas Press, 1988); William Schell Jr., *Integral Outsiders: The American Colony in Mexico City, 1876–1911* (Wilmington, DE: Scholarly Resources, 2001); David M. Pletcher, *Rails, Mines, and Progress: Seven American Promoters in Mexico, 1867–1911* (Ithaca, NY: Cornell University Press, 1958).

17. Wasserman, *Persistent Oligarchs*; Wil Pansters, *Politics and Power in Puebla: The Political History of a Mexican State, 1937–1987* (Amsterdam: CEDLA, 1990).

18. Roderic A. Camp, *Political Recruitment Across Two Centuries: Mexico 1884–1991* (Austin: University of Texas Press, 1995); Roderic A. Camp, *Mexico's Mandarins: Crafting a Power Elite for the Twenty-First Century* (Berkeley: University of California Press, 2002).

19. Moisés González Navarro, *Los extranjeros en México y los mexicanos en el estranjero, 1821–1970*, 3 vols. (Mexico City: El Colegio de México, 1993–94).

20. María del Carmen Collado, *La burguesía mexicana: El emporio Braniff y su participación política, 1865–1920* (Mexico City: Sigloveintiuno, 1987).

21. Juan Antonio Vázquez and Miguel Angel González Quiroga, "Capitalistas norteamericanos en Monterrey: Joseph A. Robertson," in Mario Cerutti, coordinator, *Monterrey, Nuevo León, el noroeste: Siete studios históricos* (Monterrey: Universidad Autónoma de Nuevo León, 1987), pp. 177–214; John Mason Hart, *The Silver of the Sierra Madre: John Robinson, Boss Shepherd and the People of the Canyons* (Tucson: University of Arizona Press, 2008), pp. 12–48. John Mason Hart, *Empire and Revolution: Americans in Mexico Since the Civil War* (Berkeley: University of California Press, 2003), pp. 7–70.

22. Mexico, Secretaría de Economía Nacional, Dirección General de Estadística, *Quinto censo de población 1930* (Mexico, 1932–36). See Moisés González Navarro, *Los extranjeros en México y los Mexicanos en el extrajero, 1821–1970*, 2 vols. (Mexico City: El Colegio de México, 1993).

23. Robert W. Dunn, *American Foreign Investments* (New York: B. W. Huebsch and the Viking Press, 1926), pp. 89–106; Luis Nicolau D'Olwer, "Las inversiones extranjeras," in *La historia moderna de México: El porfiriato, la vida económica*, vol. II, ed. Daniel Cosío Villegas (Mexico City: Editorial Hermes, 1965), pp. 973–1185.

24. Ramón Eduardo Ruíz, *The Great Rebellion, Mexico 1905–1924* (New York: W. W. Norton, 1980), p. 103.

25. John Mason Hart, *Empire and Revolution: The Americans in Mexico Since the Civil War* (Berkeley: University of California Press, 2002).

26. See Schell, *Integral Outsiders*, pp. ix–xix.

27. John Mason Hart, *Empire and Revolution*, passim, and *Revolutionary Mexico: The Coming and Process of the Mexican Revolution* (Berkeley: University of California Press, 1987); and Ruíz, *Great Rebellion*, pp. 103–5.

28. The origin of many of the tales of destruction during the Revolution was the so-called Fall Committee Report. US Congress, Senate, Committee on Foreign Relations, *Investigation of Mexican Affairs, Hearings* before a subcommittee of the Committee on Foreign Relations, Senate on S. Res. 106, 66th Congress, 2nd sess., 1919 (Washington, DC: G.P.O, 1919).

29. John Mason Hart, *Empire and Revolution: The Americans in Mexico Since the Civil War* (Berkeley: University of California Press, 2002) and *Revolutionary Mexico: The Coming and Process of the Mexican Revolution* (Berkeley: University of California Press, 1987), has argued that the Revolution was a struggle for national liberation from the economic imperialism of the United States and presents an overwhelmingly negative view of American investment and entrepreneurship in Mexico. See John E. Kicza, "Review: *Empire and Revolution*" *Business History Review* (spring 2003) for a judicious critique of Hart.

30. John H. Coatsworth, "Obstacles to Economic Growth in Nineteenth-Century Mexico," *The American Historical Review* 83 (Feb. 1978): 80–100.

31. Most notorious was the case of Rosalie Evans. Daisy Caden Pettus, ed., *The Rosalie Evans Letters from Mexico* (Indianapolis, ID: Bobbs-Merrill Company, 1926). See also Robert W. Herr, *An American Family in the Mexican Revolution* (Wilmington, DE: Scholarly Resources, 1999).

32. Friedrich Katz, *The Life and Times of Pancho Villa* (Stanford, CA: Stanford University Press, 1999).

33. See Alex Saragoza, *The Monterrey Elite and the Mexican State, 1880–1940* (Austin: University of Texas Press, 1988), p. 42.

34. Statement of Nils O. Bagge to Albert B. Fall, Albert B. Fall Collection, University of New Mexico, Center for Southwest Research Collection, Box 5, Folder 6. This statement was prepared for the congressional hearings Senator Fall chaired on the Mexican Revolution in 1919.

35. *Engineering and Mining Journal* (*EMJ*) 116 (1923): 22.

36. Morris B. Parker, *Mules, Mines, and Me, 1895–1932* (Tucson: University of Arizona Press, 1979), p. 29.

37. Otheman Stevens, "Industrial Mexico," *Cosmopolitan* 48 (1910): 734.

38. *EMJ* 118 (1924): 142.

39. Albert A. Brittingham, *Juan F. Brittingham, 1859–1940* (Np., nd.).

40. Juan Antonio Vázquez and Miguel Angel González Quiroga, "Capitalistas norteamericanos en Monterrey: Joseph A. Robertson," in *Monterrey, Nuevo León, el Noroeste*, ed. Mario Cerutti (Monterrey: UANL, 1987), pp. 177–214.

41. Not all, of course, intended to remain. For one long-term example of a successful family, see Jurgen Buchenau, *Tools of Progress: A German Merchant Family in Mexico City, 1865–Present* (Albuquerque: University of New Mexico Press, 2004).

42. C. DeKalb, "Impressions in the Mexican Highlands, III," *The Nation* 69 (Dec. 21, 1899): 464–66.

43. Sergio Valerio Ulloa, "Empresarios alemanes en Guadalajara durante el porfiriato y la revolución," *Solo Historia* 9 (July–Sept. 2000): 62.

44. W. W. Mills to David Thompson, US Ambassador to Mexico, Aug. 1, 1908, USNARG 59.

45. John H. Coatsworth, *Growth Against Development: The Economic Impact of Railroads in Porfirian Mexico* (DeKalb: Northern Illinois University Press, 1981); Sandra Kuntz Ficker, *Empresa extranjera y mercado interno* (Mexico City: El Colegio de México).

46. Whether or not foreigners (almost always from the United States or Western Europe) exploited Mexico or other developing nations is a controversial topic, to say the least. It seems to me that it boils down to the following issues. First, did the foreign enterprise extract nonrenewable resources without a fair return to the host country through a percentage of the profits, taxes, or economic linkages? Second, did the foreign enterprise pay below-market wages or provide working conditions for its employees that were less than those provided by similar, native businesses? The latter question, of course, begs the issue of whether the businesses, foreign or domestic, paid living wages or furnished safe conditions for their workers. I am arguing that the foreign businesses in Mexico mostly treated their workers better than their Mexican counterparts and at worst treated them the same as their Mexican competitors.

47. Miguel S. Wionczek, "The State and the Electric Power Industry in Mexico, 1895–1965," *Business History Review* 39:4 (winter 1965): 532.

48. Mark Wasserman, "'It's not personal. . . . It's strictly business': The Operation of Economic Enterprise in Mexico During the Nineteenth and Twentieth Centuries," *Latin American Research Review* 40:3 (Oct. 2005), provides a review of some of this scholarship. Stephen Haber, *Crony Capitalism and Development in Latin America: Theory and Evidence* (Stanford, CA: Hoover Institute Press, 2002).

49. Edward Beatty, *Institutions and Investment: The Political Basis of Industrialization in Mexico Before 1911* (Stanford, CA: Stanford University Press, 2001), pp. 9–12, provides a measured assessment of Díaz's policy toward foreigners. See Julio Moreno, *Yankee Don't Go Home: Mexican Nationalism, American Business Culture, and the Shaping of Modern Mexico, 1920–1950* (Chapel Hill: University of North Carolina Press, 2003), for the later period.

50. José Y. Limantour to Lic. Pablo Macedo, May 15, 1908, Roll 50, Archivo de José Y. Limantour, Fundación CARSO.

51. *El Correo de Chihuahua*, Oct. 11 and 12, 1906.

52. Ibid., July 15, 1904; Sandels, "Silvestre Terrazas," p. 79.

53. Testimony of Nils O. Bagge, Fall Committee, p. 1428.

54. *South American Journal,* Jan. 23, 1909, p. 99.
55. Daniel Guggenheim to Porfirio Díaz, July 24, 1908, Colección de General Porfirio Díaz, Universidad Iberoamericana, doc. 33:910813.
56. J. B. Body to Weetman Pearson, June 1, 1901, Weetman Pearson Papers.
57. Ibid., Jan. 1906, Weetman Pearson Papers. One of the more startling statements about Limantour was made by Guillermo Landa y Escandón, one of the most important insiders of the Díaz regime, who represented many foreign companies and who opined, "Limantour knows [Henry Clay] Pierce . . . well . . . , but he is afraid of the man." Guillermo Landa y Escandón to Weetman Pearson, Mar. 12, 1910, Weetman Pearson Papers. It is likely that Limantour worried more about Standard Oil of New Jersey, whose interests Pierce represented, than Pierce himself, ruthless though he may have been.
58. Ruíz, *Great Rebellion,* p. 100.
59. Alan Knight, *U.S.-Mexican Relations, 1910–1940: An Interpretation* (San Diego: Center for U.S.-Mexican Studies, University of California, San Diego, 1987), p. 22.
60. Chester Lloyd Jones and George Wyeth, "Economic Conditions in Mexico," 1928 report in USNARG 59, 812.50/16, cited in Knight, *U.S.-Mexican,* p. 25.
61. Carmon B. Hardy, "Cultural Encystment as a Cause of the Mormon Exodus from Mexico," *Pacific Historical Review* 34 (Nov. 1965): 439–54.
62. W. F. Buckley et al. to Woodrow Wilson, May 22, 1916, Weetman Pearson Papers.
63. Sandra Kuntz Ficker, *Empresa extranjera y mercado interno: El Ferrocarril Central Mexicano, 1880–1907* (Mexico City: El Colegio de México, 1995); Sandra Kuntz Ficker and Priscilla Connelly, eds., *Ferrocarriles y obras públicas* (Mexico City: Instituto Mora, 1999).
64. Cited in Edward Beatty, *Institutions and Investment: The Political Basis of Industrialization in Mexico Before 1911* (Stanford, CA: Stanford University Press, 2000), p. 5.
65. Beatty, *Institution and Investment,* pp. 5–6. Haber, Razo, and Maurer, *Politics of Property Rights.*
66. Beatty, *Institution and Investment,* pp. 11–12.
67. J. O. Crockett to H. I. Miller, July 26, 1915, Box 4, Papers of the Ferrocarril Noroeste de México. Unfortunately for the Madera Company, the inability to ship lumber and the diminishing labor force severely limited its possibilities.
68. Fred Adams to Weetman Pearson, Feb. 19, 1917, Weetman Pearson Papers.
69. For the post-1920 era, see Enrique Cárdenas, *La hacienda pública y la política económica, 1929–1958* (Mexico City: El Colegio de México, 1994); and Enrique Cárdenas, *La industrialización mexicana durante el gran depression* (Mexico City: El Colegio de México, 1987).
70. Grunstein, "Telephones," pp. 9–11. Calles seemingly ignored his prerevolutionary predecessor Díaz when he allowed ITT to buy into the Mexican market. Díaz had feared the possibility of foreign trusts taking over crucial sectors of the economy. And in fact ITT surreptitiously bought 34 percent of Ericsson's Mexican company.

71. Alan Knight, "Cardenismo: Juggernaut or Jalopy," *Journal of Latin American Studies* 26:1 (Feb. 1994).

72. Haber, Razo, and Maurer, *Politics of Property Rights*, p. 12.

73. Ibid., p. 10.

74. Ibid., p. 44.

75. Ibid., p. 47.

76. Ibid., p. 48.

77. John Womack, "The Mexican Economy During the Revolution, 1910–1920: Historiography and Analysis," *Marxist Perspectives* (winter 1978); Luis Anaya Merchant, *Colapso y reforma: La integración del sistema bancario en el México revolucionario, 1913–1920* (Mexico City: Universidad Autónoma de Zacatecas, 2002).

78. Haber, Razo, and Maurer, *Politics of Property Rights*, p. 76.

79. Paolo Riguzzi, "From Globalization to Revolution? The Porfirian Political Economy: An Essay on Issues and Interpretations," *Journal of Latin American Studies* 41:2 (May 2009): 353.

80. Peter Evans, *Dependent Development: The Alliance of Multinational, State, and Local Capital in Brazil* (Princeton, NJ: Princeton University Press, 1979). See also Mark Wasserman, "Foreign Investment in Mexico, 1876–1911: A Case Study of the Role of Regional Elites," *The Americas* 36 (July 1979): 2–21.

81. Jesús Silva Herzog, "La revolución Mexicana en crisis," *Cuadernos Americanos* (1944): 33–34, cited in Hansen, *Politics of Mexican Development*, pp. 124–25.

82. Pedro Martínez de Río to Lewis Douglass, Dec. 1, 1903, Lewis Douglas Papers, Box 126, Folder 9, University of Arizona.

83. Interestingly, Martínez del Río was scrupulously honest about his dealings with Douglas. In 1905 he pointed out that because he was doing less work for the Moctezuma Copper Company and the Nacozari Railway Company, he believed that they should reduce his remuneration from US$250 to US$150 per month. P. Martínez del Río to James Douglas, Feb. 13, 1905, Lewis Douglas Papers, Box 126, Folder 9.

84. P. Martínez del Río to James Douglas, Oct. 26, 1904, Lewis Douglas Papers, Box 126, Folder 9.

85. John B. Body to Lord Cowdray (Pearson), Apr. 15, 1912, Weetman Pearson Papers, Science Museum, London, United Kingdom.

86. T. H. Carter-Mitchell, Assistant General Manager, to Ernest M. Clarke, The Mines of El Oro, Ltd., Dec. 22, 1922, Weetman Pearson Papers, Science Museum, London, United Kingdom.

87. *EMJ* 121 (1926): 284.

88. For the classic analyses of the evolution of the Mexican state from 1920 to 1970, Frank R. Brandenburg, *The Making of Modern Mexico* (New York: Prentice-Hall, 1964); Nora Hamilton, *The Limits of State Autonomy: Post-Revolutionary Mexico* (Princeton, NJ: Princeton University Press, 1982); Roger D. Hansen, *The Politics of Mexican Development* (Baltimore, MD: The Johns Hopkins Press, 1971).

89. Peter Evans, *Dependent Development: The Alliance of Multinational, State, and Local Capital in Brazil* (Princeton, NJ: Princeton University Press, 1979) found a similar phenomenon, which he called the "triple alliance" in Brazil.

Chapter 2

1. Mark Wasserman, "Foreign Investment in Mexico, 1876–1911: A Case Study of the Role of Regional Elites," *The Americas* 36 (July 1979): 2–21.
2. E. Alexander Powell, "The Betrayal of a Nation," *The American Magazine* 70 (Oct. 1910): 717–18.
3. Powell, "Betrayal," 719. Aldo Musacchio and Ian Read, "Bankers, Industrialists, and Their Cliques: Elite Networks in Mexico and Brazil During Early Industrialization," Working Paper, 2006, lists the "Most Central Mexican Directors," which includes in order of their centrality, Pablo Macedo, Guillermo Land y Escandón, Hugo Scherer, Ernesto Brown (National Railways), Luis Elguero, Fernando Pimentel y Fagoaga, José Signoret, Enrique Creel, J. B. Body (Pearson interests), Luis Riba, Carlos Casasús, Henri Tron, Porfirio Díaz Jr., Joaquín Casasús, and Roberto Nuñez. Scherer, Body, Brown, Signoret, and Tron were foreigners (or at least foreign born). Manuel Gómez Morín was the outstanding intermediary of the postrevolutionary era.
4. Stephen H. Haber, *Industrialization and Underdevelopment: The Industrialization of Mexico, 1890–1940* (Stanford, CA: Stanford University Press, 1987).
5. Roderic A. Camp, *Entrepreneurs and Politics in Twentieth-Century Mexico* (New York: Oxford University Press, 1989).
6. Mark Wasserman, "Enrique C. Creel: Business and Politics in Mexico, 1880–1930," *Business History Review* 59:4 (winter 1985): 645–62.
7. J. Adolphus Owens, comp., *Anywhere I Wander I Find Facts and Legends Relating to the Creel Family* (Warrior, AL: n.p., 1975): pp. 520–23; Alejandro Creel Cobián, *Enrique C. Creel, Apuntes para su biografía* (Mexico City: n.p., 1974), pp. 9–26. Paz Cuilty was the sister of Carolina Cuilty de Terrazas, the wife of General Luis Terrazas.
8. Mark Wasserman, *Persistent Oligarchs: Elites and Politics in Chihuahua, Mexico, 1910–1940* (Chapel Hill: University of North Carolina Press, 1993), pp. 74–93.
9. Banco Minero de Chihuahua, Consejo de Administración, *Informe del Consejo de Administración y Comisario a la asamblea general de accionistas de 28 de marzo de 1908* (Chihuahua: n.p., 1908).
10. According to Ricardo León, "La banca chihuahuense durante el Porfiriato," Siglo XIX, Cuadernos de Historia 2 (Feb. 1992), in 1900 the major shareholders of the Banco Minero were Juan F. Brittingham (8.06%) and Sucesores de Hernández Hermanos of Monterrey (7.33%) with Luis Terrazas (6.66%) and E. C. Creel (5.33%). There were many other stockholders, including Evaristo Madero and the Banco Mercantil de Monterrey and the Banco de Nuevo León.
11. *Mexican Herald*, Jan. 22, 1906, p. 7; *Mexican Investor*, Feb. 3, 1906, p. 7.
12. Alex M. Saragoza, *The Monterrey Elite and the Mexican State, 1880–1940* (Austin: University of Texas Press, 1988), p. 49.
13. Document entitled "Negocios de Enrique C. Creel, May 10, 1922," which lists the landholdings and stockholdings and losses incurred by Creel during the Revolution. This document is to be found in the Creel papers (in the hands of

Eduardo Creel at the time when I obtained a copy of this document). My thanks to Harold D. Sims and Señor Creel for making this document available to me.

14. *El Correo de Chihuahua*, Mar. 10, 1904, 2; *Bankers' Magazine* 77 (Oct. 1908): 525–29; *Mexican Investor*, Mar. 31, 1906, 19; Nicolás D'Olwer et al., *El porfiriato: La vida económica*, 2 vols. (Mexico City: n.p., 1965), vol. 7 of *Historia moderna de México*, ed. Daniel Cosió Villegas, 2:827.

15. *Bankers' Magazine* 77 (Oct. 1908): 537–41; *El Correo de Chihuahua*, Mar. 22, 1904, 3; *Mexican Yearbook 1911*, 129.

16. *El Correo de Chihuahua*, June 3, 1903, 2; Chihuahua, Tesorería General, *Presupuestos de egresos para el ejercisio fiscal de 1907 a 1908* (Chihuahua: n.p., 1907); Chihuahua, Secretaría de Gobierno, Sección Estadistica, *Anuario estadístico del estado de Chihuahua 1908*; *1909*, 205; *El Periódico Oficial del Estado de Chihuahua*, July 17, 1910, 10.

17. Arthur Shepherd to Enrique C. Creel, Sept. 27, 1912, CD#1, file 55, Papers of Enrique C. Creel.

18. Enrique C. Creel to Joaquín Casasús, Nov. 30, 1899, CD#1, file 59, Papers of Enrique C. Creel.

19. Enrique C. Creel to Alexander Shepherd, Feb. 26, 1902, CD#1, file 55, Papers of Enrique Creel.

20. Alexander R. Shepherd to Enrique C. Creel, Dec. 9, 1912, CD#1, file 55, Papers of Enrique C. Creel.

21. Enrique C. Creel to George Rowland, Apr. 1, 1909, CD#1, file 60, Papers of Enrique C. Creel.

22. Noel Maurer, *The Power and the Money: The Mexican Financial System, 1876–1932* (Stanford, CA: Stanford University Press, 2002), pp. 93–114.

23. Ibid., p. 94.

24. Marín Falomir to Enrique C. Creel, Dec. 27, 1910, and Jan. 19, 1911, pt. 2, Silvestre Terrazas Papers.

25. *El Correo de Chihuahua*, Oct. 21, 1903, p. 1; *Boletín Comercial* (Chihuahua), Sept. 1, 1906, advertisements; William K. Meyers, *Forge of Progress, Crucible of Revolt: The Origins of the Mexican Revolution in La Comarca Lagunera, 1880–1911* (Albuquerque: University of New Mexico Press, 1994), pp. 69–72, 149–55.

26. *Mexican Yearbook, 1912*, 137; John R. Southworth, *Directorio official bancario de México* (Mexico City: n.p., 1906), p. 245.

27. *Bankers' Magazine* 77 (Oct. 1908), pp. 525–29; *El Correo*, Mar. 10, 1904, p. 2.

28. Ibid., pp. 537–41.

29. *Engineering and Mining Journal (EMJ)* 76 (Dec. 17, 1903): 918; 81 (Mar. 3, 1906): 429–30; 73 (Mar. 22, 1902): 426; and (Apr. 12, 1902): 528; 78 (Nov. 14, 1904): 950.

30. *Bankers' Magazine* 77 (Oct. 1908), p. 531; and 77 (Feb. 1903), p. 314.

31. *El Correo de Chihuahua*, May 13, 1903, p. 4.

32. *Mexican Investor*, July 1, 1905, Nov. 16 and 18, 1905, p. 3; *EMJ* 80 (Nov. 11, 1905): 900.

33. *El Correo de Chihuahua*, Mar. 1, 1906, p. 1; Feb. 9, 1905, p. 1; Jan. 25, 1905, p. 1; *Mexican Herald*, Apr. 22, 1907, p. 11; July 16, 1907, p. 11.

34. Jorge Griggs, *Mines of Chihuahua, 1907: History, Geology, Statistics, Mining Company Directory* (N.p., n.d.), pp. 80–81; *Mexican Financier*, Aug. 22, 1891, p. 541; Mar. 26, 1892, p. 15; *Mexican Herald*, May 21, 1896, p. 2; *EMJ* 72 (Nov. 30, 1901): 698; *El Correo de Chihuahua*, Oct. 21, 1902, p. 2.

35. Griggs, *Mines of Chihuahua*, pp. 81, 336; Lewis Morgan and Hubert Bankart to Enrique C. Creel, Dec. 2, 1896; Creel to William Heimke, Sept. 14, 1896; Juan A. Creel to H. C. Hollis, May 4 and 19, 1904, pt. 2, reel 17, STP; *Mexican Herald*, Sept. 16, 1905, p. 7.

36. *Siglo XX*, July 27, 1904, p. 2: *Periódico Oficial del Estado de Chihuahua*, Aug. 31, 1895, pt. 2, reel 2, STP.

37. Enrique C. Creel to Teodoro H. Swayne, July 7, 1906, CD#1, file 56, and Ernesto Madero to Enrique C. Creel, Mar. 11, 1908, CD#1, file 56; Creel to Federico Sisniega, July 23, 1908, CD#1, file 57, Papers of Enrique C. Creel.

38. Federico Sisniega to Ernesto Madero, Sept. 25, 1900, pt. 2, reel 7, STP; US Department of State, *Monthly Consular and Trade Reports*, no. 305 (Feb. 1906); *El Correo de Chihuahua*, Feb. 12, 1902, p. 1.

39. *Mexican Herald*, July 29, 1908, p. 1; July 30, 1908, p. 3; Sept. 27, 1908, p. 1; *El Correo de Chihuahua*, Sept. 20, 1902, p. 1; Apr. 27, 1904, p. 1; Federico Sisniega to E. C. Creel, July 2, 1904, pt. 2, reel 8, STP. Jeffrey Pilcher, *The Sausage Rebellion* (Albuquerque: University of New Mexico Press, 2006), pp. 89–117.

40. Wasserman, *Persistent Oligarchs*, pp. 73–83.

41. Juan A. Creel to Enrique C. Creel, Mar. 24, 1912, CD#1, file 80, Papers of Enrique C. Creel. This letter was an interesting discovery. The general view has been that the Porfirian oligarchy, in particular the Terrazas-Creels, financed the rebellion of Pascual Orozco. See Wasserman, *Persistent Oligarchs*, p. 16. This letter indicates that these funds may not have been given voluntarily.

42. Enrique C. Creel to John C. Van Cleaf, Vice President, National Park Bank, Sept. 27, 1916, DVD 2, file 115, Papers of Enrique Creel.

43. On September 29, 1915, Carranza reinstated the General Banking Act of 1897, then sent investigating commissions to the banks, eventually shutting down eighteen of the twenty-seven banks of issue, five of which the regime confiscated. Noel Maurer, *The Power and the Money*, pp. 147–48. Only the state banks in Mexico State, Nuevo León, Sinaloa, Sonora, Tabasco, Yucatán, and Zacatecas remained.

44. David J. D. Meyers, US consul Chihuahua, to Juan Creel, manager, Banco Minero, Jan. 8, 1929, file 851.6, vol. 6, 1929, RG 84, Records of the American Consulate in Ciudad Chihuahua US National Archives; "Review of Commerce in Chihuahua," compiled by Thomas McEnelly, US Consul, Chihuahua, Oct. 10, 1929, RG 84, vol. 6, 1925, US National Archives.

45. "Directory of Agricultural and Grazing Lands in Chihuahua," comp. US consulate Chihuahua, enclosure from McEnelly to Secretary of State, June 17, 1926, RG 84, vol. 6, 1926. The four were La Gallina, Puerto de Lobo, Las Orientales, and a parcel in the municipality of Guerrero.

46. Hacienda San Nicolas de la Torre, Jan. 12, 1915, CD#1, file 83, and Compañía Agrícola Colonizadora, Apr. 20, 1918, CD#1, file 84, Papers of Enrique C. Creel.

47. Francisco C. Terrazas to Banco Minero, May 19, 1917, CD#3, file 185; F. C. Terrrazas to Banco Minero, May 21, 1917, CD#3, file 186, Papers of Enrique C. Creel.

48. Enrique C. Creel to A. J. McQuatters, Nov. 22, 1918, CD#1, file 79, Papers of Enrique C. Creel. McQuatters, who would in 1922 try to purchase the landholdings of Luis Terrazas, already owed the Banco Minero a million dollars. Federico Stallforth and Company to Enrique C. Creel, Sept. 18, 1917, CD#1, file 79, Papers of Enrique C. Creel.

49. Bankers Trust to Creel, June 19, 1918, CD#3, file 181, Papers of Enrique C. Creel.

50. Juan A. Creel to Enrique C. Creel, Oct. 6, 1917, and Oct. 12, 1917, CD#3, file 194, Papers of Enrique C. Creel.

51. Enrique C. Creel to Price McKinney, Apr. 16, 1915, CD#1, file 106, Papers of Enrique C. Creel.

52. Enrique C. Creel to V. H. Goschen, June 28, 1919, CD#1, file 78, Papers of Enrique C. Creel.

53. Francisco C. Terrazas to Rafael Nieto, Apr. 29, 1917, CD#3, file 194, Papers of Enrique C. Creel.

54. Enrique C. Creel to S. W. Eccles, Vice President, ASARCO, May 5, June 3, and June 9, 1915, Papers of Enrique C. Creel. Originally, Creel requested that ASARCO buy US$500,000 worth of the company's bonds.

55. Unknown to Enrique C. Creel, Dec. 19, 1917, CD#3, file 167, and Unknown to Banco Minero, Jan. 19, 1917, CD#3, file 168, Papers of Enrique C. Creel.

56. Enrique C. Creel to Carlos A Gorozpe, Nov. 16, 1920, CD#3, file 165, Compañía Agrícola La Peregrina, S.A., to Compañía Alcoholera Nacional, Mar. 10, 1919, Unnamed to Enrique C. Creel, Jan. 8, 1919, Creel to Francisco C. Terrazas, Jan. 2, 1919, CD#3, file 166, Papers of Enrique C. Creel.

57. Enrique Krauze et al., *Historia de la revolución mexicana: Período 1924–1928: La reconstrucción económico*, (Mexico City: El Colegio de México, 1977), pp. 32–35; Lorenzo Meyer et al., *Historia de la revolución mexicana: Período 1928–1934: Los inicios de la institucionalización, la política del maximato* (Mexico City: El Colegio de México, 1978), pp. 224–25; Creel Cobián, *Enrique C. Creel*, p. 371.

58. Wasserman, *Persistent Oligarchs*, pp. 73–83.

59. *El Paso Morning Times*, May 5, 1910, p. 5.

60. Mario Cerutti, "Los Madero en la economía de Monterrey (1890–1910)," in *Burguesía y capitalismo en Monterrey, 1850–1910*, ed. Mario Cerutti (Mexico City: Claves Latinoamericanos, 1983), pp. 57–106.

61. Hugh Thompson, "The Maderos of Mexico," *Munsey's Magazine* 48 (1913): 882–87.

62. *El Paso Morning Times*, May 5, 1910, p. 5. Thompson, "The Maderos."

63. By his first wife, he had two sons, Francisco and Evaristo, and by his second wife, seven sons, Ernesto, Manuel, José, Salvador, Alberto, Benjamín, and David. There were nine daughters.

64. *El Paso Morning Times*, May 5, 1910, p. 5.

65. *El Correo de Chihuahua*, July 12, 1904, p. 1.

66. Ibid., Feb. 8, 1905, p. 1.

67. *EMJ* 73 (Feb. 8, 1902): 226.

68. *EMJ* 76 (Oct. 24, 1903): 633.

69. *Mexican Herald*, May 31, 1905, p. 7; *El Correo de Chihuahua*, May 29, 1905, p. 1. The company had 1.1 million pesos in capital. Beckman and Longe received US$600,000 in stock of the company and US$400,000 in bonds.

70. Weber to Evaristo Madero, Nov. 25, 1909, Max Weber Collection, UTEP, Roll 8.

71. *Mexican Herald*, Aug. 15, 1907, p. 11.

72. *EMJ* 80 (July 22, 1905): 131. *Mexican Herald*, Dec. 11, 1908, p. 10; *EMJ* 88 (May 16, 1908): 1029.

73. *El Correo de Chihuahua*, July 5, 1907, p. 1.

74. *Mexican Herald*, Feb. 12, 1908, p. 11; *Mexican Mining Journal* 16 (Feb. 1913): 95. Maderos owned Ramón Corona in 1913. The company shipped US$175,000 in ore in December 1907.

75. *Mexican Mining Journal* 16 (Mar. 1913): 149.

76. *Mexican Herald*, Mar. 2, 1908, p. 11. *EMJ* 85 (Mar. 28, 1908): 675.

77. *EMJ* 88 (Aug. 21, 1909): 385.

78. *Mexican Mining Journal*, Jan. 1909: 8, 24; *EMJ* 78 (Sept. 8, 1904): 403; *El Correo de Chihuahua*, Mar. 10, 1910, p. 1.

79. James H. Malcolmson, "Mexico in 1905," *EMJ* 81 (Jan. 6, 1906): 37–38.

80. *EMJ* 75 (Feb. 21, 1903): 308; *El Correo de Chihuahua*, Oct. 5, 1907, p. 2.

81. *El Correo de Chihuahua*, Oct. 5, 1907, p. 2.

82. *EMJ* 80 (July 22, 1905): 131.

83. Ibid., (Oct. 7, 1905): 658.

84. *El Paso Times*, Feb. 16, 1909, p. 1.

85. Thompson, "Maderos."

86. *El Correo de Chihuahua*, Oct. 5, 1907, p. 2.

87. Cerutti, "Los Madero," pp. 94–96.

88. Memo, Oct. 28, 1915, USNARG, 59, 312.115M44/3.

89. *Mexican Herald*, Jan. 6, 1909, p. 5.

90. Meyers, *Forge of Progress*, pp. 145–47.

91. Ibid., p. 148.

92. Doc. No. 22:001068, CGPD.

93. William K. Meyers, "Politics, Vested Rights, and Economic Growth in Porfirian Mexico: The Company Tlahualilo in the Comarca Lagunera, 1885–1911," *Hispanic American Historical Review 57:3 (1977)*.

94. Mario Cerutti, "La Compañía Industrial Jabonera de la Laguna: Comerciantes, agricultures e industria en el norte de México, 1880–1925," in *Historia de*

la grandes empresas de México, 1850–1930, ed. Carlos Marichal and Mario Cerutti (Mexico City: Universidad Autónoma de Nuevo León y Fondo de Cultura Económica, 1997), p. 169.

95. *El Correo de Chihuahua*, Feb. 10, 1903, p. 3.

96. Ibid., July 6, 1907, pp. 167–70.

97. Ibid., Mar. 27, 1909, p. 1.

98. Mario Cerutti, "La Compañía Industrial Jabonera de la Laguna," pp. 187–94; William K. Meyers, *Forge of Progress, Crucible of Revolt: The Origins of the Mexican Revolution in La Comarca Lagunera, 1880–1911* (Albuquerque: University of New Mexico Press, 1994), pp. 149–55.

99. Cerutti, "Compañía Jabonera," p. 186.

100. Meyers, *Forge of Progress*, p. 153.

101. Cerutti, "Los Madero," p. 86. The other factories were La Amistad, owned by Prince, Torres, y Prince; La Belle Unión, owned by the Compañía Industrial Saltillera, S.A.; and El Porvenir, owned by Valentín Rivero y Sucesores.

102. *El Correo de Chihuahua*, July 31, 1909, p. 1, and Aug. 1, 1909, p. 1.

103. Cerutti, "Los Madero," pp. 86–89.

104. Mario Cerutti, "Los Madero en la economía de Monterrey (1890–1910)," in *Burguesía y capitalismo en Monterrey, 1850–1910*, ed. Mario Cerutti (Mexico City: Claves Latinoamericanos, 1983), pp. 57–106; Cerutti, "Compañía Jabonera."

105. Cerutti, "Los Madero," p. 89; *Mexican Financier*, Feb. 27, 1892, p. 547. Other partners included Lic. Emeterio de la Garza, ex-governor Villarreal, General Treviño, and J. A. Robertson. This illustrated the family's extensive network of business associates.

106. Mario Cerutti, "Empresariado y banca en el norte de México (1870–1910): El Banco Refaccionario de la Laguna," in *La banca regional en México (1870–1930)*, comp. Mario Cerutti and Carlos Marichal (Mexico City: El Colegio de México and El Fondo de Cultura Económica, 2003), pp. 168–215.

107. Cerutti, "Los Madero," p. 91.

108. Ibid., "Empresariado."

109. Ibid., p. 194.

110. Ibid., p. 202.

111. La Amistad in Gómez Palacio was closed for two years in 1908 and 1909. *El Correo de Chihuahua*, Nov. 30, 1909, p. 1.

112. Revolution 1913, p. 297.

113. *El Correo de Chihuahua*, July 16, 1911, p. 4.

114. Marvin D. Bernstein, *The Mexican Mining Industry, 1890–1940* (Albany: State University of New York, 1964), p. 119.

115. Jeffrey Bortz, unpub. ms, 2:19.

116. Cobb to Secretary of State, Oct. 6, 1915, USNARG 59, 812.00/16493

117. Cobb, El Paso, to Secretary of State, Oct. 5, 1915, USNARG 59, Records of the Department of State, Internal Affairs of Mexico, 1910–1929, 812.00/16387.

118. Memo, Oct. 28, 1915, USNARG, 59, 312.115M44/3.

119. Cobb to Secretary of State, Sept. 27, 1916, USNARG 59, Records of the Department of State, Internal Affairs of Mexico, 1910–1929.

120. *Excelsior*, Nov. 10, 1919, Buckley, BLAC, UTA, 153.5.

121. Stephen H. Haber, *Industry and Development: The Industrialization of Mexico, 1890–1940* (Stanford, CA: Stanford University Press, 1989), pp. 132–33.

122. *New York Times*, Nov. 26, 1913.

123. *El Periódico Oficial del Estado de Chihuahua*, Feb. 14, 1915, p. 10.

124. *Boletín Comercial*, May 15, 1916, p. 7.

125. *EMJ* 112 (Aug. 6, 1921): 228.

126. *EMJ* 115 (Jan. 6, 1923): 34–35.

127. Haber, *Industry and Development*, p. 133.

128. Ibid., p. 145.

129. Cerutti, "Compañía Jabonera," 195–97.

130. Alejandro Suverza, "Dinamita, un polvorín sin vigilancia," *El Universal*, Aug. 7, 2007. El Universal.com.

131. *Boletín Financiero y Minero*, Feb. 26, 1921, and Mar. 10, 1921, cited in Stephen Haber, Armando Razo, and Noel Maurer, *The Politics of Property Rights: Political Instability, Credible Commitments, and Economic Growth in Mexico, 1876–1929* (Cambridge: Cambridge University Press, 2003), p. 99.

132. Mark Wasserman, *Capitalists, Caciques, and Revolution: The Native Elite and Foreign Enterprise in Chihuahua, Mexico, 1854–1911* (Chapel Hill: University of North Carolina Press, 1984).

133. Reyes in fact identified the Madero as "obstructionists." Bernardo Reyes to Porfirio Díaz, Apr. 8, 1903, Doc. No. 28:004378 CGPD.

134. William Stanley Langston, "Coahuila in the Porfiriato, 1893–1911: A Study of Political Elites" (PhD diss., Tulane University, 1980), pp. 154–55.

135. Ibid., pp. 162–63.

136. Ibid., pp. 168–70.

137. Ibid., pp. 96–97; Langston, on p. 115, maintains that Díaz "feared and disliked Evaristo Madero."

138. Ibid., p. 97.

139. Ibid., p. 140.

Chapter 3

1. Charles Edward Russell, "The Seven Kings in Mexico: A Profitable Tale from Recent Railroad History," *Cosmopolitan* 43 (July 1907): 278.

2. Ibid., p. 279; *New York Times*, Oct. 1, 1903, p. 1, pt. 1-2-1.

3. Russell, "Seven Kings," p. 279.

4. "Minister Limantour's Statement to Congress, 1908," *Mexican Yearbook, 1908*, p. 690. *New York Times*, Nov. 1, 1903, part 4, has selections of Limantour's speech justifying the merger.

5. Russell, "Seven Kings," p. 279. These are Russell's words.

6. There is a considerable body of scholarly work on Mexican railroads. Francisco R. Calderón, "Los ferrocarriles," in the *Historia moderna de México: El porfiriato, la vida económica*, vol. 7, pt. I (Mexico City: Editorial Hermes, 1965), pp. 483–634; Sandra Kuntz Ficker, *Empresa extranjera y mercado interno: El Ferrocarril Central Mexicano, 1880–1907* (Mexico City: El Colegio de México, 1995); Sandra Kuntz Ficker and Priscilla Connelly, eds., *Ferrocarriles y obras públicas* (Mexico City: Instituto Mora, 1999); John H. Coatsworth, *Growth Against Development: The Economic Impact of Railroads in Porfirian Mexico* (DeKalb: Northern Illinois University Press, 1981); Lorenzo Arrieta Ceniceros, "Importancia económica y social de los ferrocarriles en Yucatán: Empresas y grupos económicos, 1876–1915," *Estudios Políticos* 5:18–19 (Apr.–Sept. 1979): 113–87; Arturo Grunstein, "De la competencia al monopolio: La formación de los ferrocarriles nacionales de México," in *Ferrocarriles y obras públicas,* ed. Sandra Kuntz Ficker y Priscilla Connelly (Mexico City: Instituto Mora, 1999); Arturo Grunstein Dickter, "Surgimiento de los ferrocarriles nacionales de México (1900–1913): Era inevitable la consolidación monopólica," in *Historia de los grandes empresas en México, 1850–1930*, ed. Carlos Marichal and Mario Cerutti (Mexico City: Fondo de Cultura Económica, 1997); Arturo Grunstein Dickter, "A Tentative Reinterpretation of Mexican Railroad Policy in the Late Porfiriato, 1890–1911," unpub. paper, n.d.; Sandra Kuntz Ficker, "Economic Backwardness and Firm Strategy: An American Railroad Corporation in Nineteenth-Century Mexico," *Hispanic American Historical Review* 80:2 (May 2000): 267–98; Robert W. Randall, "Mexico's Pre-revolutionary Reckoning with Railroads," *The Americas* 42:1 (July 1985): 1–28; Paolo Riguzzi, "Los caminos del atraso: Tecnología, instituciones e inversion en los ferrocarriles Mexicanos, 1850–1900," in *Historia económica de México.* Enrique Cárdenas, ed., 2d ed., 2004, pp. 494–550; Paolo Riguzzi, "Inversiones extranjeras y interés nacional en los ferrocarriles mexicanos, 1880–1914," *Las inversions extranjeras en América Latina, 1850–1930*, ed. Carlos Marichal (Mexico City: Fondo de Cultura Económica, 1992); Paolo Riguzzi, "Mercados, regiones, y capitals en los ferrocarriles de propiedad Mexicana, 1870–1908," in *Ferrocarriles y obras públicas*, ed. Sandra Kuntz Ficker y Priscilla Connelly (Mexico City: Instituto Mora, 1999); Arthur P. Schmidt, "The Social and Economic Effect of the Railroad in Puebla and Veracruz, Mexico, 1867–1911" (PhD diss., Indiana University, 1974). For a short discussion of the nationalization, see Michael Matthews, *The Civilizing Machine: A Cultural History of Mexican Railroads, 1870–1910* (Lincoln: University of Nebraska Press, 2013), pp. 182–84.

7. James Creelman, *Díaz, Master of Mexico* (New York: D. Appleton and Co., 1916), p. 384.

8. David M. Pletcher, "Mexico Opens the Door to American Capital, 1877–1880," *The Americas* 16 (July 1959): 6.

9. Ibid.

10. Robert Glass Cleland, ed., *Mexican Yearbook, 1922–1924* (Los Angeles: Times-Mirror Press, 1924), p. 205; Joseph Nimmo Jr., *Commerce Between the United States and Mexico and the Construction of Railroads Connecting the Two*

Countries. Report to the US House of Representatives, Jan. 31, 1884 (Washington, DC: Government Printing Office, 1884), pp. 57–59.

11. Edgar Turlington, *Mexico and Her Foreign Creditors* (New York: Columbia University Press, 1930), pp. 227–28.

12. *The Mexican Yearbook, 1908* (London: McCorquodale & Company, 1908), pp. 653–85.

13. Mexico had been a battleground for the US railroad tycoons beginning in the 1880s, when Jay Gould and W. R. Palmer clashed over a concession to build a line from Mexico City to Laredo. The Atchison, Topeka, and Santa Fe built the Sonora Railway in 1880–82 in order to obtain an outlet to the Pacific Ocean in its rivalry with Collis P. Huntington's Southern Pacific.

14. *New York Times*, Oct. 1, 1901, sec. 3, p. 5.

15. Ibid., Apr. 27, 1903, sec. 2, p. 3; David M. Pletcher, *Rails, Mines, and Progress: Seven American Promoters in Mexico, 1867–1911* (Ithaca, NY: AHA, 1958), pp. 298–99.

16. John Kenneth Turner, *Barbarous Mexico* (Chicago: Charles H. Kerr, 1911), p. 257.

17. Carlos Díaz Dufoo, *Limantour* (Mexico City: Eusebio Gómez de la Puente, 1910), p. 124.

18. Slason Thompson, *Cost Capitalization and Estimated Value of American Railways: An Analysis of Current Falacies* (Chicago: Huntherp-Warren Printing Company, 1907), p. 61.

19. *New York Times*, Nov. 12, 1906, sec. 2, p. 1; Eliot James and Homer B. Vanderblue, eds., *Railroads: Cases and Selections* (New York: Macmillan Company, 1925), p. 598.

20. William Z. Ripley, *Railroads: Finance and Organizations* (New York: Longmans, Green, and Co., 1915), p. 513.

21. Speyer to J. Y. Limantour, May 6, 1905, Archivo de José Y. Limantour, Condumex, Roll 35.

22. Kuntz Ficker, *Empresa extranjera*, pp. 202–4.

23. Fred Wilbur Powell, *The Railroads of Mexico* (Boston: Stratford and Co.), p. 143.

24. *New York Times*, Aug. 23, 1903, p. 25; Speyer to Limantour, May 6, 1905, AJYL, Roll 33.

25. Turlington, *Mexico*.

26. *New York Times*, Apr. 1, 1901, sec. 16, p. 6.

27. Lorena May Parlee, "Porfirio Díaz, Railroads, and Development in Northern Mexico: A Study of Government Policy toward the Central and Nacional Railroads, 1876–1910" (PhD diss., University of California, San Diego, 1981), p. 244.

28. Ibid., 245.

29. Ibid.

30. Ibid., p. 246.

31. *New York Times*, Mar. 17, 1901, p. 3:2.

32. Parlee, "Railroads," p. 246.

33. Ibid., pp. 246–47.

34. Díaz Dufoo, *Limantour*, pp. 133–35.

35. Parlee, "Railroads," p. 249.

36. Ibid., citing Porfirio Díaz, *Informe de Ciudadano General Porfirio Díaz, presidente de los estados unidos mexicanos a sus compatriotas: Acerca de los actos de su administración en el periodo constitucional comprendido entre el 1 de diciembre de 1900 a 30 de noviembre de 1904* (Mexico City: n.p., 1904), pp. 161–63.

37. Parlee, "Railroads," p. 250 citing Limantour, *Apuntes*, p. 84.

38. Ibid., p. 250.

39. Ibid., pp. 250–51; Nicholas d'Olwer et al., *El porfiriato: La vida económica*, vol. VII, pts. I and II of *La historia moderna de México*, ed. Daniel Cosío Villegas (Mexico City: Editorial Hermes, 1965), p. 607.

40. D'Olwer, La vida económica, p. 608. The actual market value of the stock acquired and the price paid by the government was a little less than US$700,000. (The cost minus the market value of US$8,839,608.)

41. José Y. Limantour to Speyer & Company, Apr. 24, 1905, Archivo de José Y. Limantour (AJYL), Condumex, Roll 33.

42. Ibid., Mar. 30, 1905, AJYL, Roll 33.

43. Ibid., Apr. 24, 1905, AJYL, Roll 33.

44. Ibid., Apr. 24, 1905, and Limantour to Cleveland J. Dodge, Apr. 25, 1905, AJYL, Roll 33.

45. Speyer to Limantour, May 6, 1905, AJYL, Roll 33.

46. Ibid.

47. Ibid.

48. D'Olwer, *La vida económica* calculated the Central's debt at US$131,807,669, an enormous sum. Although the Mexican Central's gross profits had increased during the sixteen years prior to the merger, doubling from 1892 to 1902, the company, because of the devaluation of silver, was unable to service its debt. "Nationalization of Railways in Mexico," *Moody's Magazine*, June 1907, p. 42; *New York Times*, June 21, 1901, p. 10, Aug. 10, 1902, p. 30, May 8, 1902, p. 2.

49. Parlee, "Railroads," pp. 257–58. Pierce implausibly denied any plans to merge with any other carrier: "The Mexican Central has not made, and does not expect to make, any exclusive alliance with any single line or combination of roads and will continue to be conducted as an independent Mexican property...." *New York Times*, Aug. 16, 1903, p. 10. Harriman's vast acquisitions of US railroads began in June 1906.

50. *Mexican Yearbook, 1908*, pp. 689–95, contains the full text of the speech in translation.

51. James Speyer to Limantour, Feb. 24, 1906, AJYL, Roll 39.

52. Ibid., Jan. 4, 1907, AJYL, Roll 51.

53. E. L. Andrews to Enrique C. Creel, Mexican Ambassador to the United States, Aug. 5, 1907, and E. L. Andrews to Limantour, Nov. 12, 1907, AJYL, Roll 47.

54. Limantour to R. W. Vincent, Aug. 7, 1907, AJYL, Roll 46.

55. "Mexican Government's Railway Policy and the Consolidation of the Mexican Central and Mexican National Railways," *Mexican Yearbook, 1908*, pp. 689–714.

56. *Mexican Yearbook, 1914*, p. 5.

57. "Railway Financial News," *Railway Age Gazette*, July 8, 1910, p. 105; *Poor's Manual of Railroads of the United States, 1910*, pp. 1822–23.

58. "Railway Financial News," *Railway Age Gazette*, Sept. 9, 1910, p. 483.

59. The texts of all the documents are translated in the *Mexican Yearbook, 1908*, pp. 695–714.

60. Manuel López Gallo, *Economía y política en la historia de México* (Mexico City: n.p., 1988), p. 289. He cites González Roa, *El problema*, pp. 123–26, 131–33, 142.

61. *Moody's Magazine*, June 1907, pp. 44–45.

62. *Stock Exchanges Ten-Year Record of Prices and Dividends, 1898–1907* (London: Frederick C. Mathieson and Sons, 1907), pp. 105–7, 120–21, 328; D'Olwer, *La vida económica*, p. 615; González Roa, *El problema*, 121–24. For explanation of stock-watering, see Frederick Cleveland and Fred Wilbur Powell, *Railroad Finance* (New York: D. Appleton and Company, 1912), p. 337; Ripley, *Railroads: Finance and Organization*, p. 248.

63. López Gallo, *Economía*, p. 287.

64. Ibid., cites Francisco Bulnes, *El verdadero Díaz*, pp. 122–23; Carlton Beals, *Porfirio Díaz: Dictator of Mexico* (Philadelphia, PA: S. B. Lippincott Company, 1932), p. 335.

65. Beals, *Porfirio Díaz*, p. 335.

66. Turner, *Barbarous Mexico*, pp. 263–67.

67. Edward I. Bell, *The Political Shame of Mexico* (New York: McBride, Nast & Company, 1914), pp. 10–13. Neither Turner nor Bell has other than hearsay evidence. There is proof that Harriman made two trips to Mexico. The first in March 1902 included a meeting with Díaz that yielded a concession to build a railroad line from Guaymas to Guadalajara. George Kennan, *E. H. Harriman, A Biography*, vol. 1 (Boston: Houghton Mifflin Company, 1922), pp. 255–56. The second was to northern Mexico. *New York Times*, Sept. 23, 1906, sec. 3, p. 2.

68. López Gallo, *Economía*, p, 287.

69. D'Olwer, *La vida económica*, p. 620.

70. Limantour, *Apuntes*, p. 142.

71. *The Financial Review: Finance, Commerce, Railroad, 1910* (New York: William B. Dana Company, 1910), p. 94.

72. "The Mexican Railway Merger," *The Commercial and Financial Chronicle*, Apr. 11, 1908, pp. 890–91.

73. *Informe del Secretario de Hacienda y Crédito Público para la Consolidación de los Ferrocarriles Nacional de México y Central Mexicano* (Mexico City: Ministerio de Hacienda y Crédito Público, 1908), p. 39.

74. Limantour, *Apuntes*, p. 183.

75. *The Financial Review, 1907*, p. 94. The National had not yielded any dividend until 1906, when it declared a 1 percent dividend to its First Preferred holders. In 1907 it yielded 2 percent. These were the first years under government control. The Mexican Central never had declared dividends.

76. Turlington, *Mexico*, p. 243.

77. D'Olwer, *La vida económica*, p. 621.

78. Ibid., p. 611.

79. Roger W. Babson, "Analysis and Comments," *Moody's Manual of Railroads and Corporation Securities*, ed. George Hoskins (New York: Moody Manual Company, 1911), pp. 446–48.

80. D'Olwer, *La vida económica*, p. 621.

81. *Railway Age Gazette* 46 (1910): 132.

82. *Poor's Manual*, 1912, p. 1624. The FNM guaranteed the dividends on US$30 million in debentures.

83. *Poor's Manual, 1912*, p. 1602; W. Rodney Long, *Railways of Mexico. U.S. Department of Commerce, Trade Promotion Series,* no. 16 (Washington, DC: Government Printing Office, 1925), p. 31. The Mexican government sold the Veracruz lines for US$109,000 and guaranteed dividends totaling US$950,000 over three years.

84. *Third Annual Report of the National Railways of Mexico*, pp. 14–15.

85. Parlee, "Railroads," p. 271.

86. See especially Speyer to Limantour, May 6, 1905, AJYL, Roll 33.

87. *New York Times*, Oct. 19, 1904, p. 1:3. The syndicate included: the Mutual Life Insurance Company, the Equitable Life Insurance Company, Guaranty Trust Co., Union Trust Co., Central Trust Co., National City Bank, Harvey Fisk and Sons, Lazard Freres, First National Bank of Chicago, Girard National Bank of Philadelphia, Old Colony Trust of Boston, Speyer Brothers of London, Speyer-Ellison of Frankfort, Texeira Mattos Brothers of Amsterdam, and Deutsche Bank of Berlin.

88. There is some doubt, however, as to what extent the railroads implemented the order, for the government reissued the decree in 1911. The fact that American engineers employed by the FNM demanded in 1910 that no more than half of engineers and conductors should be promoted from within the ranks indicates that a significant number of Mexicans had taken over skilled positions. "General News Section," *Railway Age Gazette* 48 (Feb. 4, 1910): 265.

89. Howard Ryan, "Selected Aspects of American Activities in Mexico, 1876–1910" (PhD diss., University of Chicago, 1964), pp. 269–76.

90. Grunstein, "De la competencia al monopolio"; Grunstein Dickter, "Surgimiento"; Arturo Grunstein Dickter, "A Tentative Reinterpretation of Mexican Railroad Policy in the Late Porfiriato, 1890–1911" (unpub. paper, n.d.).

91. See also Alfred Tischendorf, *Great Britain and Mexico in the Era of Porfirio Díaz* (Durham, NC: Duke University Press, 1961), pp. 52–55.

92. Grunstein, "Tentative Reinterpretation," pp. 22–24. For the most part rate-fixing agreements held only for the shipment of export. There was some

cooperation concerning imports, but these arrangements were shakier than those about exports.

93. Grunstein, "Tentative Reinterpretation," p. 28. He cites what he calls the Dieppe Report, an *Informe* reprinted in Francisco Trentini, ed., *El florecimiento de México* (Mexico City: n.p., 1906), pp. 182–85.

94. Grunstein, "Tentative Reinterpretation," p. 34.

95. Ibid., p. 33.

96. Parlee, "Railroads," pp. 235–40.

97. Ibid., p. 254. The Central paid Creel US$50,000 to sit on its board. Moreover, Creel had considerably more ties to US-owned railroads. He set up the Chihuahua al Pacífico line in 1898, which he merged with the Kansas City, Mexico, and Orient railroad, operated by US tycoon Arthur E. Stilwell. Creel then served as vice president of the KCM&O. Creel later was vice president of the Mexico Northwestern line. Mark Wasserman, *Capitalists, Caciques, and Revolution: Native Elite and Foreign Enterprise in Chihuahua, Mexico, 1854–1911* (Chapel Hill: University of North Carolina Press, 1984), p. 64.

98. Parlee, "Railroads," p. 245.

99. Ibid., p. 265.

Chapter 4

1. John Mason Hart, *Revolutionary Mexico: The Coming and Process of the Mexican Revolution* (Berkeley: University of California Press, 1987), p. 158.

2. There are some memoirs, which I have listed in the Bibliography.

3. Ramón Eduardo Ruíz, *The People of Sonora and the Yankee Capitalists* (Tucson: University of Arizona Press, 1988), p. 63, maintains that his archival research leaves no doubt that Sonorans mistrusted the North Americans after an initial period of welcome.

4. The *Boletín Agricultura Mexicana* noted the heavy movement of North Americans into the north as early as May 1899. *Boletín Agricultura Mexicana* 22 (May 24, 1899): 378.

5. Machado, "Destruction," p. 15, citing Cobb to Lansing, March 5, 1917, 611.127/219, USNARG 59.

6. Stewart E. McMillan, American Consul, Piedras Negras, to Secretary of State, Nov. 2, 1933, 812.52/1832, USNARG 84.

7. Guy W. Ray, American Vice Consul, Guaymas, to Secretary of State, Mar. 16, 1934.

8. John J. Dwyer, *The Agrarian Dispute: The Expropriation of American-Owned Rural Land in Postrevolutionary Mexico* (Durham, NC: Duke University Press, 2008), pp. 159–60.

9. Ibid.

10. General Agrarian Report: Expropriation of American Agricultural Lands, Sept. 30, 1937, 812.52/2319, USNARG 84. This report estimated the lands expropriated from Americans at 395,000 acres. See also Dwyer, *Agrarian Dispute*.

11. For examples of large ranches in Chihuahua, see *El Periódico Oficial del Estado de Chihuahua*, Feb. 1, 1936, pp. 88–89; Feb. 20, 1936, p. 1; July 13, 1935, p. 271; Oct. 29, 1936, p. 855; July 7, 1937, p. 566.

12. The prospects of riches in Mexican land led such notables as Levi P. Morton, vice president of the United States (1889–93), and Joseph Cannon, speaker of the US House of Representatives, to invest in property in Chihuahua, *Mexican Financier*, Jan. 19, 1889, p. 396, and *Mexican Herald*, Aug. 28, 1906, p. 2.

13. *El Correo de Chihuahua*, Feb. 10, 1909, p. 1.

14. *Mexican Herald*, Sept. 17. 1907, p. 11.

15. Summary of Mexican Intelligence, Jan. 14, 1921, Albert Bacon Fall Papers, Box 5, Folder 5. The plan was to sell the land in small plots.

16. "Memorandum of W. M. Ferris," in "Land Title Difficulties in Mexico: A Memorandum Written in 1926," *Business Historical Society Bulletin* 24:1 (Mar. 1950): 15–16.

17. W. A. Swanberg, *Citizen Hearst: A Biography of William Randolph Hearst* (New York: Scribner, 1961), pp. 32, 190, 191.

18. In 1872 the price for cattle was US$13–17 per head. Pierson to Second Assistant Secretary of State, Oct. 13, 1872, USNARG 59, Consular Reports, Chihuahua.

19. W. H. Brown to Second Assistant Secretary of State, Oct. 1, 1872, USNARG 59; US State Department, *Commercial Relations of the United States, 1871*, p. 898; US State Department, *Commercial Relations of the United States, 1884–1885*, pp. 652–53.

20. *Chihuahua Enterprise*, Apr. 15, 1883, p. 77.

21. *Mexican Financier*, Feb. 23, 1884, p. 341.

22. Manuel A. Machado Jr., *The North Mexican Cattle Industry, 1910–1970: Ideology, Conflict and Change* (College Station: Texas A&M Press, 1981), p. 5.

23. US Department of State, *Reports from the Consuls*, no. 152 (May 1893), pp. 94–95.

24. Juan Manuel Romero Gil, *Minería y sociedad en el noroeste porfirista* (Culiacán: Gobierno del Estado De Sinaloa, 1991), p. 186.

25. The statistics on the export of cattle are not consistent, ranging from estimates of 400,000 for the three years 1895–97 to 620,000 in 1895 alone. *Mexican Financier*, Apr. 17, 1895, p. 133; *Mexican Herald*, Nov. 26, 1895, p. 1.

26. US State Department, *Consular Reports, Commerce and Manufacturing*, no. 210 (Mar. 1898), 300–301. The US Congress raised tariffs in response to pressure from Texas cattlemen; *Boletín de la Sociedad Agrícola Mexicana*, July 31, 1897, p. 447; *El Correo de Chihuahua*, June 30, 1904, p. 2. Luis Terrazas and Corralitos seem to have maintained a steady level of exports, however. *Mexican Investor*, Apr. 14, 1906, pp. 13–14; *Mexican Herald*, May 28, 1906, p. 3. *US Monthly Commerce and Trade Report*, no. 319 (Apr. 1907), 3; *Mexican Herald*, Feb. 9, 1906, p. 3; *El Paso Morning Times*, May 15, 1909, p. 8.

27. Hart, *Revolutionary Mexico*, p. 180.

28. Friedrich Katz, "Labor Conditions on Haciendas in Porfirian Mexico: Some Trends and Tendencies," *HAHR* 54 (Feb. 1974): 1–47.

29. Emilio Paul to Porfirio Díaz, Apr. 2, 1908, 33:00437–42, CPD.
30. Miguel Cardenas, Governor of Coahuila, to Porfirio Díaz, May 1908, 33:0005446–7, CPD.
31. President Campeche-Laguna Corporation, Feb. 7, 1919, ABF Papers, Reel 34.
32. Governor of Chiapas to Porfirio Díaz, Apr. 4, 1907, 32:004008, CPD.
33. "Informe que rende el Jefe Político del Distrito Galena con motivo de la queja que elean las vecinos de Palomas contra el representante de la Woods-Hagenbarth Land and Cattle Company," Apr. 7, 1907, 32:0080007–12, CPD.
34. Romana Falcón, *Agrarismo en Veracruz: La etapa radical (1928–1935)* (Mexico City: El Colegio de México, 1977).
35. For US relations, see Robert Freeman Smith, *The United States and Revolutionary Nationalism in Mexico, 1916–1932* (Chicago: University of Chicago Press, 1972).
36. Adrian Bantjes, *As If Jesus Walked on Earth: Cardenismo, Sonora, and the Mexican Revolution* (Wilmington, DE: Scholarly Resources, 1998); Ignacio Almada Bay, *La conexión yocupicio: Soberanía estatal y tradición cívico-liberal en Sonora, 1913–1939* (Mexico City: El Colegio de México, 2009); Dudley Ankerson, *Agrarian Warlord: Saturnino Cedillo and the Mexican Revolution in San Luis Potosí* (Dekalb: Northern Illinois University Press, 1984).
37. Josephus Daniels to Secretary of State, Oct. 15, 1936, 812.52/2027, USNARG 84.
38. *El Periódico Oficial del Estado de Chihuahua*, Feb. 3, 1934, pp. 8–9.
39. Stewart E. McMillan, American Consul, Piedras Negras, to Secretary of State, Nov. 2, 1933, 812.52/1832, USNARG 84.
40. Alberto Calzadíaz Barrera, *Dos gigantes: Sonora y Chihuahua* (Hermosillo, Sonora: Escritores Asociados del Norte, 1964), p. 201; W. W. Johnson, p. 172; *Mexican Herald*, Dec. 8, 1906, p. 11.
41. *El Periódico Oficial del Estado de Chihuahua*, Feb. 12, 1927, p. 3; and Aug. 13, 1908, p. 12; *Mexican Herald*, Mar. 25, 1907, p. 10; *El Correo de Chihuahua*, June 6, 1910, p. 1, June 7, 1910, p. 1, June 8, 1910, p. 1, July 22, 1910, p. 4; Friedrich Katz, *The Life and Times of Pancho Villa* (Stanford, CA: Stanford University Press, 1998), pp. 226–28.
42. H. C. Ferris to H. I. Miller, Feb. 22, 1912, FNO, Box 1.
43. Charles C. Cumberland, *Mexican Revolution: The Constitutionalist Years* (Austin: University of Texas Press, 1972), pp. 282–87; Katz, *Pancho Villa*, pp. 226–28.
44. There were a number of heirs. One document lists Anne M., Norman William, Ivan, and Ethel Mary Muriel. Later correspondence comes from Ian and Juan. There is also a Guillermo.
45. Los Remedios was affected by three dotaciones in 1921 and 1923 by the pueblos San Bernardino, Santa Rosalía de Cuevas, and Santa María de Cuevas, which incorporated twelve thousand acres, representing 55 percent of the agricultural land of the ranch. The Bentons lost ten thousand acres to San Lorenzo in 1926, lost another twenty-five thousand acres in 1925, and fended off yet another petition

in 1932. The ranch lost more than forty-five thousand acres to surrounding villages in 1937 and 1938.

Ian Benton to Presidente de la Comisión Local Agraria, Nov. 8, 1924, Benton File Folder 27; Ian Benton to Miembros de la Comisión Local Agraria, Jan. 24, 1925, Benton Papers, John H. McNeely Collection, University of Texas El Paso, File Folder 27. Benton contested the number of villagers eligible for land. *El Periódico Oficial del Estado de Chihuahua*, May 8, 1926, p. 9, Feb. 12, 1927, p. 3; Dec. 12, 1931, pp. 5–6; Sept. 17, 1932, p. 3; July 24, 1937, p. 587; Dec. 10, 1938, 994–95.

46. Memoranda on the Exchange of Los Remedios, Nov. 15, 1925, Benton Papers, File Folder 5.

47. Ibid.

48. Benton to Col. A. Almeida, Sept. 10, 1926, Benton Papers, File Folder 5.

49. Mary Whatley Clark, "Angus Cattle in Mexico," *The Cattleman* (Fort Worth, TX), June 1956, pp. 32–33.

50. Katz, *Pancho Villa*, p. 327.

51. Maurice F. Bauchert Correspondence, 812:5200/Bauchert, USNARG 59, Decimal Files, Internal Affairs of Mexico, 1910–1929.

52. American Investors in Land in Mexico, Chihuahua Consular District, Dec. 10, 1937, 812.52/2488, USNARG 84.

53. Reports of International Arbitral Awards, vol. 5, pp. 291–94, Captain A. B. Urmston v. United Mexican States, Aug. 6, 1931 (New York: United Nations, 2006).

54. Ibid.

55. Mark Wasserman, *Capitalists, Caciques, and Revolution: The Native Elite and Foreign Enterprise in Chihuahua, Mexico, 1854–1910* (Chapel Hill: University of North Carolina Press, 1984), p. 106. The Warren brothers owned La Palotada and another hacienda in Janos and Ascensión, hotbeds of agrarian uprisings in 1910, totaling 442,486 acres.

56. Testimony of John R. Blocker, Fall Committee Report, 1920, vol. 1, p. 1177.

57. Ibid., p. 1180.

58. Testimony of James D. Sheahan, Apr. 28, 1920, Fall Committee, vol. 2, pp. 2395–410.

59. Loucks to A. B. Fall, Sept. 22, 1919, ABFP, Reel 35; W. B. Loucks to Fall, July 18, 1919; Loucks to Fall, Sept. 22, 1919, ABF Papers, Reel 35.

60. William H. Mealy to Porfirio Díaz, Jan. 7, 1903, 28:000266–7, CPD; Mealey to Díaz, Mar. 10, 1903, 28:003224–6, CPD.

61. H. B. Tanner to Fall, Oct. 9, 1918, ABF Papers, Reel 35.

62. Louis and Edith Giroux to Secretary of State, Apr. 28, 1939, 812.5200/Louis and Edith Giroux/5, USNARG 84.

63. Frederick W. Hinke, American Consul, Mazatlán, to Secretary of State, Dec. 8, 1933, 812.614/134, USNARG 84. Morris to Secretary of State, Feb. 7, 1934, 812.614/141, USNARG 84. From his description he operated the farm with sharecroppers (for he provided loan of land, oxen, seed, and a corn ration). Letter dated July 25, 1938, 812.5200 San Cristobal Hacienda/22, USNARG 84.

64. John C. Ketcham to Secretary of State, June 23, 1928, 812.5200/796; C. K. Warren to Secretary of States, July 30, 1928, 812.5200/805, USNARG 84; *Mexican Herald*, Nov. 11, 1908, p. 5.

65. 812.52/1591, 1922, USNARG 84.

66. C. K. Warren to John C. Ketcham, Feb. 24, 1926, USNARG 84, Ciudad Juárez, 350/1926/3.

67. Dye to Secretary of State, Mar. 16, 1926, USNARG 84, 350 E. K. Warren/1926/3.

68. Ciudad Juárez, Annual Report 1926, USNARG 84.

69. Dwight Morrow to Secretary of State, Apr. 26, 1928, 812.5200/786, USNARG 84.

70. Charles P. Reiniger to Secretary of State, Nov. 9, 1938, 812.5200/Mexican American Land Co./1, USNARG 84.

71. Enclosure dated Nov. 11, 1936, American Consul Guaymas, Sonora, 812.52/2046, USNARG 84.

72. Thomas C. Romney, *The Mormon Colonies in Mexico* (Salt Lake City, UT: Deseret Book Company, 1918), pp. 45, 60; William Wallace Mills, *Forty Years in El Paso* (El Paso, TX: Carl Herzog, 1962), p. 166.

73. Florence C. Lister and Robert H. Lister, *Chihuahua: Storehouse of Storms* (Albuquerque: University of New Mexico Press, 1960), p. 194.

74. Romney, *Mormons*, p. 60; Lister and Lister, *Chihuahua*, p. 195. The Gómez de Campo were related to the Terrazas. The Gómez del Campo property was of poorer quality.

75. Romney, *Mormons*, pp. 57–59; Lister and Lister, *Chihuahua*, pp. 192–93; Annie R. Johnson, *Heartbreak of Colonia Díaz* (Mesa, AZ: Annie R. Johnson, 1972), pp. 44–46.

76. Lister and Lister, *Chihuahua*, p. 197.

77. Romney, *Mormons*, pp. 62, 65–66, 93, 95–96, 111, 113; *Mexican Herald*, Aug. 7, 1896, p. 2, and Sept. 5, 1907, p. 4.

78. Romney, *Mormons*, p. 144. B. Carmon Hardy, "Cultural Encystment as a Cause of the Mormon Exodus from Mexico," *Pacific Historical Review* 34 (Nov. 1965): 439–54, argues that the colonists' isolation caused deep resentment and led to hostility among the locals.

79. Jason Dormady, "Rights, Rule, and Religion: Old Colony Mennonites and Mexico's Transition to the Free Market, 1920–2000," in *Religious Culture in Modern Mexico*, ed. Martin Nesvig (New York: Rowman and Littlefield, 2007), pp. 157–77, provides the major source for the narrative on the Mennonites. What follows is a summary of his work, much of which is taken from Harry Leonard Sawatsky, *They Sought a Country: Mennonite Colonization in Mexico* (Berkeley: University of California Press, 1971).

80. These were the Presidential Decree of January 27, 1921, on immigration and the Provisional Law for Concession of Exemptions to Colonists.

81. The agrarians tried again in 1941 and 1947.

82. Noé G. Palomares Peña, *Proprietarios norteamericanos y reforma agraria en Chihuahua, 1917–1942* (Ciudad Juárez: Universidad Autonoma de Ciudad Juárez, 1991), pp. 111–12.

83. Agrarian Law of Chihuahua, 1922, in USNARG 84, 812.52/924.

84. James B. Barker, "The Beginnings of the Hearst Estate and the Mexican Revolution," http://www.texanculture.utsa.edu/memories/htms/Barker_transcript.htm, p 2.

85. W. A. Swanberg, *Citizen Hearst: A Biography of William Randolph Hearst* (New York: Scribner, 1961), pp. 32, 190, 191.

86. Barker, "Beginnings," p. 13.

87. Ibid., 14.

88. Machado, "Destruction," p. 12. The ranch had between twenty and sixty thousand head of cattle.

89. JJP to R, Home Smith, Oct. 3, 1916, FNOM, Box 4.

90. Dye to Secretary of State, Jan. 20, 1922, USNARG 84, 810.8/1922/5.

91. Palomares, *Proprietarios norteamericanos*, pp. 116–17.

92. Dye to Secretary of State, Oct. 17, 1922, USNARG 84 1910–1929, 862.2/1922/7. It is not clear what happened to the other fifty thousand head.

93. William M. Ferris, Manager, to Ing. Rafael Rico G., 8 Feb. 1926, USNARG 84 812.5200/Babicora/ 4; Ferris to Secretaría de Relaciones Exteriores, 25 Oct. 1926, 812.5200 /Babicora/4; "Ferris Memorandum," p. 16.

94. *El Paso Times*, June 22, 1923, p. 8.

95. Obregón to Ferris, 1924, "Ferris Memorandum," p. 18.

96. *El Periódico Oficial del Estado de Chihuahua*, Oct. 25, 1924, pp. 2–4.

97. Governor Orozco to Calles, Jan. 1, 1928, AGN-Ramo Presidentes-OC, 104-N-18.

98. "Ferris Memorandum," p. 19. The documentation necessary to prove the validity of the estate's ownership proved difficult to assemble, for they were scattered over several repositories in Chihuahua and California. Some had been destroyed.

99. R. P. Denegri to Fernando González Roa, Ferris Memorandum, p. 21.

100. Robert E. Olds to Dwight Morrow, US Ambassador, Feb. 25, 1928, USNARG 84 812.5200/Babicora/5.

101. Thomas McEnally to Morrow, Mar. 12, 1928, USNARG 84, 812.5200/Babicora/16. Fernando Orozco to Calles, Mar. 13, 1928, AGN, Ramo Presidentes-OC, 818-CH-23.

102. Machado, *North Mexican*, p. 34.

103. Ibid., p. 35.

104. Ibid.

105. Peckham to Secretary of State, USNARG 84, 812.5200/Babicora/24; W. J. McCafferty to Secretary of State, Aug. 6, 1929, USNARG 84, 812.5200/Babicora/29.

106. Palomares, *Proprietarios norteamericanos*, p. 118.

107. Ibid.
108. Rodrigo Quevedo to Cardenas, AGN, Presidentes, Cardenas, 404.1/5156.
109. Frank Dobie, "Babicora," *American Hereford Journal*, Jan. 1, 1954, p. 4.
110. *El Periódico Oficial del Estado de Chihuahua*, Feb. 23, 1935, 139.
111. Ibid., Mar. 23, 1935, p. 209.
112. Ibid., Aug. 3, 1935, p. 574.
113. Enrique Entive, Presidente de la Comité Ejidal de San Rafael de Manzanas, Matachic, to Cárdenas, Sept. 10, 1936, AGN, Cárdenas, 403/419.
114. Political Situation in Ciudad Juárez, Aug. 1938, USNARG 59, Internal Affairs of Mexico, 1930–39, 812/Chihuahua/310.
115. *El Periódico Oficial del Estado de Chihuahua*, Jan. 12, 1938, p. 52; Jan. 22, 1938, p. 16; May 21, 1938, p. 380; May 28, 1938, p. 399.
116. PSP to Richard A. Clark, Sept. 26, 1938, and PSP to Jefe de Departamento de Agraria, Aug. 20, 1938, AGN, Presidentes, Cardenas, 404.1/5156 Memorandum; Aug. 12, 1938, AGN, Presidentes, Cardenas, 404.1/5156.
117. Roberto Pliego to President, July 29, 1939, AGN, Presidentes, Cárdenas, 404.1/5156.
118. Cuauhtemoc Mendoza, Secretary Organización de Liga de Comunidades Agraria Ing. Antonio Dehesa, to President, Apr. 17, 1939, AGN, Presidentes, Cárdenas, 404.1/5156 *El Periódico Oficial del Estado de Chihuahua*, Sept. 2, 1939, p. 660.
119. Palomares, *Proprietarios norteamericanos*, p. 120.
120. Ibid., p. 130.
121. Barker, "Beginnings," p. 4.
122. Epitacio Armedariz to President, Dec. 31, 1938, AGN Presidentes, Cárdenas, 104/10271; Ferris to Obregón, Mar. 6, 1924, "Ferris Memorandum," p. 16.
123. *Mexican Herald*, Jan. 2, 1907, p. 10; *South American Journal*, Sept. 25, 1909, p. 344.
124. *Mexican Herald*, Aug. 29, 1909, p. 3.
125. Ibid. *El Periódico Oficial del Estado de Chihuahua*, Feb. 24, 1923, pp. 4ff. Luis Huller and Woods-Hagenbarth were subsequent owners.
126. *Mexican Herald*, June 19, 1906, p. 1.
127. Memorandum on Land Invasion of Palomas, Aug. 1921, AGN, Presidentes, Obregón-Calles, 811-P-22.
128. Wasserman, *Persistent Oligarchs*.
129. *El Paso Morning Times*, Oct. 14, 1921, p. 3.
130. Memorandum on Land Invasion of Palomas, Aug. 1921, AGN, Presidentes, Obregón-Calles, 811-P-22; Memorandum para Acuerdo Presidencial, 1936, AGN, Presidentes, Cárdenas, 501/744.
131. Obregón to Ramón P. Negri, Subsecretario de Agricultura, Feb. 15, 1923, AGN, Presidentes, Obregon-Calles, 818-P-24.
132. E. J. Marshall, President Palomas Land and Cattle Company, to Obregón, June 29, 1923, AGN, Presidentes, Obregón-Calles, 818-P-24.

133. *El Paso Morning Times,* Mar. 21, 1923, p. 8.

134. *El Periódico Oficial del Estado de Chihuahua,* Sept. 23, 1933, p. 2.

135. Ibid., Sept. 25, 1926, p. 3.

136. Ibid., July 7, 1926, p. 8.

137. Ibid., Oct. 8, 1932, pp. 2ff. The property had become successful by then grazing forty to fifty thousand head of cattle, shipping thirteen to fourteen thousand a year to market. George P. Shaw, American Consul, Ciudad Juárez, June 30, 1938, USNARG 84, 812.52/29012.

138. Memorandum para Acuerdo Presidencial, 1936, AGN, Presidentes, Cárdenas, 501/744.

139. *El Periódico Oficial del Estado de Chihuahua,* Mar. 2, 1938, pp. 238, 241. Resume of the Political Situation in Ciudad Juárez, Oct. 1939, 812/Chihuahua/380, USNARG 84; *El Periódico Oficial del Estado de Chihuahua,* Sept. 11, 1937, p. 737; Machado, *North Mexican,* pp. 55–56.

140. Machado, *North Mexican,* pp. 55–56. The expropriation was before the Mexican Supreme Court in 1950. Palomares Peña, *Proprietarios Norteamericanos,* p. 48.

141. Daniel Jones, *Forty Years Among the Indians* (Los Angeles: Westernlore Press, 1962), pp. 261, 335, 357, 360.

142. *El Periódico Oficial del Estado de Chihuahua,* Oct. 28, 1909, 16; *El Paso Morning Times,* Aug. 5, 1909, p. 3.

143. *Mexican Financier,* Aug. 23, 1884, p. 327.

144. Ibid., June 5, 1886, p. 156.

145. Ibid., Jan. 12, 1889, p. 365; and Mar. 22, 1890, p. 634.

146. Charles W. Kindrick to W. R. Day, Assistant Secretary of State, Jan. 11, 1898, USNARG 59, Consular Reports, Chihuahua City.

147. Lister and Lister, *Chihuahua,* p. 191; *El Correo de Chihuahua,* Apr. 27, 1904, p. 1; Lawrence Douglas Taylor Hansen, "La colonización Boer en Chihuahua," *Historia Mexicana* 52:2 (2003): 449–89.

148. *Mexican Herald,* Nov. 11, 1907, p. 9.

149. Nelson Rhodes, Vice President, Sinaloa Land Company, to Porfirio Díaz, June 1, 1908, 33:007017, CPD. And Sinaloa Land Co. to Porfirio Díaz, June 1, 1908, 33: 007023–5, CPD.

150. *El Paso Morning Times,* Sept. 21, 1909, p. 1.

151. "Data Pertinent to Titles of Properties of the Cía. Constructora Richardson," Compañía Constructora Richardson, S.A., Ms. 113, Box 1, Folder 2, University of Arizona Library.

152. Information Letter, Richardson Construction Company, May 20, 1907, Compañía Constructora Richardson, S.A., Ms. 113, Box 1, Folder 3.

153. Ibid. Richardson obtained the assets of the Sonora and Sinaloa Irrigation Company. The holdings included 330,000 acres of prime cultivable land and 80,500 acres of timberlands. The timber alone was reportedly worth US$1.5 million. The remaining 220,000 acres were excellent grazing lands.

154. Ibid.

155. "Data Pertinent to Titles of Properties of the Cía. Constructora Richardson," Compañía Constructora Richardson, S.A., Ms. 113, Box 1, Folder 2, University of Arizona Library.

156. "Background material on irrigation development of the Yaqui Valley, Sonora, Mexico, and the sale of the project to the Mexican government." Chandler P. Ward, Jan. 24, 1968, Compañía Constructora Richardson, S.A., Ms 113, Box 1, Folder 1, University of Arizona Library.

157. Ibid.

158. Ibid.

159. Ibid.

160. *Mexican Herald*, July 5, 1907, p. 11.

161. Ibid., Sept. 17, 1907, p. 3.

162. Lister, *Storehouse of Storms*, p. 178.

163. *Mexican Herald*, Sept. 18, 1907, p. 11.

164. Ibid., Feb. 11, 1908, p. 5; and Feb. 18, 1908, p. 11.

165. Ibid., Sept. 18, 1907, 11. Three hundred were North Americans, *Mexican Herald*, July 16, 1907, p. 10.

166. Leo J. Keene to Secretary of State, Dec. 2, 1909, USNA, Case no. 1416418; El Correo de Chihuahua, Aug. 3, 1908, p. 1. The company had to call in the Rurales to ensure protection; *El Correo de Chihuahua*, Aug. 3, 1908, p. 1.

167. *South American Journal*, Oct. 9, 1909, p. 399, July 23, 1910, p. 89, Apr. 23, 1910, p. 456, and Nov. 20, 1909, p. 575; *Mexican Herald*, Mar. 9, 1909, p. 10; *South American Journal*, Oct. 9, 1909, p. 399 and July 23, 1910, p. 89; *Mexican Herald*, Mar. 9, 1909, 10. The *South American Journal* concluded that Pearson's timber operations were exceedingly profitable. *South American Journal*, Oct. 9, 1909, p. 401.

168. J. F. Hulse, *Railroads and Revolutions: The Story of Roy Hoard* (El Paso, TX: Mangan Books, 1986), p. 43.

169. Ibid., pp. 44–46.

170. J. G. Crockett to H. I. Miller, Vice President, Mexico Northwestern Railway, May 15, 1915, Box 4, FNOM papers, BLAC.

171. Hulse, *Railroads and Revolution*, p. 52.

172. Ibid., pp. 68–73.

173. Ibid., pp. 87–88.

174. Ibid., pp. 106–7.

175. *El Periódico Oficial del Estado de Chihuahua*, Sept. 9, 1933, pp. 4–5.

176. Summary of Political Situation in Ciudad Juárez, Aug. 1937, 812.00/Ch/281, USNARG 84.

177. Hulse, *Railroads and Revolution*, p. 116.

178. *El Periódico Oficial del Estado de Chihuahua*, Oct. 12, 1935, p. 837. In 1935 Cargill lost 4,551 hectares.

179. Ibid., Feb. 3 1940, p. 73.

180. C. E. Sheahan to Fred Hartley, Nov. 4, 1942, 812.5200 International Land and Cattle Company/5; and Green H. Hackworth to James R. Garfield, June 10,

1939, 812.5200 International Land and Cattle Company/3, USNARG 84. This was comprised of the Hacienda de Corrales, bought by Sheahan from the Faudoa family, with 146,497 hectares. 812.52/1591, USNARG 84, 1922.

181. American Consul Durango to Secretary of State, Oct. 13, 1938, 812.5200 Durango Land and Timber Company/2, USNARG 84. The operation employed thirty-five hundred workers.

Chapter 5

1. A number of historians have explored aspects of the story of the Corralitos Company: see George E. Paulsen, "Reaping the Whirlwind in Chihuahua: The Destruction of the Minas de Corralitos, 1911–1917," *New Mexico Historical Quarterly* 58:3 (1983): 253–55; Linda B. Hall, "Obregón and the Politics of Land Reform, 1920–1924," *Hispanic American Historical Review* 60:2 (May 1980): 233–37; John Mason Hart, *Empire and Revolution: Americans in Mexico Since the Civil War* (Berkeley: University of California Press, 2002), pp. 177, 189, 291, 359–62.

2. Paulsen, "Reaping," pp. 253–55. Memorandum of E. C. Houghton to the President of the Republic of Mexico, Dec. 24, 1921, Mexico, Archivo General de la Nación, Ramo Presidentes, Obregón-Calles, 818-C-49, E. C. Houghton to Ministerio de Agricultura y Fomento, Oct. 21, 1921, AGNRP, Obregón-Calles, 818-C-49. Corralitos bought the land in 1880 and the Secretario de Fomento had approved the titles in 1885.

3. There is some confusion about when Morgan founded the Candelaria Company. According to Jane-Dale Lloyd, *Cinco ensayos sobre cultura material de rancheros y medieros de noroeste de Chihuahua, 1886–1910* (Mexico City: Universidad de Iberoamericana, 2001), p. 59, citing the *Periódico Oficial del Estado de Chihuahua*, June 7, 1884, p. 25, the company commenced operations in 1884; Paulsen, "Reaping," claims 1889.

4. Paulsen, "Reaping," p. 255.

5. Ing. José Castanedo, "El Distrito de Corralitos del Estado de Chihuahua," *Boletín Minero* 24:3 (Sept. 1927): 162–67. According to Morris B. Parker, *Mules, Mines, and Me in Mexico, 1895–1933* (Tucson: University of Arizona Press, 1979), p. 29, in 1898 Candelaria had been "slipping for some time," and US$45,000 in the red.

6. Paulsen, "Reaping," p. 257.

7. Lloyd, *Cinco ensayos*, p. 61. All the statistics were taken from Chihuahua, *Anuario estadisticas del Estado de Chihuahua*, 1905, pp. 93–95; 1906, p. 229; and 1907, pp. 136–40.

8. Lloyd, *Cinco ensayos*, p. 84.

9. Candelaria Mining Company to Olegario Molina, Ministerio de Comunicaciones y Obras Públicas, Nov. 29, 1909, Papers of Thomas W. Peirce, Box 2, Nettie Lee Benson Latin American Collection, University of Texas at Austin. That equaled a 797,453 pesos loss. Laird wrote in 1909 that the company store,

presumably for its workers, was quite profitable, returning 100 percent of the money invested in it. George A. Laird to A. S. Dwight, Feb. 26, 1909, Peirce Papers.

10. A. S. Dwight to Laird, Mar. 6, 1909, Peirce Papers, Box 2. Laird's letters in 1909 in Box 2 provide a rundown of these problems.

11. Paulsen, "Reaping," pp. 259–60.

12. Ibid., p. 260. Paulsen, working with US consular dispatches and the Records of the United States and Mexican Claims Commission provides the narrative for the years 1910 to 1920.

13. E. C. Houghton to E. D. Morgan, Oct. 10, 1915, Peirce Papers.

14. Paulsen, "Reaping," p. 261.

15. Ibid.

16. Notice of Chancery Court Decree in New Jersey, June 18, 1917, Peirce Papers.

17. Paulsen, "Reaping," p. 263.

18. E. D. Morgan to Thomas W. Peirce, Sept. 21, 1906, Peirce Papers. Greene offered US$500,000 cash and the rest over five years.

19. Peirce to Morgan, Oct. 12, 1906, Peirce Papers. Morgan claimed the property to be worth more than US$1.5 million.

20. Morgan to Peirce, Oct. 1, 1907, Peirce Papers.

21. E. C. Houghton, General Manager, the Corralitos Company to the Members of the National Association for the Protection of American Rights in Mexico, Apr. 30, 1919, Peirce Papers.

22. Charles A. Dana to Thomas W. Peirce, Mar. 27, 1911, Peirce Papers.

23. E. D. Morgan, President, Report to the Directors of the Corralitos Company, Apr. 3, 1911, Peirce Papers.

24. E. C. Houghton, General Manager, the Corralitos Company to the Members of the National Association for the Protection of American Rights in Mexico, Apr. 30, 1919. Peirce Papers.

25. E. C. Houghton to E. D. Morgan, Feb. 3, 1913, Peirce Papers 110–1.

26. Ibid.

27. The Corralitos Company, Treasurer's Report of Receipts and Disbursements, Jan. 1, 1913, to Dec. 31, 1913, Peirce Papers. J. O. Crockett to H. I. Miller, Apr. 29, 1913, Ferrocarril Noroeste de Mexico Papers, Box 3, reported that Salazar "completely looted the ranch, taking 100 horses."

28. E. D. Morgan to President and Stockholders, Apr. 3, 1914, Peirce Papers.

29. Ibid., Sept. 15, 1914, Peirce Papers.

30. Ibid., Mar. 11, 1915, Peirce Papers.

31. E. C. Houghton to E. D. Morgan, Oct. 10, 1915, Peirce Papers.

32. E. D. Morgan to T. W. Peirce, Nov. 29, 1915, Peirce Papers 155. Morgan paid the tax on only four thousand head.

33. E. C. Houghton to E. D. Morgan, Mar. 29, 1916, Peirce Papers 110. E. C. Houghton, General Manager, the Corralitos Company to the Members of the National Association for the Protection of American Rights in Mexico, Apr. 30, 1919. Peirce Papers, NLB Collection, UTA.

34. E. D. Morgan to Raynal Bolling, President, June 4, 1916, Peirce Papers.

35. Annual Report of the Corralitos Company for the Year Ended December 31, 1917, Peirce Papers, NLBC, UTA.

36. Ibid.

37. E. C. Houghton to E. Shearson, Sept. 17, 1917, Peirce Papers.

38. Ibid., Oct. 22, 1917, Peirce Papers.

39. Ibid., Dec. 13, 1917, Peirce Papers.

40. Ibid., Jan. 20, 1919, Peirce Papers.

41. Ibid., Jan. 12, 1921, Peirce Papers.

42. Memorandum of E. C. Houghton to the President of the Republic of Mexico, Dec. 24, 1921, México, Archivo General de la Nación, Ramo Presidentes, Obregón-Calles, 818-C-49. See also Linda B. Hall, "Obregón and the Politics of Land Reform, pp. 233–37.

43. Ibid. E. C. Houghton to Ministerio de Agricultura y Fomento, Oct. 21, 1921, AGNRP, Obregón-Calles, 818-C-49.

44. E. D. Morgan, Minutes of Meeting March 2, 1921, Peirce Papers; *El Paso Morning Times*, July 19, 1921, p. 12 and July 27, 1921, p. 12 reported the two hundred families of squatters on sixteen thousand acres.

45. William W. Cook to Edwin D. Morgan, Mar. 19, 1921.

46. E. C. Houghton to Shearson, Oct. 25, 1921, Peirce Papers 146.

47. E. C. Houghton to John W. Dye, American Consul in Ciudad Juárez, Nov. 10, 1921, USNARG 84, 810.81/1921/4.

48. E. C. Houghton to Shearson, Jan. 16, 1922, Peirce Papers, 110E.

49. Minutes of the Meeting of the Directors of the Corralitos Company Held at the Offices of Shearing Hammill and Company, Nov. 3, 1922, Peirce Papers. E. Shearson to Peirce, Nov. 10, 1923, Peirce Papers.

50. E. C. Houghton to Alvaro Obregón, Apr. 12, 1923: Obregón to José Acosta Rivera, Gobernador Interino del Estado de Chihuahua, Apr. 12, 1923; Acosta to Obregón, Apr. 12, 1923, AGNRP, Obregón-Calles, 818-C-49. Casas Grandes had filed its petition before the Comisión Local Agraria on Nov. 15, 1921. The *Periódico Oficial del Estado* de Chihuahua announced the provisional restitution on March 27, 1923.

51. Alvaro Obregón to Houghton, Apr. 19, 1923, AGNRP, Obregón-Calles, 818-C-49.

52. "... con absolute apego ley y que trátase de una reinvindicación terrenos que fuéron le quitados al pueblo—Casas Grandes." Alvaro Obregón to Houghton, Apr. 13, 1923, AGN, Obregón-Calles, 818-C-49. The expediente includes a copy of the *Periódico Oficial del Gobierno del Estado de Chihuahua*, March 31, 1923.

53. Private Secretary to Subsecretario de Agricultura y Fomento, June 18, 1923; Alvaro Obregón to I. C. Enríquez, June 15, 1923; Obregón to Enríquez, June 16, 1923, AGNRP, Obregón-Calles 818-C-49.

54. E. C. Houghton to Alvaro Obregón, Oct. 23, 1924; Houghton to Obregón, July 5, 1924; Obregón to Houghton, July 15, 1923, AGNRP, Obregón-Calles, 818-C-49.

55. Edward Shearson to Board, Sept. 18, 1922, Peirce Papers, Box 2. One might ask why anyone would buy the ranch, given its legal difficulties. In the case of the Newman firm, speculators were taking a calculated risk. The others, of course, were ultimately unwilling to purchase compromised property.

56. Minutes of Board of Directors, Corralitos Company, Nov. 20, 1922, Peirce Papers.

57. White and Case to Board of Directors of the Corralitos Company, Nov. 3, 1923, Peirce Papers.

58. J. Almeida, Governor of Chihuahua to Plutarco Elías Calles, Jan. 12, 1926: Fernando Orozco to Calles, Apr. 12, 1926; Orozco to Calles, Apr. 2, 1926, AGNRP, Obregón-Calles 818-C-49.

59. Plutarco Elías Calles to Fernando Orozco, Apr. 21, 1926, AGNRP, Obregón-Calles, 818-C-49.

60. *Periódico Oficial del Estado de Chihuahua*, Jan. 12, 1929, p. 24.

61. Ibid., Aug. 22, 1931, pp. 29–30.

62. Ibid., Sept. 30, 1933, p. 2.

63. US Department of State, American and Mexican Claims Commission, *Report to the Secretary of State, 1948*, pp. 201–8; *El Periódico Oficial del Estado de Chihuahua*, Feb. 3, 1934, p. 13.

64. *Periódico Oficial del Estado de Chihuahua*, Mar. 6, 1937, 205.

65. Parker, *Mules*, p. 159. Quevedo was governor of Chihuahua from 1932 to 1936. He headed the Chihuahuan underworld during the 1930s and also became one of the largest landowners in the state. See Hart, *Empire*, pp. 360–61. Wallace had been the foreman of the ranch. The Wallaces held thirty-five thousand acres at least until the 1980s.

66. Seelig to Shearson, Feb. 11, 1919, Peirce Papers.

67. Paulsen, "Reaping," p. 258.

68. Ibid., pp. 255–56.

69. E. D. Morgan to General A. Villarreal, Secretario de Agricultura y Fomento, Feb. 15, 1921, AGN-RP, Obregón-Calles, 818-C-49.

70. Parker, *Mining*, pp. 22, 150–52. Davis became president of the subsidiary Aventurera Mining Company in 1902. He resigned from Corralitos in 1906. *El Paso Times*, Apr. 15, 1935. Davis had his own property in the region and lived in El Paso. He may not have devoted all his time to the management of Corralitos.

71. Parker, *Mules*, p. 22.

72. Ibid., p. 30.

73. Manuel A. Machado Jr., *The North Mexican Cattle Industry, 1910–1975: Ideology, Conflict, and Change* (College Station: Texas A&M University Press, 1981), p. 5.

74. *Mexican Herald*, Mar. 11, 1896, p. 3.

75. Machado, *North Mexican*, p. 8.

76. Houghton to Morgan, Dec. 15, 1911, Peirce Papers, Box 2.

77. Machado, *North Mexican*, p. 28.

78. Ibid., p. 32.

79. Ibid., p. 33.

80. Ibid., pp. 39, 127–28.

81. Lloyd, *Cinco ensayos*, pp. 60–61. The RG, SM, & P was 156 miles long in 1904 and connected the Mormon colonies, ending at Estación Terrazas. The successor company built the line from Casas Grandes to Madera in 1910. C. L. Sonnichsen, *Colonel Greene and the Copper Skyrocket* (Tucson: University of Arizona Press, 1974), pp. 156–57. Francisco R. Calderón, "Los ferrocarriles," El porfiriato, *La vida económica*, vol. 7, pt. 1, *Historia moderna de México*, ed. Daniel Cosío Villegas (Mexico City: Editorial Hermes, 1965), pp. 563–64.

82. Paulsen, "Reaping," 258; *Engineering and Mining Journal* 57 (Apr. 28, 1894): 400; 86 (Nov. 21, 1908): 1031; 87 (June 5, 1909): 1159; 91 (Jan. 7, 1911): 72; *Mexican Mining Journal*, May 1910.

83. Calderón, "Ferrocarriles," 582–83.

84. Candelaria Mining Company to Olegario Molina, Ministerio de Comunicaciones y Obras Públicas, Nov. 29, 1909, Peirce Papers.

85. Ibid.

86. Parker, *Mules*, p. 32.

87. Lloyd, *Cinco ensayos*, pp. 59–60.

88. Parker, *Mules*, p. 33.

89. Paulsen, "Reaping," p. 257; Donald F. Roberts, "Mining and Modernization: The Mexican Border States during the Porfiriato, 1876–1911" (PhD diss., University of Pittsburgh, 1974), p. 245.

90. Lloyd, *Cinco ensayos*, pp. 62–63.

91. Ibid., p. 65.

92. Parker, *Mules*, 33–34.

93. E. D. Morgan to General A. Villarreal, Secretario de Agricultura y Fomento, February 15, 1921, AGN-RP, Obregón-Calles, 818-C-49.

94. Parker, *Mules*, 32, 34.

95. Dwight to Morgan, May 21, 1909, Peirce Papers, Box 2.

96. Laird to Dwight, July 30, 1909, Peirce Papers, Box 2.

97. Parker, *Mules*, p. 33.

98. George A. Laird to Dwight, Feb. 23, 1910, Peirce Papers, Box 2.

99. The Corralitos Company Treasurer's Report of Receipts and Disbursements, Jan. 1, 1911, to Dec. 31, 1911, Peirce Papers.

100. E. D. Morgan to Raynal Bolling, President, June 4, 1916, Peirce Papers.

101. Houghton to Ministro de Agricultura y Fomento, Oct. 21, 1921, AGNRP, Obregón-Calles, 818-C-49.

102. C. I. Reeves to Peirce, Jan. 20, 1914, Peirce Papers.

103. *Mexican Financier*, Dec. 15, 1888, p. 157.

104. Lloyd, *Cinco ensayos*, p. 60.

105. Parker, *Mules*, p. 43.

106. George A. Laird, Manager, to Dwight, Feb. 17, 1910, Peirce Papers, Box 2.

107. Report of E. D. Morgan to the Board of Directors of The Corralitos Company, Nov. 8, 1911. Peirce Papers. The second half of the report covers from 1900 to 1911.

108. C. S. Reeves to Peirce, Nov. 21, 1910, and Jan. 25, 1911, Peirce Papers.
109. E. C. Houghton to E. D. Morgan, Feb. 3, 1913, Peirce Papers 110–1.
110. Ibid.
111. Houghton to Morgan, Jan. 7, 1914, attached to Reeves to Peirce, Jan. 20, 1914, Peirce Papers.
112. E. E. Morgan to the President and Stockholders, Sept. 15, 1914, Peirce Papers.
113. E. C. Houghton to Shearson, Jan. 20, 1919, Peirce Papers.
114. Report of E. D. Morgan to the Board of Directors of The Corralitos Company, Nov. 8, 1911, Peirce Papers. This includes a report from Houghton covering 1895 to 1900.
115. E. D. Morgan, President, Report to the Directors of the Corralitos Company, Apr. 3, 1911, Peirce Papers.
116. Ibid.
117. Ibid.
118. John W. Peirce to John Mason Hart, Apr. 9, 1984, John Mason Hart Collection.
119. E. C. Houghton to Edward Shearson, Jan. 17, 1921, Peirce Papers.
120. Memorandum of E. C. Houghton to the President of the Republic of Mexico, Dec. 24, 1921, AGNRP, Obregón-Calles, 818-C-49. The pueblo, according to Houghton had only 120 heads of household and was thus claiming far more land than allowed by law.
121. Ibid.
122. John W. Peirce to John Mason Hart, Apr. 9, 1984, John Mason Hart Collection.
123. E. C. Houghton to Edward Shearson, Jan. 17, 1921, Peirce Papers.
124. E. C. Houghton to John W. Dye, American Consul in Ciudad Juárez, Nov. 10, 1921, USNARG 84, 810.81/1921/4.
125. Memorandum of E. C. Houghton to the President of the Republic of Mexico, Dec. 24, 1921, AGNRP, Obregón-Calles, 818-C-49.
126. E. C. Houghton to Edward Shearson, Jan. 17, 1921, Peirce Papers.
127. E. D. Morgan, Minutes of Meeting Mar. 2, 1921, Peirce Papers.
128. Ibid.
129. E. C. Houghton to Edward Shearson, Jan. 16, 1922, Peirce Papers, 110E.
130. Ibid.
131. Ibid.
132. Ibid.
133. Hall, "Land Reform," p. 235.
134. Ibid., p. 236. The *El Paso Times*, Dec. 13, 1923, reported that the company requested that the state government remove the squatters, who had settled the land three years ago.
135. Hall, "Land Reform," p. 236.
136. Ibid.; Orozco to Calles, Apr. 2, 1926, AGNRP, Obregón-Calles, 818-C-49.

137. Meeting of Directors of the Corralitos Company, Aug. 7, 1922, Peirce Papers, 110E.

138. William Phillips, Acting Secretary of State to the Corralitos Company, Sept. 14, 1922, Peirce Papers.

139. John W. Peirce to John Mason Hart, Apr. 9, 1984, John Mason Hart Collection.

140. Mark Wasserman, *Capitalists, Caciques, and Revolution: The Native Elite and Foreign Enterprise in Chihuahua, Mexico, 1854–1911* (Chapel Hill: University of North Carolina Press, 1984), p. 44.

Chapter 6

1. The standard study of Mexican mining remains Marvin D. Bernstein, *The Mexican Mining Industry, 1890–1950: A Study of the Interaction of Politics, Economics, and Technology* (Albany: State University of New York Press, 1964). See also Donald F. Roberts, "Mining and Modernization: The Mexican Border States during the Porfiriato, 1876–1911" (PhD diss., University of Pittsburgh, 1974).

2. *Engineering and Mining Journal* (*EMJ*) 89 (Jan. 8, 1910): 117; *Mining Magazine, Feb.* 1910, p. 112.

3. C. L. Sonnichsen, *Colonel Greene and the Copper Skyrocket* (Tucson: University of Arizona Press, 1974).

4. *EMJ* 89 (Jan. 8, 1910): 117.

5. This was according to Ramón Corral, a leader of the hated triumvirate that ruled the state of Sonora during the last decade of the Porfiriato; see Ramón Eduardo Ruíz, *The People of Sonora and the Yankee Capitalists* (Tucson: University of Arizona Press, 1988), p. 71.

6. Ruíz, *Sonora*, p. 71.

7. Ibid.

8. Marvin D. Bernstein, *The Mexican Mining Industry, 1890–1950* (Albany: State University of New York Press, 1964).

9. "The Effect of the Revolution on American-Mexican Mining Interests: May Operations Be Resumed?" Memorandum submitted on behalf of forty-five companies to the American-Mexican Claims Commission, Sept. 1916, pp. 9–10.

10. Ibid., pp. 11–12.

11. Ibid., p. 14.

12. Ibid, p. 15.

13. Ibid.

14. Ibid., p. 8.

15. Ibid., p. 15.

16. J. D. Hubbard to Stockholders, Dec. 20, 1909, Box 15, Folder 4, Papers of Frank O. Lowden, Regenstein Library, University of Chicago.

17. R. B., "The Situation in Mexico," *EMJ* 95 (Jan. 25, 1913): 241–42.

18. Arnold Hoffman, "Towne Mines Corporation: A Short History" (unpub. manuscript, 1954), p. 12.

19. E. P. Ryan, General Manager, to C. V. Brennan, Britannia Mining and Smelting Company, May 15, 1930, El Potosi Mining Company, Box 2, Folder 9, Correspondence 1929–30.

20. *EMJ* 115 (1923): 504.

21. John Leroy Drug, "Engineer Tells of Prospects in Yaqui Country," *EMJ* 116 (Oct. 27, 1923): 719–20.

22. *EMJ* 99 (1915): 463.

23. *EMJ* 122 (1926): 940–41.

24. "The High Cost of Mining in Nayarit," *EMJ* 127 (Feb. 23, 1929): 524.

25. Anonymous, "Bolshevism in Mexico," *EMJ* 109:21 (May 22, 1920): 1152–53.

26. *EMJ* (May 22, 1915): 912.

27. John E. Kelly, "The Naica Controversy," *EMJ* 111 (Feb. 12, 1921): 320–21; Rafael Martínez Carrillo to *EMJ*, *EMJ* 111 (Apr. 2, 1921), 576–77; "The Naica Case," *EMJ* 111 (July 1921): 816; Henry Bruere to *EMJ*, *EMJ* 111:24 (July 1921): 976.

28. *Chihuahua Enterprise*, July 13, 1907, and July 20, 1907 in CGPD, Doc. 32:007534–5; Memorandum to Porfirio Díaz about the Minas de Dolores, CGPD, Docs. 32:007837–4. See also the court documents in Doc. 32:0078747–58.

29. *Mexican Financier*, Aug. 1, 1885, p. 285, and Oct. 24, 1891, p. 105; *EMJ* 35 (1883): 116; 43 (1887): 101; 47 (1889): 98; and 53 (1892): 387.

30. W. Frisbee Jr., San Carlos Copper Company, to Porfirio Díaz, Dec. 2, 1902, Colección General Porfirio Díaz (CGPD), Universidad Iberoamericana, Mexico City, Document 27:015444.

31. Eusebio Carrillo to Porfirio Díaz, Mar. 6, 1908, CGPD, Doc. 33:003959–60.

32. *Mexican Herald*, Apr. 9, 1896, p. 7.

33. Ibid., Nov. 6, 1910, p. 2.

34. John R. Southworth, *Official Directory of Mines and Estates of Mexico* (Mexico City: John R. Southworth, 1910), p. 76; *Mexican Herald*, Feb. 24, 1910, p. 913; *Mexican Mining Journal* XI (Aug. 1910): 10.

35. Fletcher Toomer, *Report on the Parral and Durango Railroad Company's Properties and the Hidalgo Mining Company's Properties Parral, Mexico* (London: Waterlow Brothers and Layton, 1905), p. 92.

36. *EMJ* 53 (Feb. 6, 1892): 191. The mill earned US$54,000 and the mines US$62,000.

37. *Mexican Herald*, Mar. 9, 1896, p. 2.

38. S. E. Gill, "Mineral District of Hidalgo de Parral," *EMJ* 63 (May 22, 1897): 509.

39. *EMJ* 71 (June 22, 1901): 794.

40. *EMJ* 78 (Dec. 8, 1904): 924.

41. Toomer, *Report*, p. 36. James I. Long to W. W. Mills, Apr. 15, 1905, USNARG 59, Dispatches of US Consuls, Chihuahua City. W. W. Mills to Francis B. Loomis, Assistant Secretary of State, Mar. 23, 1903, USNARG 59, Dispatches of the Consuls of the United States, 1854–1906, Ciudad Chihuahua.

42. Toomer, *Report*, p. 91. *EMJ* 72 (Oct. 12, 1901): 456.

43. W. W. Mills to Francis B. Loomis, Assistant Secretary of State, Mar. 23, 1903, USNARG 59, Dispatches of the Consuls of the United States, 1854–1906, Ciudad Chihuahua.

44. Southworth, *Directory*, p. 72.

45. W. W. Mills to Francis B. Loomis, Apr. 18, 1905, USNARG 59, Dispatches from the US Consuls, Chihuahua City.

46. Toomer, *Report*, p. 92.

47. *Mexican Herald*, May 15, 1908, p. 11.

48. *El Correo de Chihuahua*, Dec. 18, 1905, p. 1; *Mexican Herald*, Jan. 15, 1906, p. 7; *EMJ* 81 (Feb. 3, 1906): 251; *Mexican Herald*, Jan. 15, 1906, p. 7; *EMJ* 81 (Feb. 3, 1906): 251; *Mexican Herald*, Apr. 9, 1906, p. 3; *EMJ* 81 (Apr. 28, 1906): 827; *Mexican Mining Journal* (Nov. 1908): 30.

49. *South American Journal*, Jan. 9, 1909, pp. 34–35.

50. Ibid.

51. *EMJ* 90 (Oct. 15, 1910): 787; *Mexican Mining Journal* XI (Nov. 1910): 35. *Mexican Herald*, Nov. 6, 1910, p. 2.

52. *Mexican Herald*, Nov. 6, 1910, p. 2.

53. Ibid.

54. Franklin W. Smith, "Mining at Parral," *EMJ* 95 (Jan. 11, 1913): 138.

55. *EMJ* 96 (Aug. 30, 1913): 426.

56. *EMJ* 101 (June 3, 1916): 1004.

57. Ibid., 101 (Apr. 22, 1916): 754.

58. *EMJ* 109 (Mar. 20, 1920): 721; *EMJ* 109 (Apr. 24, 1920): 987; *EMJ* 109 (June 12, 1920): 1333.

59. James I. Long to W. W. Mills, Apr. 15, 1905, USNARG 59, Dispatches of US Consuls, Chihuahua City.

60. The entire story of the Dos Estrellas is from José Alfredo Uribe Salas, "Un enclave minero en Michoacán: La formación de una empresa 1898–1912," *Tzintzun: Revista de Estudios Históricos* 8 (Jan. –Dec. 1987): 57–71. See also Henry R. Wagner, *Bullions to Books: Fifty Years Of Business and Pleasure* (Los Angeles: The Zamorano Club, 1942), p. 32.

61. The profits were US$656,345 in 1902; US$1,235,650 in 1903; no information for 1904; US$2,1155,482 in 1905; US$3,882,372 in 1906; US$21 million 1907–10; and US$6 million in 1911.

62. Uribe Salas, "Un enclave," p. 60.

63. El Potosí Mining Company, *Annual Report 1931*, pt. 1, p. 10, Jan. 27, 1932, Box 1, Folder 1, Benson Latin American Collection, University of Texas at Austin.

64. Ibid., p. 11.

65. Ibid., p. 13.

66. Ibid.

67. Ibid.

68. El Potosí Mining Company, *Annual Report 1932*, pt. 1, Box 1, Folder 5, Benson Latin American Collection, University of Texas at Austin, p. 11.

69. Ibid., *Annual Report 1933*, pt. 1, Box 1, Folder 3, Benson Latin American Collection, University of Texas at Austin.

70. Ibid., *Annual Report 1934*, pt. 1, Box 1, Folder 7, Benson Latin American Collection, University of Texas at Austin.

71. Ibid.

72. El Potosí Mining Company, *Annual Report 1935*, Box 1, Folder 7, Benson Latin American Collection, University of Texas at Austin.

73. Ibid., *Annual Report 1936*, Box 1, Folder 9, Benson Latin American Collection, University of Texas at Austin.

74. Ibid., *Annual Report 1937*, Box 2, Folder 1, Benson Latin American Collection, University of Texas at Austin.

75. Bernstein, *Mexican Mining*, p. 224.

76. Ruíz, *Sonora*, p. 108. Ruíz cites US consular reports.

77. John Mason Hart, *The Silver of the Sierra Madre: John Robinson, Boss Shepherd, and the People of the Canyons* (Tucson: University of Arizona, 2008), passim.

78. Hart, *Silver*, p. 98.

79. David M. Pletcher, *Rails, Mines, and Progress: Seven American Promoters in Mexico, 1867–1911* (Ithaca, NY: Cornell University Press, 1958), p. 183.

80. Ibid., p. 183.

81. Ibid., p. 194.

82. Ibid., p. 195.

83. Hart, *Silver*, pp. 144, 192.

84. Pletcher, *Rails, Mines*, pp. 200–201.

85. Hart, *Silver*, p. 102. Hart points out that information about the Yaquis is in the company records.

86. Pletcher, *Rails, Mines*, pp. 202–3.

87. Hart, *Silver*, p. 99.

88. Pletcher, *Rails, Mines*, pp. 205–6.

89. Ibid., p. 217.

90. Ibid., p. 194.

91. Hart, *Silver*, p. 103.

92. Hulse, *Railroads and Revolution*, p. 62.

93. Pletcher, pp. 213–14.

94. Marvin D. Bernstein, "Colonel William C. Greene and the Cananea Copper Bubble," *Bulletin of the Business Historical Society* 26:4 (Dec. 1952): 179–98. The other major sources on his career in Mexico are Sonnichsen, *Colonel Green*, and Pletcher, *Rails, Mines*.

95. Pletcher, *Rails, Mines*, p. 223, tells the story of the founding of the Greene empire. Greene was to get back the mines because the parties had to register the transaction in Mexico and he was able to get a cooperative court to return the property. Litigation ensued, but Greene eventually settled.

96. Pletcher, *Rails, Mines*, p. 235.

97. A. Frederick Mignone, "A Fief for Mexico: Colonel Greene's Empire Ends," *Southwest Review* 44 (Aug. 1959): 335.

98. He sold the line to the Southern Pacific of Mexico in 1903. Pletcher, *Rails, Mines*, p. 230.

99. David M. Pletcher, "American Capital and Technology in Northwest Mexico, 2876–2922" (PhD diss., University of Chicago, 1946), p. 172.

100. *Mexican Herald*, Mar. 7, 1906, p. 574.

101. Ibid., Feb. 16, 1907, p. 2; Feb. 28, 1907, p. 11.

102. Ibid., Feb. 7, 1908, p. 10.

103. Ibid., Feb. 10, 1908, p. 4.

104. *Mexican Mining Journal* 8 (Mar. 1908), p. 29.

105. *Mexican Herald*, July 22, 1908, p. 11, Aug. 2, 1908, p. 10; *EMJ* 86 (Sept. 8, 1908): 494.

106. *EMJ* 86 (Oct. 17, 1908): 786, notes that he paid off his Mexican workers and the proceeds from the sale of merchandise and machinery were in the hands of Governor Creel.

107. *The Mining Magazine*, Oct. 1909, pp. 102–3.

108. "Statement of the Cananea Consolidated Copper Company, S.A.: How the Company Has Been Affected by Mexican Revolutionary Conditions, Taxation, etc." G. W. Young, Secretary and Treasurer, Sept. 28, 1916. Torrance, Box 2, No. 172.

109. Pletcher, *Rails, Mines*, p. 229.

110. Ibid., p. 220 citing the *EMJ* 82 (Oct. 6, 1906): 623.

111. Pletcher, *Rails, Mines*, pp. 237–38.

112. Pletcher, p. 167.

113. *Mexican Herald*, Dec. 12, 1907, 11.

114. Federico Sisniega to Enrique C. Creel, Aug. 5, 1908, Silvestre Terrazas Papers, Bancroft Library, II, 10.

115. Mignone, "A Fief," p. 336.

116. Arnold Hoffman, "Towne Mines Corporation: A Short History" (unpub. manuscript, 1954) provides most of the information for the following section.

117. Ibid., p. 43.

118. Ibid., p. 13.

119. Ibid., p. 8.

120. Ibid., pp. 15–16.

121. Compañía Metalúrgica Mexicana, Box 6, File 21, BLAC.

122. Hoffman, "Towne Mines," p. 57. The company lost approximately US$2.25 million in those ten years or US$225,000 a year on average. From 1933 to 1939 it earned more than US$3 million.

123. Memo for journal entry, Jan. 31, 1940, CMM, Box 6, File 22.

Chapter 7

1. The best histories of the American Smelting and Refining Company in Mexico are Horace D. Marucci, "The American Smelting and Refining Company in Mexico, 1900–1925" (PhD diss., Rutgers University, 1995); R. F. Manahan,

"Mining and Milling Operations of American Smelting and Refining Company in Mexico, 1899 to 1948" (unpub. manuscript, 1948); Marvin Bernstein, *The Mexican Mining Industry, 1890–1950* (Albany: State University of New York, 1964). I have taken the historical information that is not cited in the notes from these sources.

2. Marucci, "American Smelting," p. 83.

3. Ibid., pp. 90–91. The family purchased the mines through M. Guggenheim and Sons, the Guggenheim Smelting Company, the Guggenheim Exploration Company, the Aguascalientes Metal Company, the Asientes Mining Company, and Solomon Guggenheim (as an individual).

4. Marucci, "American Smelting," p. 164, citing *Engineering and Mining Journal (EMJ)* 76 (Nov. 22, 1903): 802. For the formation of ASARCO, see Isaac F. Marcosson, *Metal Magic: The Story of the American Smelting and Refining Company* (New York: Farrar, Strauss, & Co., 1949), pp. 57–84.

5. Marucci, "American Smelting, p. 171, citing *EMJ* 77 (May 13, 1904): 817.

6. Marucci, "American Smelting," pp. 192–96, discusses the impact of the laws.

7. Ibid., pp. 224–26.

8. Ibid., p. 231, citing the *Mexican Mining Journal* (Mar. 1909): 31.fz3.

9. Marucci, "American Smelting," p. 279.

10. Wagner, *Bullion to Books*, p. 155. See also Bernstein, *Mexican Mining*, p. 99; and Marucci, "American Smelting," p. 284.

11. ASARCO, *Fifteenth Annual Report of the American Smelting and Refining Company*, Dec. 31, 1913, p. 7, cited by Marucci, "American Smelting and Refining," p. 308.

12. *EMJ* 95 (Feb. 8, 1913): 350; and (Feb. 15, 1913): 394.

13. *EMJ* 96 (July 19, 1913): 140.

14. *EMJ* 97 (May 1914): 928; S. W. Eccles, "American Smelting and Refining Company in Mexico in 1916," *EMJ* 103 (Jan. 6, 1917): 22.

15. R. R. Manahan, "Historical Sketch of Mining and Milling Operations of American Smelting and Refining Company in Mexico, 1899 to 1948" (n.d., n.p.), p. 29.

16. *EMJ* 97 (May 2, 1914): 928.

17. S. W. Eccles, "The American Smelting and Refining Company in Mexico in 1914," *EMJ* 99 (Jan. 9, 1915): 130.

18. Manahan, "Historical Sketch," p. 29.

19. Ibid.

20. S. W. Eccles, "The American Smelting and Refining Company in Mexico in 1916," *EMJ* 103 (Jan. 6, 1917): 22.

21. Ibid.; *EMJ* 103 (May 5, 1917): 813; 104 (Sept. 22, 1917): 540.

22. S. W. Eccles, "The American Smelting and Refining Company in Mexico in 1917," *EMJ* 105 (Jan. 1918): 67; 109 (Feb. 21, 1920): 527.

23. Manahan, "Historical Sketch," p. 30.

24. *El Monitor*, Dec. 22, 1919, William F. Buckley Collection, 153.5, BLAC.

25. C. C. Baker to Plutarco Elías Calles, May 17, 1930, Asarco, G8/Expediente 28, Fideicomiso Plutarco Elías Calles y Fernando Torreblanca (FPEC); *EMJ* 109 (Feb. 21, 1920): 527.

26. *EMJ* 112 (July 23, 1921): 150; Ricardo E. Mora, Representativo de Asarco to Secretario de Industria, Comercio y Trabajo, Feb. 28, 1921, Archivo General de la Nación, Ramo Presidentes, Obregón-Calles (AGN-OC), 731-O-4.

27. A. B. Parsons, "New A. S. and R. Projects in Mexico Involve $10,000,000 for Construction," *EMJ* 118 (Nov. 15, 1924): 786–87; *EMJ* 120 (July 18, 1925): 105; *EMJ* 124 (Dec. 3, 1927): 1021.

28. *El Paso Times*, Nov. 16, 1926, p. 1.

29. Parsons, "New A. S. and R. Projects in Mexico Involve."

30. *EMJ* 127 (Jan. 19, 1929): 122–23; *La Voz de Parral*, Feb. 2, 1929.

31. Francis Styles, "American Consul, Chihuahua City, Notes on the Economic Situation in the Chihuahua Consular District," July 17, 1930, 850, US National Archives, State Department, Record Group 84, Dispatches from the American Consul Chihuahua City, 1930: 6; El Correo de Chihuahua, June 12, 1930, p. 1.

32. Daniel Guggenheim to Porfirio Díaz, July 24, 1908, Colección de General Porfirio Díaz, Document 33:010813.

33. Marucci, "American Smelting," pp. 74–75.

34. Manahan, "The Mining Operations of the American Smelting and Refining Company in Mexico" (unpub. manuscript, n.d.), p. 4.

35. Manahan, "Mining Operations," p. 12.

36. Ibid., p. 16.

37. Ibid., p. 5.

38. Bernstein, *Mexican Mining*, p. 38; Marucci, "American Smelting," p. 80.

39. *EMJ* 80 (July 22, 1905): 131; and (October 7, 1905): 658; *Mexican Herald*, Feb. 11; Henry R. Wagner, *Bullion to Books: Fifty Years of Business and Pleasure* (Los Angeles: The Zamorano Club, 1942), pp. 124–25. Because ASARCO built the smelter in order to forestall competitors from establishing a plant, company executives initially had no intention of operating it. Creel, however, pressured the company. Wagner, who was in charge of the smelter, eventually got it running, though it took some years for it to operate profitably.

40. Marucci, "American Smelting," pp. 88–89.

41. Ibid., p. 90.

42. Manahan, "Historical Sketch," p. 25.

43. Wagner, *Bullion to Books*, p. 135.

44. Ibid., p. 145.

45. Ibid., p. 146.

46. Ibid., p. 151.

47. Ibid., p. 152.

48. Ibid., pp. 173–74.

49. Cable from Ward Pearson, Jan. 2, 1914, Box 4, Ferrocarriles Noroeste de Mexico.

50. *EMJ* 97 (May 2, 1914): 928.

51. *EMJ* 98 (July 11, 1914): 92.
52. Wagner, *Bullion to Books*, p. 168.
53. "More Mexican Mining Law," *EMJ* 100 (Oct. 23, 1915): 688; and (Oct. 30, 1915): 736.
54. Marucci, "American Smelting," pp. 394–95.
55. Report of Gus T. Jones, Special Agent in Charge, Aug. 21, 1920, Albert Bacon Fall Papers, Box 5, Folder 3.
56. C. C. Baker to Calles, May 17, 1920, ASARCO, G8/Expediente 28, Fideicomiso Plutarco Elías Calles; *EMJ* 109 (Feb. 21, 1920): 527.
57. Ricardo E. Mora, Representativo de ASARCO, to Secretaría de Industria, Comercio y Trabajo, Feb. 28, 1921, AGN-OC, 731-O-4.
58. *EMJ* 112 (July 23, 1921): 150.
59. *EMJ* 113 (May 20, 1922): 887.
60. Ricardo F. Mora, Representativo General de ASARCO, to Obregón, Feb. 14, 1924, AGN-OC, 802-F-11.
61. *EMJ* 110 (Aug. 7, 1920): 277.
62. Mitchell to Secretary of State, Sept. 19, 1923, and Mc Enelly to Secretary of State, Jan. 2, 1924, USNARG 84, ACCCC, Confidential, 1922–28.
63. Dudley Ankerson, *Agrarian Warlord: Saturnino Cedillo and the Mexican Revolution in San Luis Potosí* (DeKalb: Northern Illinois University Press, 1984), pp. 112–13.
64. *El Paso Times*, Nov. 16, 1926, p. 1.
65. *El Periódico Oficial del Estado de Chihuahua*, Nov. 12, 1932, p. 1.
66. Manahan, "Historical Sketch," p. 36.
67. Lee R. Blohm, US Consul, Chihuahua City, to Secretary of State, Aug. 12, 1935, 812.5041/95, USNARG 59.
68. "Resume of Conditions in Chihuahua," Mar. 1939, 812.00/719, USNARG 59.
69. *El Paso Times*, Mar. 25, 1939, p. 2.
70. William F. Blocker, Ciudad Juárez, to Secretary of State, May 25, 1939, 812.63/962, USNARG 59. "Resume of Political Situation in Ciudad Juárez," May 1939, 812.00/Chihuahua/350, USNARG 59.
71. Manahan, "Historical Sketch," pp. 22–26.
72. Manahan, "American Smelting," pp. 7–8.
73. J. C. Pickering, "Mexico a Field for Investment," *EMJ* 120 (Dec. 5, 1925): 92–95.
74. Manahan, "Historical Sketch."
75. *EMJ* 111 (June 4, 1921): 963; and (June 11, 1921): 1003.
76. *EMJ* 112 (Aug. 27, 1921): 353.
77. *EMJ* 113 (May 20, 1922): 887.
78. Henry B. Ott, American Vice Consul, Chihuahua, to Secretary of State, "Report on Safety and Protection of Americans in Parral," Mar. 27, 1924, USNARG 84, Confidential File, 1922–1928.
79. *EMJ* 118 (Dec. 13, 1924): 948; Parsons, "New A.S.and R. Projects in Mexico," *EMJ* 118 (Nov. 15, 1924): 786–87; *Boletín Comercial* (Chihuahua), Oct. 15,

1924, pp. 23–24. The *EMJ* set the figures at US$10 million for new construction overall.

80. *EMJ* 123 (June 18, 1927): 907; 124 (Dec. 3, 1927): 1021; *Boletín Comercial*, Dec. 15, 1928, 21.

81. Jesús Gómez Serrano, *Aguascalientes: Imperio de los Guggenheims* (Mexico City: Sep/80, 1982), pp. 330–31.

82. *EMJ* 91 (June 17, 1911): 1229; 92 (July 29, 1911): 227.

83. Ankerson, *Agrarian Warlord*, p. 86.

84. *EMJ* 109 (June 20, 1920): 1333; 110 (July 31, 1920): 228–20.

85. *EMJ* 110 (Aug. 7, 1920): 277.

86. J. B. Stewart, American Consul, "Economic Report for September," Oct. 19, 1920, 812.50/77, J. B. Stewart, "Economic Report October, Chihuahua Consular District, Nov. 5, 1920, 812.50/78, USNARG 59.

87. *EMJ* 110 (Nov. 13, 1920): 960.

88. Enríquez to Obregón, Feb. 28, 1921, AGN-OC, 407-A-6; Howard Burks, Vice Superintendent, American Smelters' Securities Corporation, to Secretaría de Industria, Comercio y Trabajo, June 29, ANG, Trabajo 311/16; *EMJ* 111 (Mar. 26, 1921): 562; (Jan. 15, 1921): 116; Luis Gutiérrez, Governor of Coahuila, to President, Oct. 25, 1921, AGN-OC, 422- F1-C11.

89. *EMJ* 115 (Apr. 21, 1923): 728.

90. *El Paso Times*, Sept. 28, 1923, p. 8; and Oct. 1, 1923, p. 10; Mitchell to Secretary of State, Sept. 19, 1923, American Consul Chihuahua City, Confidential, 1922–28, USNARG 84.

91. Mitchell to Secretary of State, Sept. 19, 1923, USNARG 84, Confidential, 1922–1928.

92. Dudley Ankerson, *Agrarian Warlord: Saturnino Cedillo and the Mexican Revolution in San Luis Potosí* (DeKalb: Northern Illinois University Press, 1984), pp. 112–13.

93. Francis Styles, "Notes on the Economic Situation in the Chihuahua Consular District," July 17, 1930, 850, USNARG 84, ACCC, 1930: 6.

94. *El Correo de Chihuahua*, June 12, 1930, 1, 4.

95. "Political Conditions in Chihuahua," Dec. 1932, 812.00/Chihuahua/160, USNARG 59.

96. Harold G. Wood, American Vice Consul Piedras Negras, to Secretary of State, July 12, 17, and 25, 1934, 812.5045/174, 175, 178 and Samuel Sorobkin, Saltillo, to Secretary of State, July 19, 1934, 812.5045/177, USNARG 59.

97. Ankerson, *Agrarian Warlord*, p. 86.

98. *EMJ* 135 (Feb. 1934): 83–84.

99. Lee R. Blohm, US Consul, Chihuahua City, to Secretary of State, Aug. 12, 1935, 812.5041/95, USNARG 59.

100. *EMJ* 136 (Jan. 1935): 45. ASARCO employed ten thousand at its Santa Eulalia (Aquiles Serdán), La Prieta, Parral, Tecolotes, and Santa Bárbara facilities with a daily payroll of $M 30,000. *EMJ* 136 (Feb. 1936): 88.

101. "Political Conditions in Chihuahua," Aug. 1935, 812.00/Chihuahua/229 and "Political Conditions in Chihuahua," Sept. 1935, 812.00/Chihuahua/231,

USNARG 59; "Political Conditions in Chihuahua, "Aug. 1935, USNARF 84, ACCC, 800, 1935:4; "Political Conditions in Chihuahua," Oct. 1935, 800, 1935:14; *El Correo de Chihuahua*, Aug. 14, 1935, p. 1, and Aug. 16, 1935, p. 1.

102. Lee R. Blohm, to Secretary of State, Sept. 20, 1935, and Oct. 9, 1935, 812.5045/241 and 245.

103. *EMJ* 136 (Oct. 1936): 525.

104. Ibid., (Dec. 1935): 626–27.

105. Ibid., (Dec. 1936): 627.

106. Montgomery, San Luis Potosí, Secretary of State, Dec. 27, 1936, 812.5045/362, and Montgomery to Secretary of State, Dec. 27, 1946, 812.5045/362, USNARG 59; "Resume of Conditions in Mexico," Nov. 1936, 812.00/30424, USNARG 59. According to Ankerson, *Agrarian Warlord*, p. 160, ASARCO's plants and mines in San Luis Potosí had a payroll of approximately a million pesos a month and had a considerable impact on the local economy.

107. "Resume of Conditions in Mexico," Nov. 1937, 812.00/30520, USNARG 59.

108. *EMJ* 138 (Mar. 1937): 155.

109. "Resume of Conditions in Mexico," Oct. 1938, 812.00/30648, USNARG 59.

110. Ibid., Mar. 1938, 812.00/30559, USNARG 59; *El Paso Times*, Mar. 20, 1938, p. 1. Seventeen hundred went on strike.

111. Blohm to Secretary of State, Mar. 21, 1938, 812.00/5045/711, USNARG 59.

112. G. R. Vilbon, "Political Report," Sept. 30, 1938, Piedras Negras, Coahuila, 812.00/Ch313, USNARG 59.

113. J. B. Stewart, US Consul General, Mexico City, "Political Report for October, 1938," 812.00/30642, USNARG 59. "Political Report for December, 1938," 812.00/30668, USNARG 59.

114. *EMJ* 140 (Apr. 1939): 78–79.

115. Blohm, "Summary of Political Developments in Chihuahua, March, 1939," 812.00/Chihuahua/328, USNARG 59; *El Paso Times*, Mar. 25, 1939, p. 2.

116. *EMJ* 140 (Apr. 1939): 78–79.

117. *EMJ* 141 (Mar. 1940): 78–79.

118. "Chihuahua City and Environs," G-2, 9677, USNARG 165, US Military Intelligence, Reel 5.

119. R. C. Tanis to Dugan, Mar. 2, 1938, 812.504/1712, USNARG 59.

Chapter 8

1. There were also considerable investments in banking, petroleum, and industry.

2. There is a large body of research on the postrevolutionary state in Mexico. The concept of the Leviathan state emerged from the success of the so-called Mexican economic miracle after 1940. Observers came to overemphasize the power held by the federal government in Mexico City. See Nora Hamilton, *The Limits*

of State Autonomy: Post-Revolutionary Mexico (Princeton, NJ: Princeton University Press, 1982); Roger D. Hansen, *The Politics of Mexican Development* (Baltimore, MD: Johns Hopkins University Press, 1971); and Thomas Benjamin, "The Leviathan on the Zócalo: Recent Historiography of the Post-Revolutionary Mexican State," *LARR* 20:3 (1985): 195–217.

Bibliography

Archives

Mexico

Archivo General de la Nación de México, Ramo Presidentes, Obregón-Calles
Colección de General Porfirio Díaz, Universidad Iberoamerica, Mexico City
Fideicomiso Archivos Plutarco Elías Calles y Fernando Torreblanca, Archivo Plutarco Elías Calles, Mexico City
Papers of Enrique C. Creel, CARSO (Condumex), Mexico City
Archivo de José Y. Limantour, CARSO, Mexico City

United States

Roland Anderson Collection, University of Texas, El Paso (UTEP)
Archivo del Ferrocarril Noroeste de México, Nettie Lee Benson Collection (NLB), University of Texas at Austin
Ian A. Benton Collection, UTEP
Buckley Collection, NLB
Compañía Constructora Richardson, S.A., University of Arizona
George Crane Collection, Baker Library, Harvard University
John Mason Hart Collection, Houston, Texas
Lewis Douglas Papers, University of Arizona
Albert B. Fall Collection, Center for Southwest Research Collection, University of New Mexico
James H. Hyslop Collection, UTEP
Papers of Frank O. Lowden, University of Chicago
Mexico Northwestern Collection, UTEP
El Potosí Mining Company, NLB
Silvestre Terrazas Papers, Bancroft Library, University of California, Berkeley
Papers of Thomas W. Peirce, NLB
United States, National Archives, Record Group 59, General Records of the Department of State, Consular Despatches, Chihuahua City, Ciudad Juárez

United States, National Archives, General Records of the Department of State, Record Group 59, Decimal Files, 1910–29
United States, National Archives, General Records of the Department of State, Record Group 59, Minor Files, 1906–10
United States, National Archives, General Records of the Department of State, Record Group 59, Numerical Files, 1906–10
United States, National Archives, Record Group 76, Records of the United States and Mexican Claims Commission
United States, National Archives, Record Group 84, General Records of the Department of State, Records of the American Consular Post in Chihuahua City, 1918–35
United States, National Archives, Record Group 84, Records of the American Consular Post in Ciudad Juárez, 1918–35
Max R. Weber Collection, UTEP

United Kingdom

Weetman Pearson Papers, Science Museum, London

Periodicals and Newspapers

Bankers' Magazine
Boletín Agricultura Mexicana
Boletín Comercial
Boletín Financiero y Minero
Chihuahua Enterprise
El Correo de Chihuahua (Ciudad Chihuahua)
El Paso Morning Times
Engineering and Mining Journal
Mexican Herald
Mexican Investor
Mexican Yearbook, 1908–1912
Moody's Manual of Railroads and Corporations
El Periódico Oficial del Estado de Chihuahua
Poor's Manual
Railway Age Gazette
New York Times
South American Journal

Books

Aboites Aguilar, Luis. *Norte precario: Poblamiento y colonización en México (1760–1940)*. Mexico City: El Colegio de México, 1995.

Almada Bay, Ignacio. *La conexión yocupicio: Soberanía estatal y tradición cívico-liberal en Sonora, 1913–1939*. Mexico City: El Colegio de México, 2009.
Altamirano, Graziella, ed. *Prestigio, riqueza y poder: Las elites en México, 1821–1940*. Mexico City: Instituto Mora, 2000.
Anaya Merchant, Luis. *Colapso y reforma: La integración del sistema bancario en el México revolucionario, 1913–1920*. Mexico City: Universidad Autónoma de Zacatecas, 2002.
Ankerson, Dudley. *Agrarian Warlord: Saturnino Cedillo and the Mexican Revolution in San Luis Potosí*. DeKalb: Northern Illinois University Press, 1984.
Bantjes, Adrian. *As If Jesus Walked on Earth: Cardenismo, Sonora, and the Mexican Revolution*. Wilmington, DE: Scholarly Resources, 1998.
Barragán, Juan Ignacio, and Mario Cerutti. *Juan F. Brittingham y la industria en México, 1859–1940*. Monterrey: Urbis Internacional, 1993.
Beals, Carleton. *Porfirio Díaz. Dictator of Mexico*. Philadelphia, PA: S. B. Lippincott Co., 1932.
Beatty, Edward. *Institutions and Investment: The Political Basis of Industrialization in Mexico Before 1911*. Stanford, CA: Stanford University Press, 2001.
Bell, Edward I. *The Political Shame of Mexico*. New York: McBride, Nast & Company, 1914.
Bernecker, Walther L. *De agiotistas y empresarios: En torno de la temprana industrialización mexicana (Siglo XIX)*. Mexico City: Universidad Iberoamericana, 1992.
———. *Contrabando: Ilegalidad y corrupción en el México del siglo XIX*. Mexico City: Universidad Iberoamericana, 1994.
Bernstein, Marvin D. *The Mexican Mining Industry, 1890–1950*. Albany: State University of New York Press, 1964.
Bortz, Jeffrey L., and Stephen Haber, eds. *The Mexican Economy, 1870–1930: Essays on the Economic History of Institutions, Revolution, and Growth*. Stanford, CA: Stanford University Press, 2002.
Brandenburg, Frank R. *The Making of Modern Mexico*. New York: Prentice-Hall, 1964.
Buchenau, Jurgen. *Tools of Progress: A German Merchant Family in Mexico City, 1865–Present*. Albuquerque: University of New Mexico Press, 2004.
Bulwer-Thomas, Victor. *The Economic History of Latin America Since Independence*. Cambridge: Cambridge University Press, 1994.
Bunker, Steven B. *Creating Consumer Culture in the Age of Porfirio Díaz*. Albuquerque: University of New Mexico Press, 2012.
Burnes Ortiz, Arturo. *La minería en la historia económica de Zacatecas (1546–1876)*. Zacatecas: Universidad Autónoma de Zacatecas, 1987.
Butler, William. *Mexico in Transition*. New York: Hunt & Eaton, 1893.
Calzadíaz Barrera, Alberto. *Dos gignates: Sonora y Chihuahua*. Hermosillo, Sonora: Escritores Asociados del Norte, 1964.
Camp, Roderic Ai. *Entrepreneurs and Politics in Twentieth Century Mexico*. New York: Oxford University Press, 1989.

———. *Mexico's Leaders: Their Education and Recruitment.* Tucson: University of Arizona Press, 1980.

———. *Mexico's Mandarins: Crafting a Power Elite for the Twenty-first Century.* Berkeley: University of California Press, 2002.

———. *Political Recruitment Across Two Countries, Mexico, 1884–1991.* Austin: University of Texas Press, 1995.

Cárdenas, Enrique. *La industrialización mexicana durante la gran depresión.* Mexico City: El Colegio México, 1987.

Cárdenas García, Nicolás. *Empresas y trabajadores en la gran minería mexicana (1900–1929).* Mexico City: INEHRM, 1998.

———. *La quimera del desarrollo: El impacto ecónomco y social de la minería en el oro, Estado de México (1900–1930).* Mexico City: INEHRM, 1996.

Cárdenas Sánchez, Enrique. *Cuando se origió el atraso económico de México: La economía mexicana en el largo siglo XIX, 1780–1920.* Madrid: Fundación José Ortega y Gasset, 2003.

Ceceña, José Luis. *México en la orbital imperial: Las empresas transnacionales.* Mexico City: Editorial El Caballito, 1979.

Cerda González, Luis C. *Historia financiera del Banco Nacional de México.* 2 vols. El Porfiriato, 1884–1910. Mexico City: Fomento Cultural Banamex, 1994.

Cerutti, Mario, ed. *Agua, tierra, y capital en el noroeste de México: La región citrícola de Nuevo León, 1850–1940.* Monterrey: Universidad Autónoma de Nuevo León, 1991.

———, ed. *De los Borbones a la revolución: Ocho estudios regionales.* Mexico City: GV Editores, 1986.

———. *Burguesía y capitalismo en Monterrey, 1850–1910.* Mexico City: Claves Latinoamericanas, 1983.

———, ed. *Durango (1840–1915): Banca, transportes, tierra y industria.* Monterrey: Universidad Autónoma de Nuevo León, 1995.

———. *Empresarios españoles y sociedad capitalista en México (1840–1920).* Asturias: Archivo de Indianos, 1995.

———, ed. *Monterrey, Nuevo León, el noroeste: Siete estudios históricos.* Monterrey: Universidad Autónoma de Nuevo León, 1987.

———, et al. *Vascos, agricultura y empresa en México.* Mexico City: Universidad Iberoamericana La Laguna, 1999.

Cerutti, Mario, and Oscar Flores, eds. *Españoles en el norte de México: Proprietarios, empresarios, Y diplomacia (1850–1920).* Monterrey: Universidad Autónoma de Nuevo León, 1997.

Cerutti, Mario, and Carlos Marichal, eds. *La banca regional en México (1870–1910).* Mexico City: El Colegio de México and El Fondo de Cultura Económica, 2003.

Chandler, Alfred D., Jr. *The Visible Hand: The Managerial Revolution in American Business.* Cambridge, MA: Harvard University Press, 1977.

Chandler, Alfred D., Jr., and Herman Daems, eds. *Managerial Hierarchies: Comparative Perspectives on the Rise of Modern Industrial Enterprise.* Cambridge, MA: Harvard University Press, 1980.

Coatsworth, John H. *Growth Against Development: The Economic Impact of Railroads in Porfirian Mexico.* DeKalb: Northern Illinois University Press, 1981.
Coleman, D. C., and Peter Mathias, eds. *Enterprise and History.* Cambridge: Cambridge University Press, 1984.
Collado, María del Carmen. *La burguesía mexicana: El emporio Braniff y su participación política, 1865–1920.* Mexico City: Siglo Veintiuno Editores, 1987.
———. *Empresarios y politicos, entre la restauración y la revolución, 1920–1924.* Mexico City: Instituto Nacional de Estudios Históricos de la Revolución Mexicana, 1996.
Connolly, Priscilla. *El contratista de don Porfirio: Obras públicas, deuda y desarollo desigual.* Mexico City: El Colegio de México, 1997.
Cosío Villegas, Daniel. *Historia moderna de México: El porfiriato: La vida económica.* Vol. 7, pt. 2. Mexico City: Editorial Hermes, 1965.
Creel Cobián, Alejandro. *Enrique C. Creel: Apuntes para su biografía.* Mexico: n.p., 1974.
Creelman, James. *Díaz, Master of Mexico.* New York: D. Appleton and Co., 1916.
Cumberland, Charles C. *Mexican Revolution: The Constitutionalist Years.* Austin: University of Texas Press, 1972.
Dale-Lloyd, Jane. *Cinco ensayos sobre cultura material de rancheros y medieros de noroeste de Chihuahua, 1886–1910.* Mexico City: Universidad Iberoamericana, 2001.
———. *El proceso de modernización capitalista en el noroeste de Chihuahua (1880–1910).* Mexico City: Universidad Iberoamerica, 1987.
Davis, John H. *The Guggenheims: An American Epic.* New York: William Morrow and Co., 1978.
Díaz Dufoo, Carlos. *Limantour.* Mexico City: Eusebio Gómez de la Puente, 1910.
Dumont, Raymond E., ed. *Gentlemanly Capitalism and British Imperialism: The New Debate on Empire.* London: Longman, 1999.
Dunn, Frederick Sherwood. *The Diplomatic Protection of Americans in Mexico.* New York: Columbia University Press, 1933.
Dunn, Robert W. *American Foreign Investments.* New York: B. W. Huebsch and the Viking Press, 1926.
Dwyer, John J. *The Agrarian Dispute: The Expropriation of American-Owned Land in Post-Revolutionary Mexico.* Durham, NC: Duke University Press, 2008.
Evans, Peter. *Dependent Development: The Alliance of Multinational, State, and Local Capital in Brazil.* Princeton, NJ: Princeton University Press, 1979.
Falcón, Romana. *Agrarismo en Veracruz: La etapa radical (1928–1935).* Mexico City: El Colegio de México, 1977.
Flores Clair, Eduardo. *Conflictos de trabajo de una empresa minera: Real del Monte y Pachuca 1872–1877.* Mexico City: INAH, 1991.
Garner, Paul. *British Lions and Mexican Eagles: Business, Politics, and Empire in the Career of Weetman Pearson in Mexico. 1889–1919.* Stanford, CA: Stanford University Press, 2011.

Gauss, Susan M. *Made in Mexico: Regions, Nation, and the State in the Rise of Mexican Industrialization, 1920s–1940s*. University Park: Penn State University Press, 2010.

Gómez Serrano, Jesús. *Aguascalientes: Imperio de los Guggenheim*. Mexico City: Secretaría de Educación Pública, 1982.

González, Luis. *Historia de la revolución mexicana, 1934–40: Los días del presidente Cárdenas*. Mexico City: El Colegio de México, 1981.

González Navarro, Moisés. *Los extranjeros en México y los mexicanos en el estranjero, 1821–1970*. 3 vols. Mexico City: El Colegio de México, 1993–94.

González Pacheco, Cuauhtémoc. *Capital extranjero en la selva de Chiapas, 1863–1982*. Mexico City: Universidad Autónoma de México, 1983.

González Salazar, Roque, ed. *La frontera del norte: Integración y desarollo*. Mexico City: El Colegio de México, 1981.

Guzmán, José Napoleón. *Michoacán y la inversion extranjera, 1880–1891*. Michoacán: Universidad de Michoacán San Nicolás de Hidalgo, 1982.

Haber, Stephen, ed. *Crony Capitalism and Economic Growth in Latin America: Theory and Evidence*. Stanford, CA: Hoover Institution Press, 2002.

———. *How Latin America Fell Behind*. Stanford, CA: Stanford University Press, 1997.

———. *Industry and Development: The Industrialization of Mexico, 1890–1940*. Stanford, CA: Stanford University Press, 1989.

Haber, Stephen, Armando Razo, and Noel Maurer. *The Politics of Property Rights: Political Instability, Credible Commitments, and Economic Growth in Mexico, 1876–1929*. Cambridge: Cambridge University Press, 2003.

Hamilton, Nora. *The Limits of State Autonomy: Post-Revolutionary Mexico*. Princeton, NJ: Princeton University Press, 1982.

Hansen, Roger D. *The Politics of Mexican Development*. Baltimore, MD: Johns Hopkins University Press, 1971.

Hart, John Mason. *Empire and Revolution: Americans in Mexico Since the Civil War*. Berkeley: University of California Press, 2002.

———. *Revolutionary Mexico: The Coming and Process of the Mexican Revolution*. Berkeley: University of California Press, 1987.

———. *The Silver of the Sierra Madre*. Tucson: University of Arizona Press, 2008.

Heidenheimer, Arnold J., ed. *Political Corruption*. New York: Holt, Rinehart, and Winston, 1970.

Hernández Chávez, Alicia. *Historia de la revolución mexicana, 1934–1940: La mecánica cardenista*. Mexico City: El Colegio de México, 1979.

Holden, Robert H. *Mexico and the Survey of Public Lands: The Management of Modernization, 1876–1911*. DeKalb: Northern Illinois University Press, 1994.

Hulse, J. F. *Railroads and Revolutions: The Story of Roy Hoard*. El Paso, TX: Mangan Books, 1986.

James, Eliot, and Homer B. Vanderblue, eds. *Railroads: Cases and Selections*. New York: Macmillan and Co., 1915.

Katz, Friedrich. *The Life and Times of Pancho Villa.* Stanford, CA: Stanford University Press, 1999.
———. *The Secret War in Mexico.* Chicago: University of Chicago Press, 1984.
Knight, Alan. *The Mexican Revolution.* 2 vols. Cambridge: Cambridge University Press, 1984.
———. *U.S.-Mexican Relations, 1910–1940: An Interpretation.* San Diego: Center for Mexican Studies, University of California San Diego, 1987.
Knowles, L. C. A. *Economic Development in the Nineteenth Century: France, Germany, Russia, and the United States.* London: Routledge and Kegan Paul, Ltd., 1932.
Krauze, Enrique, et al. *Historia de la revolución mexicana: Período 1924–1928: La reconstrucción económica.* Mexico City: El Colegio de México, 1979.
Kuntz Ficker, Sandra. *Empresa extranjera y mercado interno: El Ferrocarril Central Mexicano, 1880–1907.* Mexico City: El Colegio de México, 1995.
Kuntz Ficker, Sandra, and Priscilla Connelly, eds. *Ferocarriles y obras públicas.* Mexico City: Instituto Mora, 1999.
Leal, Juan Felipe, and Mario Huacuja Rountree. *Economía y sistema de haciendas en México: La hacienda pulquería en cambio, siglos XVIII, XIX, y XX.* Mexico City: Ediciones Era, 1981.
Lewis, Cleona. *America's Stake in International Investments.* Washington, DC: The Brookings Institution, 1938.
Lida, Clara E., ed. *Tres aspectos de la presencia espannõla en México durante el porfiriato.* Mexico City: El Colegio de México, 1981.
Lister, Florence C., and Robert H. Lister. *Chihuahua: Storehouse of Storms.* Albuquerque: University of New Mexico Press, 1960.
Lizama Silva, Gladys. *Zamora en el porfiriato: Familias, fortunas, y economía.* Zamora, Michoacán: El Colegio de Michoacán, 2000.
Lopes, María Aparecida de S. *De costumbres y leyes: Abigeato y derechos de propriedad en Chihuahua durante el porfiriato.* Michoacán: El Colegio de México, 2005.
López Gallo, Manuel. *Economía y política en la historia de México.* Mexico City: n.p., 1988.
Machado, Manuel A., Jr. *The North Mexican Cattle Industry, 1910–1970: Ideology, Conflict and Change.* College Station: Texas A&M Press, 1981.
Manero, Antonio. *La revolución bancaria en México, 1865–1955.* Mexico City: Talleres Gráficos de la Nación, 1957.
Marcosson, Isaac F. *Metal Magic: The Story of the American Smelting and Refining Company.* New York: Farrar, Strauss, & Co., 1949.
Marichal, Carlos, ed. *Las inversions extranjeras en América Latina, 1850–1930.* Mexico City: Fondo de Cultura Económica, 1992.
Marichal, Carlos, and Mario Cerutti, eds. *Historia de los grandes empresas en México, 1850–1930.* Mexico City: Fondo de Cultura Económica, 1997.
Martínez Moctezuma, Lucía. *Iñigo Noriega Lazo: Un emporio empresario:*

Imigración y crecimiento economic (1868–1913). Mexico City: Universidad Autónoma Iztapalapa, 2001.
Maurer, Noel. *The Power and the Money: The Mexican Financial System, 1876–1932*. Stanford, CA: Stanford University Press, 2002.
McCaleb, Walter F. *Present and Past Banking in Mexico*. New York: Harper & Brothers, 1920.
———. *The Public Finances of Mexico*. New York: Harper & Brothers Publishers, 1921.
Meyer, Lorenzo. *Historia de la revolución mexicana, 1924–1928: Estado y sociedad con Calles*. Mexico City: El Colegio de México, 1977.
———. *Historia de la revolución mexicana, 1928–1934: El conflict social y los gobiernos del maximato*. Mexico City: El Colegio de México, 1978.
———, et al. *Historia de la revolución mexicana, período 1928–1934: Los inicios de la institucionalización, la política del maximato*. Mexico City: El Colegio de México, 1978.
Meyers, William K. *Forge of Progress, Crucible of Revolt: The Origins of the Mexican Revolution in La Comarca Lagunera, 1880–1911*. Albuquerque: University of New Mexico, 1994.
Miranda Arrieta, Eduardo. *Economía y comunicaciones en el Estado de Guerrero, 1877–1910*. Michoacán: Universidad Michoacana de San Nicolás de Hidalgo, 1994.
Mora-Torres, Juan. *The Making of the Mexican Border: The State, Capitalism, and Society in Nuevo León, 1848–1910*. Austin: University of Texas Press, 2001.
Moreno, Julio. *Yankee Don't Go Home: Mexican Nationalism, American Business Culture, and the Shaping of Modern Mexico, 1920–1950*. Chapel Hill: University of North Carolina Press, 2003.
Nickel, Herbert J., ed. *Paternalismo y economía moral en las haciendas mexicanas del porfiriato*. Mexico City: Universidad Iberomaericana, 1989.
North, Diane M. T. *Samuel Peter Heintzelman and the Sonora Exploring and Mining Company*. Tucson: University of Arizona Press, 1980.
Ocasio Meléndez, Macial. *Capitalism and Development: Tampico Mexico, 1876–1924*. New York: Peter Lang, 1998.
Olveda, Jaime, ed. *Inversiones y empresarios en el noroccidente de México, siglo XIX*. Zapapopan: El Colegio de Jalisco, 1996.
Oñate, Abdiel. *Banqueros y hacendados: La quimera de la modernización*. Mexico City: Universidad Autónoma Metropolitana, 1991.
Ortiz Hernán, Sergio. *Los ferrocarriles de México: Una visión social y económica*. Mexico City: Secretaría de Cominicaciones y Transportes, 1974.
Owens, J. Adolphus, Comp. *Anywhere I Wander I Find Facts and Legends Relating to the Creel Family*. Warrior, AL: n.p., 1975.
Palomares Peña, Noé. *Proprietarios norteamericanos y reforma agraria en Chihuahua, 1917–1942*. Ciudad Juárez: Universidad Autónoma de Ciudad Juárez, 1991.
Pansters, Wil. *Politics and Power in Puebla: The Political History of a Mexican State, 1937–1987*. Amsterdam: CEDLA, 1990.

Pérez Acevedo, Martin. *Empresarios y empresas en Morelia, 1860–1910*. Michoacán: Universidad Michoacana de San Nicolás de Hidalgo, 1994.

Pérez Rosales, Laura. *Familia, poder, riqueza y subversión: Los fagoaga noohispanos, 1730–1830*. Mexico City: Universidad Iberoamericana, 2003.

Pilcher, Jeffrey M. *The Sausage Rebellion: Public Health, Private Enterprise, and Meat in Mexico City, 1890–1917*. Albuquerque: University of New Mexico Press, 2006.

Plana, Manuel. *El reino del Algoodón en México: La estructure agrarian de la Laguna (1855–1910)*. Torreón: Universidad Autónoma de Nuevo León, 1984.

Pletcher, David M. *Rails, Mines, and Progress: Seven American Promoters in Mexico, 1867–1911*. Ithaca, NY: Cornell University Press, 1958.

Ramírez Bautista, Elia. *Estadísticas bancarias: Recopilación de estadísticas económicas del siglo XIX*. 2 vols. Mexico City: Instituto Nacional de Antropología y Historia.

Razo, Armando. *Social Foundations of Limited Dictatorship: Network and Private Protection During Mexico's Early Industrialization*. Stanford, CA: Stanford University Press, 2008.

Ripley, William Z. *Railroads: Finance and Organization*. New York: Macmillan and Company, 1925.

Rippy, J. Fred. *British Investments in Latin America, 1822–1949*. Hamden, CT: Archon Books, 1966.

Romero Gil, Juan Manuel. *Mineria y sociedad en el noroeste porfirista*. Culiacán: Gobierno del Estado De Sinaloa, 1991.

Romero Ibarra, María Eugenia, and Pablo Serrano, eds. *Regiones y expansion capitalista en México durante el siglo XIX*. Mexico City: Universidad Autónoma de México, 1998.

Ruíz, Ramón Eduardo. *The Great Rebellion, Mexico 1905–1924*. New York: W. W. Norton, 1980.

———. *The People of Sonora and the Yankee Capitalists*. Tucson: University of Arizona Press, 1988.

Saragoza, Alex. M. *The Monterrey Elite and the Mexican State, 1880–1940*. Austin: University of Texas Press, 1988.

Sawatzky, Harry Leonard. *They Sought a Country: Mennonite Colonization in Mexico*. Berkeley: University of California Press, 1971.

Schell, William, Jr. *Integral Outsiders: The American Colony in Mexico City, 1876–1911*. Wilmington, DE: Scholarly Resources, 2001.

Schneider, Ben Ross. *Business Politics and the States in Twentieth-Century Latin America*. Cambridge: Cambridge University Press, 2004.

Smith, Peter H. *Labyrinths of Power: Political Recruitment in Twentieth-Century Mexico*. Princeton, NJ: Princeton University Press, 1979.

Smith, Robert Freeman. *The United States and Revolutionary Nationalism in Mexico, 1916–1932*. Chicago: University of Chicago Press, 1972.

Sonnichsen, C. L. *Colonel Greene and the Copper Skyrocket*. Tucson: University of Arizona Press, 1974.

Swanberg, W. A. *Citizen Hearst: A Biography of William Randolph Hearst.* New York: Scribner, 1961.
Thompson, Slason. *Cost Capitalization and Estimated Value of American Railways: An Analysis of Current Falacies.* Chicago: Huntherp-Warren Printing Company, 1907.
Tinker Salas, Miguel. *In the Shadow of the Eagles: Sonora and the Transformation of the Border During the Porfiriato.* Berkeley: University of California Press, 1997.
Tischendorf, Alfred. *Great Britain and Mexico in the Era of Porfirio Díaz.* Durham, NC: Duke University Press, 1961.
Turlington, Edgar. *Mexico and Her Foreign Creditors.* New York: Columbia University Press, 1930.
Turner, John Kenneth. *Barbarous Mexico.* Chicago: Charles H. Kerr, 1911.
Valdés Ugalde, Francisco. *Autonomía y legitimidad: Los empresarios, la poítica, y el estado en México.* Mexico City: Siglo Veintiuno, 1997.
Vargas-Lobsinger, María. *La Hacienda de La Concha: Una empresa algonera de la Laguna, 1883–1917.* Mexico City: UNAM, 1984.
Wasserman, Mark. *Capitalists, Caciques, and Revolution: The Native Elite and Foreign Enterprise in Chihuahua, Mexico, 1854–1910.* Chapel Hill: University of North Carolina Press, 1984.
———. *Everyday Life and Politics in Nineteenth-Century Mexico: Men, Women, and War.* Albuquerque: University of New Mexico Press, 2000.
———. *Persistent Oligarchs: Elites and Politics in Chihuahua, Mexico, 1910–1940.* Durham, NC: Duke University Press, 1993.
Weiner, Richard. *Race, Nation, and Market: Economic Culture in Porfirian Mexico.* Tucson: University of Arizona Press, 2004.
Wilken, Paul H. *Entrepreneurs: A Comparative and Historical Study.* Norwood, NJ: Ablex Publishing Co., 1979.
Wright, Harry K. *Foreign Enterprise in Mexico.* Chapel Hill: University of North Carolina Press, 1971.

Articles

Armstrong, Christopher, and H. V. Nelles. "A Curious Capital Flow: Canadian Investment in Mexico, 1902–1910." *Business History Review* 58:2 (summer 1984): 178–203.
Arrieta Ceniceros, Lorenzo. "Importancia económica y social de los ferrocarriles en Yucatán: Empresas y grupos económicos, 1876–1915." *Estudios Políticos* 5:18–19 (Apr.–Sept. 1979): 113–87.
Benjamin, Thomas. "The Leviathan on the Zócalo: Recent Historiography of the Post-Revolutionary Mexican State." *LARR* 20:3 (1985): 195–217.
Bernstein, Marvin D. "Colonel William C. Greene and the Cananea Copper Bubble." *Bulletin of the Business Historical Society* 26:4 (Dec. 1952): 179–98.

Calderón, Francisco. "Los ferrocarriles." In *Historia moderna de México: El porfiriato. La vida económica*, ed. Daniel Cosió Villegas. Mexico City: Editorial Hermes, 1965. Tomo 7.

Cerutti, Mario. "La Compañía Industrial Jabonera de la Laguna: Comerciantes, agricultores e industria en el norte de México, 1880–1925." In *Historia de los grandes empresas en México, 1850–1930*, ed. Carlos Marichal and Mario Cerutti. Mexico City: Fondo de Cultura Económica, 1997.

———. "Empresariado y banca en el norte de México (1870–1910): El Banco Refaccionario de la Laguna." In *La banca regional en México (1870–1910)*, ed. Carlos Marichal and Mario Cerutti. Mexico City: El Colegio de México and El Fondo de Cultura Económica, 2003.

———. "Guerra y comercio en torno al Río Barvo (1855–1867), linea fronteriza, espacio economic común." *Historia Mexicana* 40:2 (Oct. 1990): 217–52.

———. "Los Madero en la economía de Monterrey (1890–1910)." In *Burguesía y capitalismo en Monterrey, 1850–1910*. Mexico City: Claves Latinoamericanas, 1983.

Clark, Mary Whatley. "Angus Cattle in Mexico." *The Cattleman* (Fort Worth, TX), June 1956, pp. 32–33.

Coatsworth, John H. "Obstacles to Economic Growth in Nineteenth-Century Mexico." American Historical Review.

D'Olwer, Luis Nicolau. "Las inversions extranjeras." In *La historia moderna de México: El porfiriato. La vida económica*, vol. II, ed. Daniel Cosío Villegas. Mexico City: Editorial Hermes, 1965, pp. 973–1185.

Dormady, Jason. "Rights, Rule, and Religion: Old Colony Mennonites and Mexico's Transition to the Free Market." In *Religious Culture in Modern Mexico*, ed. Martin Nesvig. New York: Rowman and Littlefield, 2007, pp. 157–77.

Eccles, S. W. "The American Smelting and Refining Company in Mexico in 1914." *Engineering and Mining Journal* 99 (Jan. 9, 1915): 130.

———. "The American Smelting and Refining Company in Mexico in 1916." *Engineering and Mining Journal* 103 (Jan. 6, 1917): 22.

———. "The American Smelting and Refining Company in Mexico in 1917." *Engineering and Mining Journal* 105 (Jan. 1918): 67; 109 (Feb. 21, 1920): 527.

French, William E. "Business as Usual: Mexican North Western Railway Managers Confront the Mexican Revolution." *Mexican Studies/Estudios Mexicanos* 5 (1989): 221–38.

García Avila, Sergio. "Institucioned bancarias y agricultura, una perspective de desarrollo capitalista en Michoacán, 1880–1910." *Tzintzun* 8 (Jan.–Dec. 1987): 47–56.

Garner, Paul. "The Politics of National Development in Late Porfirian Mexico: The Reconstruction of the Tehuantepec National Railway." *The Bulletin of Latin American Research* 14:3 (Sept. 1995): 339–66.

Gómez-Galvarriato, Aurora. "Networks and Entrepreneurship: The Modernization of the Textile Business in Porfirian Mexico." *Business History Review* 82:3 (autumn 2008).

Gómez-Galvarriato, Aurora, and Gabriela Recio. "The Indispensable Service of Banks: Commercial Transactions, Industry and Banking in Revolutionary Mexico." *Enterprise & Society* 8:1 (2007): 68–105.

Gómez-Galvarriato, Aurora, and Jeffrey G. Williamson. "Was It Prices, Productivity or Public Policy?: Latin American Industrialisation After 1870." *Journal of Latin American Studies* 41:4 (Nov. 2009): 663–94.

Grunstein, Arturo. "De la competencia al monopolio: La formación de los ferrocarriles nacionales de México." In *Ferocarriles y obras públicas,* ed. Sandra Kuntz Ficker and Priscilla Connelly. Mexico City: Instituto Mora, 1999.

Grunstein Dickter, Arturo. "In the Shadow of Oil: Francisco J. Múgica vs Telephone Transnational Corporations in Cardenista Mexico." *Mexican Studies/Estudios Mexicanos* 21:1 (winter 2005): 1–32.

———. "Surgimiento de los ferrocarriles nacionales de México (1900–1913): Era inevitable la consolidación monopólica." In *Historia de los grandes empresas en México, 1850–1930,* ed. Carlos Marichal and Mario Cerutti. Mexico City: Fondo de Cultura Económica, 1997.

Haber, Stephen H. "Assessing the Obstacles to Industrisation: The Mexican Economy, 1830–1940." *Journal of Latin American Studies* 24:1 (Feb. 1992): 1–32.

Hall, Linda B. "Obregón and the Politics of Land Reform, 1920–1924." *HAHR* 60:2 (May 1980).

Hardy, Carmon B. "Cultural Encystment as a Cause of the Mormon Exodus from Mexico," *Pacific Historical Rreview* 34 (Nov. 1965): 439–54.

Katz, Friedrich. "Labor Conditions on Haciendas in Porfirian Mexico: Some Trends and Tendencies." *HAHR* 54 (Feb. 1974): 1–47.

Koch, Charles R. "Beef Below the Border." *Farm Quarterly* 24 (summer 1969): 45–49.

Kuntz Ficker, Sandra. "Economic Backwardness and Firm Strategy: An American Railroad Corporation in Nineteenth-Century Mexico." *Hispanic American Historical Review* 80:2 (May 2000): 267–98.

———. "La historiografía económica reciente sobre el México decimonómico." *Mexican Studies/Estudios Mexicanos* 21:2 (summer 2005): 461–92.

Lizama Silva, Gladys. "Zamora: Las grandes fortunas familiars del porfiriato." *Siglo XIX* 6:16 (Sept.–Dec. 1996): 39–68.

Lopes, María-Aparecida, and Paolo Riguzzi. "Borders, Trade and Politics: Exchange Between the United States and Mexican Cattle Industries, 1870–1947." *Hispanic American Historical Review* 92:4 (2012): 603–35.

Márquez, Graciela. "Tariff Protection in Mexico, 1892–1909: Ad Valorem Tariff Rates and Sources of Variation." In *Latin America and the World Economy Since 1800,* ed. John H. Coatsworth and Alan M. Taylor. Cambridge, MA: Harvard University Press, 1998, pp. 409–42.

Martínez Moctezuma, Luis. "La compañía agrícola colonizadora mexicana: Proyecto modernizadora de un empresario porfirista." In *Regiones y expansion capitalista en México durante el siglo XIX,* ed. María Eugenia Romero Ibarra

and Pablo Serrano. Mexico City: Universidad Autónoma de México, 1998, pp. 423–54.
Meyers, William K. "Pancho Villa and the Multinationals: United States Mining Interests in Villista Mexico, 1913–1915." *Journal of Latin American Studies* 23 (1991): 339–63.
———. "Politics, Vested Rights and Economic Growth in Porfirian Mexico: The Company Tlahualilo in the Comarca Lagunera, 1885–1911." *HAHR* 57:3 (1977).
Mignone, A. Frederick. "A Fief for Mexico: Colonel Greene's Empire Ends." *Southwest Review* 44 (Aug. 1959).
Passinanti, Thomas. "Dynamizing the Economy in a *façon irrégulière*: A New Look at Financial Politics in Porfirian México." *Mexican Studies, Estudios Mexicanos* 24:1 (winter 2005).
———. "Nada de Papeluchos: Managing Globalization in Early Porfirian Mexico." *Latin American Research Review* 42:3 (Oct. 2007).
Paulsen, George E. "Reaping the Whirlwind in Chihuahua: The Destruction of Minas Corralitos, 1911–1917." *New Mexico Historical Quarterly* 58:3 (1983).
Pérez Acevedo, Martín. "Juan Basagoiti: Un empresario vasco en Michoacán (1870–1905)." *Siglo XIX* 6:16 (Sept.–Dec. 1996): 69–88.
Pickering, J. C. "Mexico a Field for Investment." *Engineering and Mining Journal* 120 (Dec. 5, 1925): 92–95.
Pletcher, David. "An American Mining Company in the Mexican Revolution of 1911–1920." *Journal of Modern History* 20 (Mar. 1948): 19–25.
———. "The Fall of Silver in Mexico, 1870–1910 and Its Effect on American Investments." *Journal of Economic History* 18 (1958): 33–55.
———. "México, campo de inversions norteamericanos, 1867–1880."
———. "Mexico Opens the Door to American Capital, 1877–1880." *The Americas* 16 (July 1959).
Powell, E. Alexander "The Betrayal of a Nation." *The American Magazine* 70 (Oct. 1910): 717–18.
Randall, Robert W. "British Company and Mexican Community: The English Real del Monte, 1824–1849." *Business History Review* 59:4 (winter 1985): 622–44.
———. "Mexico's Pre-revolutionary Reckoning with Railroads." *The Americas* 42:1 (July 1985): 1–28.
Riguzzi, Paolo. "Los caminos del atraso: Tecnología, instituciones e inversion en los ferrocarriles Mexicanos, 1850–1900." In *Historia económica de México*, ed. Enrique Cárdenas, 2d ed. Mexico City: Fondo de Cultura Económica, 2004, pp. 494–550.
———. "From Globalization to Revolution? The Porfirian Political Economy: An Essay on Issues and Interpretations." *Journal of Latin American Studies* 41:2 (May 2009).
———. "Inversiones extranjeras y interés nacional en los ferrocarriles mexicanos,

1880–1914." In *Las inversions extranjeras en América Latina, 1850–1930,* ed. Carlos Marichal. Mexico City: Fondo de Cultura Económica, 1992.

———. "Mercados, regiones, y capitals en los ferrocarriles de propiedad mexicana, 1870–1908." In *Ferocarriles y obras públicas,* ed. Sandra Kuntz Ficker and Priscilla Connelly. Mexico City: Instituto Mora, 1999.

Rosenzweig, Fernando. "Inversión extranjera y desarrollo de manufacturas." *Estudios* 19–20 (spring 1990): 139–46.

Russell, Charles Edward. "The Seven Kings in Mexico: A Profitable Tale from Recent Railroad History." *Cosmopolitan* 43 (July 1907): 278.

Sariego Rodríguez, Juan Luis. "Historia minera de Chihuahua: Interpretaciones." *Siglo XIX* 5:13 (Sept.–Dec. 1995): 7–26.

Silva Herzog, Jesús. "La revolución Mexicana en crisis." *Cuadernos americanos* (1944).

Uribe Salas, José Alfredo. "Un enclave minero en Michoacán: La formación de una empresa, 1898–1912." *Tzintzun* 8 (Jan.–Dec. 1987): 57–72.

Valerio Ulloa, Sergio. "Empresarios alemanes en Guadalajara durante el porfiriato y la revolución." *Solo Histori*a 9 (July–Sept. 2000): 62.

Vázquez, Juan Antonio, and Miguel Antonio González Quiroga. "Capitalistas norteamericanos en Monterrey: Joseph A. Robertson." In *Monterrey, Nuevo León, el noroeste: Siete estudios históricos,* ed. Mario Cerutti. Monterrey: Universidad Autónoma de Nuevo León, 1987.

Wasserman, Mark. "Enrique C. Creel: Business and Politics in Mexico, 1880–1930." *Business History Review* 59:4 (winter 1985): 645–62.

———. "Foreign Investment in Mexico, 1876–1911: A Case Study of the Role of Regional Elites." *The Americas* 16 (July 1979): 2–21.

———. "'It's not personal. . . . It's strictly business': The Operation of Economic Enterprise in Mexico During the Nineteenth and Twentieth Centuries." *Latin American Research Review* 40:3 (Oct. 2005).

———. "Strategies for Survival of the Porfirian Elite in Revolutionary Mexico: Chihuahua During the 1920s." *HAHR* 67:1 (Feb. 1987): 87–107.

Wionczek, Miguel S. "The State and the Electric Power Industry in Mexico, 1895–1965." *Business History Review* 39:4 (winter 1965).

Womack, John. "The Mexican Economy During the Revolution, 1910–1920: Historiography and Analysis." *Marxist Perspectives* (winter 1978).

Unpublished Works

Brittingham, Albert A. *"Juan F. Brittingham, 1859–1940."* No date.

Grunstein Dickter, Arturo. "A Tentative Reinterpretation of Mexican Railroad Policy in the Late Porfiriato, 1890–1911." No date.

Hoffman, Arnold. "Towne Mines Corporation: A Short Report." 1954.

Manahan, R. R. "Historical Sketch of Mining and Milling Operations of American Smelting and Refining Company in Mexico, 1899 to 1948." 1948.

———. "The Mining Operations of the American Smelting and Refining Company in Mexico." No date.

Memoirs

Barker, James B. "The Beginnings of the Hearst Estate and the Mexican Revolution." Available at http://texanculture.utsa.edu/memories/htms/Barker_transcript.htm, p. 2.

Hammond, John Hays. *The Autobiography of John Hays Hammond*. 2 vols. New York: Farrar & Rinehart, 1935.

Herr, Robert Woodmansee. *An American Family in the Mexican Revolution*. Wilmington, DE: Scholarly Resources, 1999.

Johnson, Annie R. *Heartbreak of Colonia Díaz*. Mesa, AZ: Annie R. Johnson, 1972.

Limantour, José Yves. *Apuntes de mi vida pública*. Mexico City: Editorial Porrúa, 1965.

Marett, R. H. K. *An Eyewitness of Mexico*. London: Oxford University Press, 1939.

McKellar, Margaret Maud. *Life on a Mexican Ranch*. Ed. Dolores L. Latorre. Bethlehem, PA: Lehigh University Press, 1994.

Mills, William Wallace. *Forty Years in El Paso*. El Paso, TX: Carl Herzog, 1962.

O'Hea, Patrick. *Reminiscences of the Mexican Revolution*. London: Sphere Books, 1981.

Parker, Morris B. *Mules, Mines, and Me in Mexico, 1895–1932*. Ed. James M. Day. Tucson: University of Arizona Press, 1979.

Romney, Thomas C. *The Mormon Colonies in Mexico*. Salt Lake City, UT: Deseret Book Company, 1918.

Wagner, Henry R. *Bullions to Books: Fifty Years of Business and Pleasure*. Los Angeles: The Zamorano Club, 1942.

Government Documents

Mexico. Departamento de la Estadistica Nacional. *Exposición numérica y gráfica sobre censo, demografía, producción, y circulación*. Mexico City: Antigua Imprenta de Murguía, 1924.

United States. Department of State, American Mexican Claims Commission. *Report of the Secretary of State with Decisions Showing the Reasons for the Allowance or Disallowance of the Claims*. Washington, DC: Government Printing Office, 1948.

PhD Dissertations

Langston, William S. "Coahuila in the Porfiriato, 1893–1911: A Study of Political Elites." PhD diss., Tulane University, 1980.

Marucci, Horace D. "The American Smelting and Refining Company in Mexico, 1900–1925." PhD diss., Rutgers University, 1995.
Parlee, Lorena May. "Porfirio Díaz, Railroads, and Development in Northern Mexico: A Study of Government Policy Toward the Central and National Railroads, 1876–1910." PhD diss., University of California, San Diego, 1981.
Pletcher, David M. "American Capital and Technology in Northwest Mexico, 1876–1922." PhD diss., University of Chicago, 1946.
Roberts, Donald F. "Mining and Modernization: The Mexican Border States During the Porfiriato, 1876–1911." PhD diss., University of Pittsburgh, 1974.
Ryan, Howard. "Selected Aspects of American Activities in Mexico, 1876–1911." PhD diss., University of Chicago, 1964.
Schmidt, Arthur P. "The Social and Economic Effect of the Railroad in Puebla and Veracruz, Mexico, 1867–1911." PhD diss., Indiana University, 1974.

Index

Acosta Rivera, José, 118
Adams, Fred, 20
agriculture, 3, 182; colonization schemes and, 104–5; foreign investment, 77–131; irrigation, 82, 105; Mexican entrepreneurs, 42, 47–51; Revolution and, 27, 54, 90, 116; sharecroppers, 95, 117, 123, 124, 209n63. *See also* ranching
Aguirre, Mariano, 113
Ahumada, Miguel, 55
Almada, Francisco R., 89
Almeida family, 6, 103, 108
Alvarado, Pedro, 138
Alvarado Mining and Milling Company, 142–44
American investors, 7–19, 39, 84–179, 190n29, 207n12; landowners, 77, 81, 84–111; mining, 7, 36–38, 90, 132–36, 147–79; oil, 8, 15, 18, 62–66, 152, 192n57; railroads, 59–73, 75. *See also* United States; *individual Americans and companies*
American Smelting and Refining Company (ASARCO), 15, 24, 62–63, 132, 135, 143, 155–79, 182–83, 226n3; Chihuahua, 40, 43, 47, 161–65, 170; labor, 157, 162–63, 169–70, 173–76, 177*table*; laws and, 17, 160, 171, 179; Mexican entrepreneurs and, 40, 43, 47–48, 54; profitability, 177, 178*table*, 183; San Luis Potosí, 155, 160, 169–76, 230n106
Angel, Candelaria, 113
Ankerson, Dudley, 5
Arriola, Lorenzo, 139
ASARCO. *See* American Smelting and Refining Company (ASARCO)

Babícora, 82–83, 88, 99–102, 129, 183
Babson, Roger W., 70–71

Bagge, Nils O., 10
Bancaria (Compañía Bancaria de Obras y Bienes Raíces), 33
banking: Creel, 34–43, 51, 53, 55, 194n10; Maderos, 51–53, 55; railroads, 66–68, 72, 73
banks: Banco Central Mexicano, 36, 39, 43; Banco de México, 23; Banco de Nuevo León, 49, 51, 55, 194n10; Banco Hipotecario, 36, 39, 42, 93; Banco Mercantil de Monterrey, 36, 39, 49, 51, 55, 194n10; Banco Minero de Chihuahua, 36–38, 37*table*, 40–43, 194n10, 197n48; Banco Nacional, 36, 69; Banco Refaccionario de la Laguna, 49, 53, 56
Barker, James B., 99, 101
Batopilas Company, 36, 37–38, 90, 134, 147–51, 184
Bauchert, M. F., 90–91
Beals, Carlton, 69
Beatty, Edward, 19
Beckman, Guillermo, 46, 138, 198n69
Belden, Francisco, 49
Bell, Edward I., 69, 204n67
Benton family land, 9, 30, 88–90, 185, 208–9n45
Blocker, John R., 92
Body, John B., 25, 194n3
Boletín Financiero y Minero, 55
Brittingham, Juan F., 14, 39–40, 44, 49–50, 53–54, 194n10
Bruce, Ruben, 87
Bumsted, E. J., 138–39

Calles, Plutarco Elías (Maximato, 1924–34), 5, 32, 80; ASARCO and, 168, 169–70, 174; economy, 20–23, 28, 119, 128; elite-foreign enterprise system, 2, 23, 28, 29,

192n70; and land issues, 80, 81, 87, 89, 90, 100, 102–3, 106, 108, 119, 128
camarillas, 6, 32–33, 55–57, 93, 110
Cananea mining camp, 102, 115, 151–54
Candelaria Mining, 113–15, 120–25, 129, 215–16nn3,5,9
capital, 11, 181, 183; mining, 113, 120, 143, 147, 155, 156, 171–73, 177, 179, 183–84; railroad, 68–72; ranching, 78, 82, 83, 103–4, 113, 120, 183. *See also* investment
Cárdenas, Lázaro, 21, 87–89, 187n1; elite-foreign enterprise system, 2, 21, 27, 29, 48; and landowners, 21, 79–80, 81, 87–88, 91, 97–98, 101, 103, 119; and mining companies, 163, 170, 175
Cárdenas, Miguel, 48, 56
Cargill Lumber, 82, 108, 214n178
Carranza, Venustiano, 20, 21; banking, 41–42, 55, 196n43; civil war with Villa, 114–15, 162, 168; Creel and, 41–42; and landowners, 93, 106; vs. Maderos, 53; overthrown, 172
Casasús, Joaquín, 33, 36, 39, 105, 194n3
Catholic Church, persecution by Calles, 28
cattle, 12, 79–92; Cattle Raisers Association, 87–88; Corralitos Company, 115–18; market, 83–84, 91, 113, 121–22, 130, 207n18; Palomas Land and Cattle Company, 79, 95, 102–3, 111, 116, 213n137. *See also* ranching
centralization: economic, 72, 75, 182–83; political, 4, 13, 27–28, 75, 147
Chavero, Alfredo, 60
Chihuahua: ASARCO, 40, 43, 47, 161–65, 170; banking, 35, 36–38, 37*table*, 40–43, 194n10; Creel-Terrazas family, 34–43, 37*table*, 47, 55, 76, 165; electric company, 39, 43; foreigners resented in, 17; foreign population, 6–7; Madera Company, 20, 107–8, 109, 192n67; Mormon settlers, 18, 96, 119, 210n78; periodicals, 17, 83, 119, 217n50; Quevedos and Almeidas, 6; railroads, 106, 149, 206n97
Chihuahua governors, 141, 145; Acosta Rivera (interim), 118; Ahumada, 55; Almada, 89; Almeida, 103; Creel, 32, 37, 40, 143, 165, 225n106; Enríquez, 108, 118–19, 126–28, 169; Gutiérrez (acting), 42; León, 101, 108; Orozco, 100; Pacheco, 96; Quevedo, 101, 119, 218n65; Talamantes, 101, 170; Terrazas, 32, 34, 36, 55, 76; Villa, 42

Chinese, 18, 123
científicos, 4, 24, 32–33, 39, 56–57, 69, 105
CIJL (Compañía Industrial Jabonera de la Laguna), 39, 42, 49–54
civil wars: centralist Conservatives losing out to federalist Liberals, 4; economic policies, 19–20, 22; elite-foreign enterprise system, 2, 4, 9, 11, 13, 26–27; and foreign landowners, 86–87; Mexican entrepreneurs, 33; mining companies and, 114–15, 162, 163, 167–68, 172–73
Cloete, W. B., 48
Coahuila: ASARCO, 163, 172–73; foreign landowners, 80, 82, 85–88, 92, 93; foreign population, 6–7; Governor Miguel Cárdenas, 48, 56; Mexican and American Cattle Raisers Association, 87–88; Mexican entrepreneurs, 32, 39, 43–56, 75; railroads, 64, 75–76
colonization: religion-based, 96–98, 109, 110; schemes, 104, 110
"commitment problem," 21–23
Compañía Industrial de Parras, S.A., 51, 54
Compañía Industrial Jabonera de la Laguna (CIJL), 39, 42, 49–54
Compañía Industrial Mexicana, Creel-Terrazas, 41, 184
Compañía Metalúrgica de Torreón, Madero family's, 41, 45–47, 47*table*, 49, 53, 165–67
Compañía Metalúrgica Mexicana (CMM), Towne's, 155–56
Compañía Nacional Mexicana de Dinamita y Explosiva, 30, 39
Confederación Regional de Obreros Mexicanos (CROM), 20–21, 28
Constitution (1917), 1, 11, 20, 21, 187n1; and labor, 1, 11, 20, 21, 162, 163; and landowners, 1, 11, 21, 87, 97, 103, 108; and mining, 1, 21, 135, 156, 162–63, 171, 179
Constitutionalists, 20, 42, 116, 143, 162. *See also* Carranza, Venustiano; Obregón, Alvaro
Continental Rubber Company, Rockefellers, 48
Conventionalists, 20. *See also* Villa, Pancho
Corral, Ramón, 32–33, 221n5
Corralitos Company, 12, 82, 112–31, 207n26, 215n2, 218nn55,70
corruption: elite-foreign enterprise system, 24–28, 79, 125; landowners and, 89,

125; mining, 25–26, 125, 137–41, 153; railroad, 68, 69–70
Cosmopolitan, 58
cottonseed, 39, 49–50, 53, 54
Creel, Enrique C., 33–43, 57, 194n3; Aguila Oil Company, 25; banking, 34–43, 51, 53, 55, 194n10; CIJL, 49; Díaz government roles, 33, 34, 38–39, 57, 76; governor of Chihuahua, 32, 37, 40, 143, 165, 225n106; and land ownership, 104, 110; and mining, 46, 141, 143, 150, 165, 227n39; railroads, 75, 206n97; and Rockefellers's Continental Rubber Company, 48
Creel family: and ASARCO, 165, 227n39; entrepreneurs, 6, 32, 33–45, 47, 49–53, 55; landowners, 90; and Orozco rebellion, 196n41; Revolution and, 34, 41–43, 57, 194–95n13; Shepherd close with, 147. *See also* Terrazas family

Davis, Britton, 13–14, 39, 113, 121, 125, 218n70
Davis, Lee, 95
de Iturbe, Miguel, 75
de la Garza, Emeterio, 164, 165, 171, 199n105
de la Huerta, Adolfo, 5, 43, 80, 168, 169
depression (1890s), 11–12, 135
depression (1907), 17, 67, 107, 113, 114, 142–43, 147, 153, 160–61
Depression, Great (1930s and 1940s), 84, 87, 110, 122, 163, 173, 174–75
Díaz, Porfirio/Porfiriato (1876–1911), 5, 185–86; and banking, 36–37, 53; *científicos*, 4, 24, 32–33, 39, 57, 105; economic policies, 19–23, 60, 72, 182–83; elite-foreign enterprise system, 1–11, 24–29, 48, 57, 59–60, 72, 185–86; and foreign investment and entrepreneurship, 6–11, 16–18, 25, 33, 48, 60–72, 77–79, 85, 109, 112–14, 124–31, 135, 147, 150, 155–56, 164–66, 182, 204n67; and landowners, 77–79, 85–86, 88, 92, 93, 99–114, 124–31; Mexican entrepreneurs and, 6, 32–40, 44, 50–57, 76; and mining, 135, 138, 141, 147, 150, 159, 161, 164, 165–66, 179, 183; "order and progress," 6, 22; and railroads, 58–75, 134, 182, 204n67; rebellions against, 55, 57, 74, 161, 173, 196n41; religion-based colonies and, 96. *See also* Limantour, José Yves
d'Olwer, Nicolas, 70

Douglas mining, 25, 193n83
Drug, John Leroy, 137–38
Durango Land and Timber Company, 108–9, 215n181
Dwyer, John J., 80
dynamite manufacture, 40, 54

economy, 16, 19–23, 119, 181–82; controlled by Mexicans, 3–15, 23–30, 72, 75, 181–83, 186; Díaz policies, 19–23, 60, 72, 182–83; elite-foreign enterprise system, 23–30; foreign exploitation issue, 7–15, 30, 115, 133, 146, 151, 157, 181, 183–84, 191n46; mining most important to, 133, 156–57, 166, 184; Obregón and, 20–23, 28, 55, 97; railroads and, 60, 72, 75; vertical political integration (VPI), 22–23. *See also* agriculture; depression; elite-foreign enterprise system; entrepreneurs; industry; revolutionary reconstruction (1920–40)
electric power industry, 15–16, 39, 43
elite-foreign enterprise system, 1–13, 23–30, 57, 181, 185–86, 187n2; consistent treatment by elites toward foreigners, 78, 95–96, 182, 185; Corralitos Company, 112, 131; corruption, 24–28, 79, 125; credible commitment, 21–23; land issues, 77–78, 90, 110–11; mining, 132, 146–48, 156–57; railroads, 59–60, 72, 75; "triple alliance," 187n2, 193n89. *See also* economy; elites; entrepreneurs; foreign investors; government
elites, national, 4–6, 12, 23–24, 29–30, 31–33, 128–29, 159, 182; *científicos*, 4, 24, 32–33, 39, 56–57, 69, 105. *See also* elite-foreign enterprise system; government; local/state elites; politics; *individual national elites*
El Paso Morning Times, 44
Engineering and Mining Journal, 10, 14, 47, 132, 133, 136–40, 153–54
Enkeball, Alf, 138
Enríquez, Ignacio, 108, 118, 127–28, 169
entrepreneurs: Mexican, 6, 31–57, 75–76, 146, 194n3. *See also* foreign investors; industry; mining; ranching
La Equidad, S.A., 41–42
Ericsson, 20, 192n70
Escobars, 141
"La Estrella" (Fábrica de Hilados y Tejidos), 51, 53, 54

Estrada, Roque, 140–41
Europe: banking, 39, 53; French entrepreneur Donato Chapeaurouge, 39; German immigrants, 14–15, 85–86; and Maximilian's debts, 61; Mexican business law and, 8–9; mining, 46, 132, 135, 139, 144; World Wars, 12, 81, 84, 93, 135, 156
Evans, Peter, 187n2, 193n89
Evans, Rosalie, 30, 185
exploitation issue, foreign, 7–15, 30, 115, 133, 146, 151, 157, 181, 183–84, 191n46
expropriations: land, 2–3, 8, 42–43, 79–81, 87–110, 116, 119, 165–66, 171, 185; oil industry, 1–2, 15, 29, 182

family, 6, 31–33, 35. *See also* marriage; *individual families*
Felton, S. M., 69, 70
Ferris, William M., 82–83, 102
Ficker, Sandra Kuntz, 19
Flores, Guadalupe, 139
Follansbee, Jack, 83, 99
foreign investors, 6–30, 35, 39, 46, 53, 182; consistent treatment by elites, 78, 95–96, 182, 185; exploitation issue, 7–15, 30, 115, 133, 146, 151, 157, 181, 183–84, 191n46; government and, 16–21, 23–29; and labor, 15, 78, 79, 84–85, 109–11, 123–24, 148–50, 154, 162–63, 169–70, 184, 191n46, 192n67; local/state elites and, 12, 27–32, 85–101, 124–59, 164–69, 184; Mexican entrepreneurs and, 33–41, 44, 48–49, 146; mining, 11–12, 15, 17, 25–26, 36–40, 112–57, 183–84, 215–16nn3,5,9; railroads, 59–73, 75; ranching, 77–131. *See also* American investors; banking; elite-foreign enterprise system; Europe; landowners; profitability
Foster, E. B., 14
Fournier, Francisco J., 144
Fox, Joseph L., 94–95
Fundición Hierro de Monterrey steel mill, 17

García, Ernesto, 91
García Teruel, Luis, 102
Garza, Isaac, 49
Garza Galán, José María, 57
Germans, 14–15, 85–86
Giroux, Gideon, 94

glycerin, 39, 50, 54
Gómez Morín, Manuel, 194n3
González, Manuel, 61, 104
González Roa, Fernando, 100
González Treviño family, 44, 45
Gould, Jay, 58, 64, 202n13
government, 16–23; ASARCO and, 159, 168–71, 182; credible commitment, 16, 21–23; elite-foreign enterprise system and, 23–30; favoritism/discrimination, 16–19; landowner relations with, 85–88, 96–99, 150; Leviathan state, 182, 230n2; one-party state, 2, 25, 28–30; railroad consolidation, 2, 17, 29, 58–76, 182. *See also* Chihuahua governors; Constitution (1917); economy; elites; expropriations; laws; politics; Revolution (1910–20)
Grant, Ulysses S., 60
Greene, William C., 40, 82, 102, 106, 115, 146–54, 224n95
Grunstein, Arturo, 73–75
guayule, 47–48, 53
Guggenheim, Daniel, 17, 164, 183
Guggenheim family, 15, 47, 62, 155, 158–79, 226n3. *See also* American Smelting and Refining Company (ASARCO)
Gutiérrez, Felipe, 42

Harriman, E. H., 62, 63, 64, 69, 203n49, 204n67
Hart, John Mason, 7, 8, 77, 80, 84, 147–51, 184, 224n85
Hayes, Rutherford B., 60–61
Hearst estate/William Randolph Hearst, 98–102, 109, 119, 129, 151; Babícora, 82–83, 88, 99–102, 129, 183; expropriations, 99–101, 111, 185
Heinz, Augustus, 141
Hernández, Juan, 141
Hidalgo Mining Company, 142–43
Hill, Benjamin, 140–41
Hoard, Roy, 107–8
Hoffman, Arnold, 155
Houghton, E. C., 113, 116–19, 121, 124–28, 220n120
Hubbard, J. D., 136
Huerta, Victoriano, 89, 114, 161
Husk, Charles E., 166
Hutchinson, J. P., 141

industry: electric power, 15–16, 39, 43; glycerin, 39, 50, 54; lumber, 20, 82,

106–9, 154, 214nn167,178, 215n181; Maderos, 51, 52*table*, 53–54, 56–57; soap, 39, 49–50, 54, 62; steel, 17. *See also* mining; oil industry
"insider lending," 38
International Telephone and Telegraph Company (ITT), 20, 192n70
investment: Mexican entrepreneurs, 36, 38, 45. *See also* banking; capital; foreign investors; profitability; property rights
Irigoyen, Francisco, 119
irrigation, 82, 105
Ivins, A. W., 115

Jabonera (Compañía Industrial Jabonera de la Laguna/CIJL), 39, 42, 49–54

Katz, Friedrich, 9, 84–85, 184
Knight, Alan, 18

labor, 27–28; Constitution (1917) and, 1, 11, 20, 21, 162, 163; foreigners and, 15, 78, 79, 84–85, 109–11, 123–24, 148–50, 154, 162–63, 169–70, 184, 191n46, 192n67; landowners and, 78, 79, 84–85, 99, 101–2, 107, 109–11, 123–24, 148–50, 153–54, 192n67; mining, 123–24, 134, 144–46, 148–50, 153–54, 157, 162–63, 169–70, 173–76, 177*table*; railroads, 73, 205n88; for religion-based colonies, 96, 97; sharecroppers, 95, 117, 123, 124, 209n63; unions, 20–21, 28, 136, 144–45, 150, 159, 163, 169–70, 173–76
Laguna (Coahuila and Durango), entrepreneurs, 32, 39, 42–44, 49–56, 75–76
Laird, George A., 113, 114, 121, 123, 125, 215–16n9
Landa y Escandón, Guillermo, 33, 144, 192n57, 194n3
landowners, 77–131; colonization schemes, 104, 110; consistent treatment by elites, 78, 95–96, 182, 185; government relations with, 85–88, 96–99, and labor, 78, 79, 84–85, 99, 101–2, 107, 109–11, 123–24, 148–50, 153–54, 192n67; land reform and expropriations, 1–3, 8, 11, 21, 28, 42–43, 79–81, 86–131, 165–66, 171, 185, 217n44; land titles, 85, 100, 108, 125–28; large operations, 98–103; six requisites for success, 77–78, 81, 88, 94, 109, 112–13, 120, 129, 130; speculators, 103–6, 110; squatters, 87, 97, 99, 101–3, 117–18, 127–28, 217n44, 220n134; writs of *inafectabilidad*, 88, 101. *See also* mining; property rights; ranching
Langley, Mary, 103
Langston, W. S., 56
laws, 8–9; mining, 17, 160, 171, 179; Monetary Reform Law (1905), 160. *See also* Constitution (1917); property rights
Lawson, Thomas W., 152
León, Luis, 89, 101, 108
Leviathan state, 182, 230n2
Limantour, José Yves, 2, 33, 35–36, 76; and ASARCO, 164–65; and banking, 53; brother, 69; *científicos*, 24, 33, 56, 69; elite-foreign enterprise system, 8, 9, 17–18; entrepreneur son, 40; Maderos and, 48, 56; railroads, 58–75, 182; and trusts, 62–63, 76; and US, 61, 192n57
local/state elites: *camarillas*, 6, 32–33, 55–57, 93, 110; and foreign investors, 12, 27–32, 85–101, 124–59, 164–69, 184; "obedezco pero no cumplo" (I obey but do not comply), 3. *See also individual elites and investors*
Long brothers, 142–43
Longe, Arturo, 46, 198n69
Luján, Manuel L., 53
lumber companies, 20, 82, 106–9, 154, 214nn167,178, 215n181

Macedo, Pablo, 33, 69, 194n3
Machado, Manual, 83
Madera Company, 20, 107–8, 109, 192n67
Madero, Francisco I., 9, 25, 29–30, 198n63; assassinated, 53, 161; Club Democrático Benito Juárez, 56; entrepreneur, 39, 46, 48; land reform, 86, 105–6; and mining, 114, 166–67; Orozco rebellion vs., 91; overthrown, 89, 92, 161; rebellion against Díaz, 161, 173; Revolution, 42, 53, 86, 89
Madero family, 54, 75, 198n63; Compañía Metalúrgica, 41, 45–47, 47*table*, 49, 53, 165–67; entrepreneurs, 6, 32, 33–34, 39, 41, 43–57; Ernesto, 51, 52*table*, 54, 75, 198n63; Evaristo, 32, 33–34, 44–57, 194n10, 198n63; and foreign landowners, 85–86, 92, 165–67; Gustavo, 53, 166–67
Manahan, R. F., 161
Manrique, Aurelio Jr., 169–70, 174

marriage: elite families, 35, 44, 45; intermarriage, 14
Martínez del Río, Pablo, 69, 75
Martínez del Río, Pedro, 25, 193n83
Maurer, Noel, 38
Maximato (1924–34), 80. *See also* Calles, Plutarco Elías
Maximilian, 61
McKinley Tariff (1890), US, 83–84, 135, 159
McQuatters, A. J., 110, 143, 197n48
Mealy, William H., 93
Mendrichaga, Tomás, 39, 49
Mennonites, 96–98, 109, 110
Mexican Herald, 106, 142
Mexican Telegraph and Telephone Company, 20, 192n70
Mexico City: banking and investment, 35–36, 40; cattle, 12; entrepreneurs, 39, 43; national elite based in, 4, 24, 25, 32; railroads, 65–66, 75. *See also* government
middle class, 5
military, railroad transport, 60
Milmo (Mullins), Patricio (Patrick), 6, 14, 44, 49
mining, 3, 112–57, 182; Candelaria Mining, 113–15, 120–25, 129, 215–16nn3,5,9; Compañía Metalúrgica, 41, 45–47, 47*table*, 49, 53, 155–56, 165; corruption, 25–26, 125, 137–41, 153; *Engineering and Mining Journal*, 10, 14, 47, 132, 133, 136–40, 153–54; foreigners, 7–17, 25–26, 36–40, 112–57, 184; history, 134–37, 172; labor, 123–24, 134, 144–46, 148–50, 153–54, 157, 162–63, 169–70, 173–76, 177*table*; large operators, 36, 37–38, 90, 134, 143–56, 184; laws, 17, 160, 171, 179; management, 121, 134; market, 133; Mexican entrepreneurs, 37–43, 45–47, 53–54, 146; most important to Mexico's economy, 133, 156–57, 166, 184; profitability, 45–46, 115, 122, 129–61, 171, 176–79, 178*table*, 183, 216–17n9, 225n122; six requisites for success, 120, 132–34, 143–46, 149, 158–59, 179; small operators, 137–43; speculators, 134; subsoil rights, 136, 157, 162. *See also* American Smelting and Refining Company (ASARCO)
Molina, Olegario, 32
Molina family, 6, 32, 33
Moling, J. B., 119

Monetary Reform Law (1905), 160
Monterrey elite and entrepreneurs, 6, 14, 32, 33, 34, 57; American, 10; banking, 35, 36, 39, 44, 49, 51, 55, 194n10; families, 6, 43–44, 45, 49, 51, 75; Fundición Hierro steel mill, 17; mining and smelting, 159–60, 161, 164, 176; railroads, 64, 75–76
Montes family, 6, 32, 33
Moody's Magazine, 68
Moody's Manual, 70–71
Morgan (Edwin D.) family, 113–14, 115, 116, 120, 125–27, 215n3, 216nn19,32
Mormons, 18, 96, 109, 115, 117, 119, 210n78, 219n81
Morones, Luis, 20, 28
Morris, Gaston, 94, 209n63
Morrow, Dwight, 100

Navarro, Juan N., 75
Newhouse, Edgar, 164
Newman Investment Company, 119, 218n55
New York Times, 62, 63–64

"obedezco pero no cumplo" (I obey but do not comply), 3
Ober, Frederick, 10
Obregón, Alvaro, 2, 4, 5, 32, 187n1, 188–89n13; assassinated, 28; Creel roles, 34, 43; de la Huerta rebellion against, 80, 169; economic policies, 20–23, 28, 55, 97; elite-foreign enterprise system, 23, 28, 29; and land issues, 80, 81, 87, 100, 102–3, 106, 110, 118, 127, 185; and Mennonites, 97, 98, 110; and mining companies, 163, 168, 172; Villa and, 107, 163
oil industry, 15, 25; American, 8, 15, 18, 62–66, 152, 192n57; expropriation, 1–2, 15, 29, 182
Orozco, Fernando, 100
Orozco, Manuel Rodríguez, 170–71
Orozco, Pascual/Orozco rebellion, 42, 91, 161, 167, 196n41

Pacheco, Carlos, 96
Palmer, W. R., 60, 202n13
Palomas Land and Cattle Company, 79, 95, 102–3, 111, 116, 213n137
Parker, Morris B., 14, 121, 123, 125
Parlee, Lorena May, 72, 75
parties, 1, 4, 28–29; one-party state, 1, 2, 4, 25, 28–30; Partido Nacional

INDEX 255

Revolucionario (PNR), 1, 4, 28–29; Partido Revoluciónario Institucional (PRI), 29; Partido Revolucionario Mexicano (PRM), 28–29
Paul family, 85–86
Pearson, F. S., 107, 214n167
Pearson, Weetman, 17–18, 20, 25
Pershing Expedition (1916), 9, 18–19, 117, 161, 162
peso, decline, 63
Pierce, Henry Clay, 64, 66, 69, 192n57, 203n49
Pimentel y Fagoaga, Fernando, 33, 39, 194n3
Piñeda, Rosendo, 33
Pletcher, David, 149, 150, 224n95
politics: centralist Conservatives losing out to federalist Liberals, 4; centralized, 4, 13, 27–28, 75, 147; corruption, 25–28, 125; elite-foreign enterprise system, 25–27, 57, 147–48; foreigners and, 13–14, 124–30, 147–48, 150, 166; Mexican entrepreneurs, 31–40, 44, 55–57; railroads, 60, 75. *See also* elites; government; parties; Revolution (1910–20)
Porfiriato. *See* Díaz, Porfirio/Porfiriato
postrevolutionary state. *See* revolutionary reconstruction (1920–40)
El Potosí Mining Company, 144–45
Powell, E. Alexander, 33
Prieto, Manuel, 125, 127, 128
Pritchard, W. A., 141
profitability: ASARCO, 143, 159–61, 171, 176–79, 178*table*, 183; Corralitos Company, 112–16, 121–22, 129–30; foreign investments (general), 10, 30, 78, 83, 181, 183; landowning, 98, 111, 112–16, 121–22, 129–30; lumber companies, 108; Mexican entrepreneurs, 45–46, 50, 146; mining, 115, 122, 129–61, 171, 176–79, 178*table*, 183, 216–17n9, 225n122; railroads, 68, 108, 142, 203n48
property rights, 21–23, 128–29, 162; subsoil, 136, 157, 162; water, 48–49, 53, 79, 94, 105, 117, 127. *See also* expropriations; landowners

Quevedo, Rodrigo, 101, 108, 119, 218n65
Quevedo family, 6
Quijano, Francisco, 89

railroads, 3, 12, 58–76; charters, 61; Chihuahua al Pacífico, 106, 149, 206n97; consolidation (1902–10), 2, 17, 29, 58–76, 182; elite-foreign enterprise system, 24, 59–61; International, 64–65, 67–68, 72; Interoceanic, 58, 63, 64–65, 75; labor, 73, 205n88; landowners and, 79, 104, 122–23; Mexican Central, 40, 49, 58, 61, 63–75, 83, 134–35, 149, 159, 203nn48,49, 205n75, 206n97; Mexican National, 58, 61, 63–75, 159, 205n75; Mexican Northwestern (Ferrocarril Noroeste de México), 106, 113, 122–23, 206n97; Mexican Pacific, 58, 71; Mexican Southern, 61, 72; and mining, 122–23, 134–35, 142, 147–49, 153–69, 172; National Railways (Ferrocarril Nacional de México/FNM), 17, 64–76, 134–35, 169, 205nn82,88; official language of, 73; Pan American, 68, 72; Parral & Durango, 142; regulations, 62, 73, 74; Revolution and, 12, 70, 71, 76, 107, 123, 131; Río Grande, Sierra Madre y Pacífico (RG, SM & P), 106, 122, 152, 219n81; soap for, 50; Southern Pacific, 64, 69, 105, 202n13, 225n98; Tehuantepec, 18, 58; US, 58–63, 67, 76, 182, 202n13, 203n49, 206n97; Veracruz lines, 72, 205n83
ranching, 11–12, 47–49, 77–131; capital, 78, 82, 83, 103–4, 113, 120, 183–84; management, 82–83, 121; market, 83–84, 91, 113, 121–22, 130, 207n18. *See also* cattle; landowners
rebellions: vs. Díaz, 55, 57, 74, 161, 173, 196n41; 1920s, 28, 80, 87, 102–3, 169; Orozco (1912), 91, 161. *See also* civil wars; Revolution (1910–20)
reconstruction period. *See* revolutionary reconstruction (1920–40)
Reiniger, Charles P., 95–96
religion-based colonies, 96–98, 109, 110. *See also* Mormons
Requena, José Luis, 144
Revolution (1910–20), 1–5, 18, 25–29, 187n1, 190n29; *camarillas*, 6, 32–33, 55–57, 93, 110; cattle market, 84, 91, 121–22; Creel-Terrazas families, 34, 41–43, 57, 194–95n13; economic policies, 18–23, 181–83; elite-foreign enterprise system, 25–27, 31–32, 185–86; and foreigners, 6–18, 25, 26,

77–117, 121–39, 143–49, 155–57, 159, 166, 182; "freebooters," 5; and landowners, 77–119, 121, 124, 125, 126, 129–31, 185; Maderos, 53–55, 57, 166–67; and mining, 114, 133, 135, 139, 143–49, 155–57, 159, 166–67, 171–73; railroads, 12, 70, 71, 76, 107, 123, 131, 161. *See also* civil wars; Constitution (1917)
revolutionary reconstruction (1920–40), 1, 3, 5–6, 187n1, 230–31n2; economic policies, 19, 22–23, 29, 30, 183; elite-foreign enterprise system, 29, 30, 31–32; and foreigners, 9–11, 77–78, 83, 88, 90, 112, 113, 117–18, 136, 159, 168; and landowners, 77–78, 83, 88, 90, 112, 113, 117–18; Maderos, 54–55; Mexican entrepreneurs, 31, 32, 33, 38–39; and mining, 136, 159, 168, 182. *See also* Obregón, Alvaro
Reyes, Bernardo, 33, 56, 76, 93, 164, 200n133
Richardson Construction, 82, 105–6, 213n153
Ricketts, Louis D., 153
rights. *See* Constitution (1917); laws; property rights
Ripley, William Z., 63
Robertson, Joseph A., 6, 14, 164, 199n105
Robinson, John R., 6
Rockefellers, Continental Rubber Company, 48
Rock Island, 58–59
Rodríguez, Abelardo, 5, 29–30, 32, 87
Roever, Luis, 93
Romney, Thomas, 96
Rotan, E., 95
Rubio, Manuel Romero, 2
Ruiz, Ramón Eduardo, 8, 206n3
Russell, Charles Edward, 58–59, 72, 200n5

Saenz, Aarón, 32
Salazar, José Ínes, 114, 125, 216n27
San Luis Potosí: mining companies, 144, 155, 160, 169–76, 230n106; Río Tamasapo Sugar Company, 93–94
Scherer, Hugo, 33, 46, 69, 194n3
Schwab, Charles M., 141
Secretaría de Comunicaciones y Obras Públicas, 73–74
Sheahan, James D., 92, 214–15n180
Shepherd, Alexander/Batopilas Company, 36, 37–38, 90, 134, 146–51, 184
Sierra Madre Land and Lumber Company (SML&LC), 106–9, 154

Silva Herzog, Jesús, 25
Sinaloa Land Company, 105
Smith, D. Bruce, 121
Smith, Harry, 119
soap, 39, 49–50, 54, 62
Sonoran triumvirate, 5, 27, 32–33, 36. *See also* Calles, Plutarco Elías; de la Huerta, Adolfo; Obregón, Alvaro
South American Journal, 17
Spaniards, 18, 53, 139
Speyer & Company/James Speyer, 64, 65–66, 67, 70, 73
Standard Oil, 62–66, 152, 192n57
steel industry, 17
Steinkampf, John, 119
Stevens, Otheman, 14
Stilwell, Arthur, 40, 206n97
Stopelli, Santiago, 140–41
sugar, 62, 93–94
Summerfeld, Felix, 166–67
Symon, Roberto, 48

Tabasco Plantation Company, 93
Tabor, Henry, 141
Talamantes, Gustavo, 101, 127, 170
Tanner, H. B., 93–94
telephone company, 20, 192n70
Terrazas, Luis, 32, 44, 45; banking, 36, 194n10; Creel marriage to daughter of, 35; vs. Díaz, 55; governor of Chihuahua, 32, 34, 36, 55, 76; land and cattle owner, 34, 45, 75, 98, 130; McQuatters and, 110, 197n48; and mining, 141, 165; ranching, 207n26
Terrazas family, 35, 76, 185; and ASARCO, 40, 47, 165, 182–83; entrepreneurs, 6, 32–57; landownership, 87, 90, 96, 103, 110, 130, 185; and mining, 141, 147, 154, 165, 184; and Orozco rebellion, 196n41. *See also* Creel family
Tlahualilo Company, 48–49, 57
Towne, Robert S., 146, 154–56, 225n122
transportation: Revolution and, 27, 54. *See also* railroads
trusts, 17, 59–63, 76, 192n70. *See also* American Smelting and Refining Company (ASARCO)
Turner, John Kenneth, 69, 204n67

United States, 7, 151, 190n29; banking, 35, 38, 55; cattle market, 83–84, 99, 121–22; Civil War, 44; invasions of Mexico, 9, 18–19, 60, 117, 161, 162; labor, 12, 153;

land reform in Mexico and, 79, 81, 87; McKinley Tariff, 83–84, 135, 159; Mexican elites and, 34, 42, 57, 60–61, 76, 87, 114, 185, 188–89n13; mining, 11, 133, 135, 153, 159; railroads, 58–63, 67, 76, 182, 202n13, 203n49, 206n97; Revolution and, 81, 99, 190n29; trusts, 17, 62–63, 76. *See also* American investors

Urmston, A. B., 91–92, 95

Valenzuela family, 150
Vázquez del Mercado, Alejandro, 165
vertical political integration (VPI), 22–23
Vidaurri, Santiago, 44–45
Villa, Pancho, 9, 20, 168; Chihuahua governor, 42; civil war with Carranza, 114–15, 162, 168; and landowners/agriculture, 42, 54, 87–89, 107, 113, 116–17, 125, 129, 185; and mining companies, 155, 162, 163, 167–68

Wagner, Henry R., 166–67, 227n39
Wallace, William W. "Billy," 119, 218n65
Warren, Charles Beecher, 100
Warren, C. K., 91–92, 95
Warren, E. K., 119
Warren Lackey, Edna, 95
water rights, 48–49, 53, 79, 94, 105, 117, 127. *See also* irrigation
Wells Fargo, 72, 94, 148
Wilson, Woodrow, 18
Wionczek, Miguel S., 15–16
World Wars, 12, 81, 84, 93, 135, 156
Wright, W. L., 105

Yaqui Indians, 106, 149–50, 224n85
Yocupicio, Román, 87

Zempleman, George, 113–14
Zuloaga family, 48, 97, 113